W9-BAJ-408

ALSO BY STEPHEN KINZER

A Thousand Hills:
Rwanda's Rebirth and the Man Who Dreamed It

All the Shah's Men:
An American Coup and the Roots of Middle East Terror

Overthrow:
America's Century of Regime Change from Hawaii to Iraq

Blood of Brothers:
Life and War in Nicaragua

Bitter Fruit:
The Story of the American Coup in Guatemala
(with Stephen Schlesinger)

CRESCENT AND STAR

CRESCENT AND STAR

TURKEY BETWEEN TWO WORLDS

{REVISED EDITION}

STEPHEN KINZER

FARRAR, STRAUS AND GIROUX

NEW YORK

Farrar, Straus and Giroux
18 West 18th Street, New York 10011

Distributed in Canada by Douglas and McIntyre Ltd.
Printed in the United States of America
First edition published in 2001 by Farrar, Straus and Giroux
First revised edition, 2008

Library of Congress Cataloging-in-Publication Data

Kinzer, Stephen.
Crescent and star : Turkey between two worlds / Stephen Kinzer.—Rev. paperback ed.
p. cm.
Includes index.
ISBN-13: 978-0-374-53140-9 (pbk. : alk. paper)
ISBN-10: 0-374-53140-4 (pbk. : alk. paper)
1. Turkey—Politics and government—20th century. 2. Turkey—Ethnic relations—History—20th century. 3. Civil society—Turkey—History—20th century. 4. Turkey—Armed Forces—Political activity—History—20th century. 5. Turkey—Social life and customs—20th century. I. Title.

DR576 .K56 2008
956.1—dc22

2008016211

Designed by Jonathan D. Lippincott
Maps by Jane Simon

www.fsgbooks.com

1 3 5 7 9 10 8 6 4 2

Support from the Keyman Modern Turkish Studies Program of the Roberta Buffett Center for International and Comparative Studies at Northwestern University is gratefully acknowledged.

TO THE PEOPLE OF TURKEY

The past has vanished,
Everything that was uttered belongs there.
Now is the time to speak of new things.

—Jelaluddin Rumi (1207–73)

CONTENTS

Note on Turkish Pronunciation xi
Preface to the Revised Edition xiii

Meze 3
1. Dreaming in Turkish 9
Meze 27
2. The Hero 33
Meze 51
3. Call to Prayer 57
Meze 83
4. Ghosts 87
Meze 109
5. The Kurdish Puzzle 115
Meze 145
6. Freedom Rising 151
Meze 165
7. Guardians 171
Meze 187
8. Death by Earthquake 193
Meze 207
9. Strategic Depth 213
Meze 229
10. The Prize 235
Meze 249

Index 253

NOTE ON TURKISH PRONUNCIATION

The Turkish alphabet uses Latin letters, and most words are pronounced as they look. There are a few peculiarities, however:

c is spoken as the English j, so *cirit* is pronounced "jirit."

ç is spoken as ch, so *Çiller* is pronounced "Chiller."

ı is spoken as a short u, like the u in sun, so *rakı* is pronounced "raku."

ğ is silent but slightly extends the preceding vowel, so *Çırağan* is pronounced "Churaan."

ş is spoken as sh, so *Ateş* is pronounced "Atesh."

ö is spoken as in German or like the French eu, so *Özal* is pronounced "Oezal."

ü is spoken as in German or like the French u (*lune*), so *Atatürk* is pronounced "Atatuerk."

PREFACE TO THE REVISED EDITION

☪

When the first edition of this book appeared in 2001, Turkey was the most fascinating country in the world. It still is. Other than that, almost everything about it has changed.

I described Turkey at the end of the twentieth century as "defined by its taboos and its fears" and immersed in a "titanic conflict between the geriatric establishment and the growing number of Turks determined to re-invent their country." Its people were trying to pull the reins of power away from the "tired old elite," but their "remarkably poor leaders" were fiercely resisting their "growing clamor for democracy." "Their desire for a breakthrough to modernity is reaching critical mass," I wrote. "If their leaders do not respond to it, there may be trouble."

In the years since then, Turkey has changed as quickly and profoundly as any country on earth. Part of the change is economic, a boom produced by the explosion of foreign investment in Turkey and the growing reach of Turkish business. Part is diplomatic. A large part is psychological. At its core, though, this transformation is political.

Turks have at long last begun winning the civic revolution they have been waging for decades. Turkey's democratic institutions have proven strong enough to contain and guide this revolution, allowing it to proceed peacefully and within the bounds of law. This is a transcendent vindication of the system shaped by revolutionaries of the 1920s, and of the Turkish Republic they created.

Rare are the modern nations whose histories begin with one-party dictatorship and then flower into democracy. That is what is happening in Turkey. During the early years of the twenty-first century it has become a more open society than it has ever been.

Two factors make this process especially interesting and important to people beyond Turkey's borders. First, the party leading it has its roots in Islamic politics. This upsets the stereotype that in Muslim countries, secular parties are democratic while those whose leaders practice traditional Islam are insular and narrow-minded. It also offers a new paradigm for Islamic political movements around the world.

Second, the same regime that has led Turkey toward resolving its domestic challenges also has global ambitions. It believes it has a positive message for the world. Already its diplomatic ambitions in the Middle East, the Balkans, the Caucasus and Central Asia have palpably increased. Turkey has broken free of the United States and Europe and become an independent force on the world stage.

A government rooted in Islamic belief that also embraces democracy offers a vitally important model. When it actively seeks to engage in regional and global politics, it shows that such a nation can have influence and power. Never since the Turkish Republic was founded in 1923 has it been better positioned to fulfill its citizens' dreams and project itself out into the wider world.

Turkey's democratic revolution, like most revolutions, remains incomplete. Taboos that limit the freedom of ethnic groups and other minorities remain strong. Laws that restrict free expression are still in force. A dangerously militant strain of ultra-nationalism has emerged to oppose the growing power of freethinkers like feminists, environmentalists and those who press for greater minority rights. Turkey is finally being shaped by its hopes rather than its fears, but the fears have not disappeared. In fact, reactionary opposition to democracy becomes intense, even violent, as democrats become outspoken and effective.

No episode in recent Turkish history better expresses this tension than the emergence of the dazzlingly original novelist Orhan Pamuk. During the 1990s he had already attracted international attention for his provocative interpretations of Turkish identity and, by extension, the multi-faceted nature of identity itself. He also spoke out against injustices in Turkish society. When he won the Nobel Prize in 2006, he became a symbol of modern Turkey's integration into world culture. Many Turks cheered. Others, however, complained that Pamuk was a "bad Turk" because he dared to think for himself and give voice to democratic ideas. The fact that Turkey's first Nobel Prize winner could not be unconditionally celebrated by his compatriots, and that the legal system even allowed him to be prosecuted for speaking his mind, showed that Turkey's civic revolution is still incomplete.

A new regime has emerged in Turkey that is likely to govern for years to come. That is good, because this regime draws its strength from the people's will, but it is also disturbing. Turkey's old political system, in which weak and corrupt factions were kept in line by generals, has been replaced by one in which a single party dominates all branches of government and is also increasingly powerful in private business. Many citizens deeply mistrust the new ruling group. They fear that by catering to pious Muslims and to the steadily increasing pool of nationalist voters, it may in the end prove even less democratic than the old military-dominated system. "*Yağmurdan kacarken doluya tutulduk,*" they lament. We have escaped the rain only to be pelted by hail.

This debate is intense because the transformation of Turkey is one of the most important processes now under way in the world. It is the central focus of this reconceived book, every chapter of which has been updated and several completely rewritten. In this book as in Turkey, much has changed from what it used to be.

CRESCENT AND STAR

It is late at night when a royal messenger rouses Othello from his marriage bed to tell him that his sovereign, the duke of Venice, is in counsel with other Venetian lords and demands to see him immediately. Walking briskly toward the palace, he wonders what business could be so urgent as to bring these "most potent, grave, and reverend signors" to gather at such an extraordinary hour. He arrives to find them waiting for him. Before he has a chance to ask what the matter is, the duke speaks: "Valiant Othello, we must straight employ you / Against the general enemy Ottoman."

In Shakespeare's day and for centuries thereafter, Christians in Europe could hear no more urgent summons. Generations of them considered "the general enemy Ottoman," better known simply as "the Turk," to be the scourge of civilization. His chief characteristics were thought to include mendacity, unbridled lust, sudden violence and a passion for gratuitous cruelty. Religion was fundamental to this stereotype. Few Europeans knew anything about Islam, but nearly all considered it a satanic affront to everything a Christian held sacred.

Arabs had conquered the Holy Land in the seventh century and were later displaced by another Muslim people, the Turks, who swept into the region from Central Asia. As the age of chivalry dawned, tens of thou-

sands of Europeans found themselves so profoundly outraged by Islamic control of the places where Christ was born and died that they joined the Crusades, bloody campaigns that gave an entire continent an image of Muslims, especially Turkish Muslims, as God's enemy. The first Crusade began in 1095 at the call of Pope Urban II; when the last one ended two centuries later, Turks were still ascendant and the balance of political and religious power was essentially unchanged. But in the course of these wars, Europeans came to perceive Turks as the epitome of evil. They were presumed to be not only bent on destroying Christianity but also determined to kill or enslave every man, woman and child in Christendom. "The Turks," Martin Luther declared, "are the people of the wrath of God."

Had the Turks been simply a faraway focus of evil, they would not have struck any more fear in the European heart than did the heathen Chinese. What made them such an awful thing to contemplate was that their forces were battering down doors across Europe itself. When the most successful Turkish clan, founded by Sultan Osman and known in English as the Ottomans, conquered Constantinople in 1453, it won possession of a Christian city that had once been capital of the Roman Empire and then, for more than a thousand years, capital of the Byzantine Empire. That conquest made Turks at least the geographic heirs to two of the most powerful and culturally influential kingdoms in all human history. Not just Greeks, who were once the rulers of Byzantium, but countless other European and Middle Eastern Christians have had great trouble coming to grips with this truth. Many of them still consider Constantinople, which the Turks renamed Istanbul, to be under lamentable but perhaps reversible occupation by a hostile people.

With this incomparable prize in their hands, the Ottoman Turks set out to build a great empire of their own. They captured Athens in 1458, Tabriz in 1514, Damascus in 1516, Cairo in 1517, Belgrade in 1521, Rhodes in 1522, Baghdad in 1534, Buda in 1541, Tripoli in 1551 and Cyprus in 1571. They nearly took Vienna in 1529 and continued to threaten it for more than a century. Muslim pirates captured European seamen in the Mediterranean and raided towns in Italy, Spain, France, even Britain. For many years the great question hanging over Europe was not whether Protestantism or Catholicism would prevail, but

Turks were thought to be violent thieves, feared by europeans.

whether the Ottomans would sweep into Paris and claim the entire continent for Islam. They never did, but the fears they aroused in their military campaigns, some of which were marked by episodes of barbarous cruelty on both sides, left a deep impression on the European consciousness.

Turks consider the Ottoman period to have been a golden age of ethnic harmony and cultural diversity. In many ways it was. Ottoman sultans allowed their subject nations almost complete religious freedom and considerable political autonomy. While much of Europe was being shaken by anti-Semitic pogroms, the Ottomans were accepting thousands of Jews from Spain and other oppressive nations, allowing them not only to live peacefully but also to rise to positions of wealth and influence. But the Ottoman age was also one of almost unbroken warfare, first as Turks fought to capture territory in Europe and then as they fought to keep from losing it. In the more than six centuries between the coronation of the first Ottoman sultan around 1300 and the fall of the last one in 1922, the longest period of peace lasted just twenty-four years. Older people in some parts of Europe can still remember being warned as children that if they did not behave, Turks would come to get them.

For centuries European literature overflowed with dire warnings of the Turkish peril. King James VI of Scotland, later James I of England, wrote a vivid poem describing the world as locked in conflict "betwixt the baptiz'd race and circumcised Turban'd Turks." The sixteenth-century Italian historian Augustino Curio warned that "even at our doors and ready to come into our houses, we have this arrogant and bragging hellhound." Christopher Marlowe, in his play Tamburlaine the Great, saw the same peril for the nations of Europe: "Now Turks and Tartars shake their swords at thee / Meaning to mangle all thy provinces."

Europeans considered the Ottomans cruel sinners even after the tide of history began to turn against them. "I shall always hate the Turks," Voltaire wrote to King Frederick II of Prussia. "What wretched barbarians!" Jane Austen mused in one of her novels about "the turban'd Turk who scorns the world." In The Brothers Karamazov one brother tells another: "These Turks, among other things, have also taken a delight in tor-

turing children, starting with cutting them out of their mothers' wombs with a dagger and ending with tossing nursing infants up in the air and catching them on their bayonets before their mothers' eyes. The main delight comes in doing it before their mothers' eyes."

Yet throughout the long period when the Turk was considered to embody everything savage and unholy, many Westerners also found him an object of fascination. He seemed to have a wholly different approach to life, symbolized most vividly by the harem, which was seen as a seat of depravity but also of pleasure. Here began the duality of the Western view of Turks, the creeping suspicion that for all their savagery, they might have something to teach the Christian world.

This view spread as more Europeans began to visit Istanbul and Ottoman provinces. Many came back with startlingly positive reports. "There are many in Christendom who believe that the Turks are great devils, barbarians, and people without faith, but those who have known them and have talked with them have quite a different opinion," a French traveler wrote in 1652. "It is certain that the Turks are good people who follow very well the commandment given to us by nature, only to do to others what we would have done to us."

Another Frenchman, the philosopher Jean Bodin, returned home several decades later to tell his countrymen that the Turkish sultan "constrains no one, but on the contrary permits everyone to live as his conscience dictates. What is more, even in his seraglio at Pera he permits the practice of four diverse religions, that of the Jews, the Christians according to both the Roman and Greek rites, and that of Islam."

Perhaps the most perceptive of all the Europeans who wrote about Turkish life was Lady Mary Wortley Montagu, whose husband became British ambassador to the Ottoman court in 1716. She immersed herself in her "new world" and recorded her impressions in a series of witty and incisive letters that were published in England in 1763 and are still read today.

"Thus you see, sir, these people are not as unpolish'd as we represent them," she wrote at the end of one letter. "Tis true their magnificence is of a different taste from ours, and perhaps of a better. I am almost of the opinion they have a right notion of life; while they consume it in music, gardens, wine and delicate eating, we are tormenting our brains with

some scheme of politics or studying some science to which we can never attain, or if we do, cannot persuade people to set that value upon it we do our selves . . . I allow you to laugh at me for the sensual declaration that I had rather be a rich Effendi with all his ignorance, than Sir Isaac Newton with all his knowledge."

Among those who were struck by Lady Mary's letters was the French painter Ingres, who after reading them began to produce brilliant works depicting the harem as a haven of pure and uplifting beauty. Soon afterward Mozart wrote his opera Abduction from the Seraglio, *whose plot was equally subversive of conventional stereotypes. In the climactic scene the Turkish sultan is revealed to be tender and benevolent despite having been grossly abused by Europeans.*

This confusion of images persisted through the nineteenth century. Lord Byron's impossibly romantic death in Greece, where he was fighting against Ottoman forces in the cause of Greek independence, set off a new wave of anti-Turkish feeling throughout Europe, especially because it was accompanied by reports that the Turks had committed atrocities during their campaign. But only five years after Byron died, the future British prime minister Benjamin Disraeli was able to describe Istanbul in terms that made the Turks seem the most civilized people on earth.

"I confess to you that my Turkish prejudices are very much confirmed by my residence in Turkey," Disraeli wrote home to a friend. "The life of this people greatly accords with my taste, which is naturally somewhat indolent and melancholy, and I do not think would disgust you. To repose on voluptuous ottomans, and smoke superb pipes, daily to indulge in the luxuries of a bath which requires half a dozen attendants for its perfection, to court the air in a curved caique by shores which are a continual scene and to find no greater exertion than to canter on a barb, is I think a far more sensible life than all the bustle of clubs, and all the boring of saloons—all of this without coloring and exaggeration is the life which may be here commanded accompanied by a thousand sources of calm enjoyment and a thousand modes of mellow pleasure, which it would weary you to relate, and which I leave to your own lively imagination."

Pit of barbarism or seat of wisdom and tolerance? As the Ottoman Empire gave way to the Turkish Republic in the early years of the twen-

tieth century, the outside world was uncertain which of these two perceptions to believe. It still is. Many people, including more than a few statesmen, view modern Turkey as a backward land plagued by vast social inequalities, grotesque human-rights violations and a callous, corrupt and militaristic regime. Others, believing that Turks have contributed to civilization rather than having sought to destroy it, hope they will overcome their problems and soon emerge as a powerfully modern nation. And the Turks themselves? For centuries they shaped world history, and the not-so-distant memory of Ottoman glory allows them to believe they can again.

• ONE •

DREAMING IN TURKISH

☪

My favorite word in Turkish is *istiklal*. The dictionary says it means "independence," and that alone is enough to win it a place of honor in any language. It has special resonance in Turkey because Turkey is struggling to become independent of so much. It wants to break away from its autocratic heritage, from its position outside the world's political mainstream and from the stereotype of the terrifying Turk and the ostracism which that stereotype encourages. Most of all, it is trying to free itself from its fears—fear of freedom, fear of the outside world, fear of itself.

But the real reason I love to hear the word *istiklal* is because it is the name of Turkey's most fascinating boulevard. Jammed with people all day and late into the night, lined with cafés, bookstores, cinemas and shops of every description, it is the pulsating heart not only of Istanbul but of the Turkish nation. I go there every time I feel myself being overwhelmed by doubts about Turkey. Losing myself in Istiklal's parade of faces and outfits for a few minutes, overhearing snippets of conversation and absorbing the energy that crackles along its mile and a half, is always enough to renew my confidence in Turkey's future. Because Istanbul has attracted millions of migrants from other parts of the country—several hundred new ones still arrive every day—this street is the ultimate melting pot. The country would certainly take a huge leap forward if people could be grabbed there at random and sent to Ankara to replace the members of Parliament. Istiklal is perfectly named because its human panorama reflects Turkey's drive to break away from claustrophobic provincialism and allow its people to express their magnificent diversity.

That drive has been only partly successful. Something about the concept of diversity frightens Turkey's ruling elite. It triggers the deep insecurity that has gripped Turkish rulers ever since the Republic was founded in 1923, an insecurity that today prevents Turkey from taking its proper place in the modern world.

No nation was ever founded with greater revolutionary zeal than the Turkish Republic, nor has any undergone more sweeping change in such a short time. In a very few years after 1923, Mustafa Kemal Atatürk transformed a shattered and bewildered nation into one obsessed with progress. His was a one-man revolution, imposed and steered from above. Atatürk knew that Turks were not ready to break violently with their past, embrace modernity and turn decisively toward the West. He also knew, however, that doing so would be the only way for them to shape a new destiny for themselves and their nation. So he forced them, often over the howling protests of the old order.

The new nation that Atatürk built on the rubble of the Ottoman Empire never could have been built democratically. Probably not a single one of his sweeping reforms would have been approved in a plebiscite. The very idea of a plebiscite, of shaping a political system according to the people's will, would have struck most Turks of that era as not simply alien but ludicrous.

In the generations that have passed since then, Turkey has become an entirely different nation. It is as vigorous and as thirsty for democracy as any on earth. For years its leaders, acting to safeguard what they considered Atatürk's legacy, fiercely resisted change. They believed that Turks could not be trusted with the fate of their nation, and that an elite should make key decisions because the people were not wise or mature enough to do so. Only at the beginning of the twenty-first century did voters find a way to rebel against this stifling order.

Their rebellion is the defining episode of modern Turkish history. It marks the beginning of the end for the class that dominated Turkey for its first eighty years, and for the suffocating ideology it preaches. It is an epochal turning point not only for Turkey but for Islam. Nonetheless it fills many Turks with dread.

Atatürk's infant Turkish Republic was a very fragile creation. Sheiks and leaders of religious sects considered its commitment to secularism a direct assault on all they had held sacred for centuries. Tribal chieftains and local warlords realized that a strong centralized state would undermine their authority. Kurds who dominated eastern provinces sought to take advantage of the new state's weakness by staging military uprisings. European powers hoped it would collapse so that they could divide its territory among themselves. The new Soviet Union actively sought to subvert it and turn it into a vassal state.

In this hostile climate, Atatürk and his comrades came to think of themselves as righteous crusaders slashing their way through a world filled with enemies. They ruled by decree and with a rubber-stamp Parliament, equating criticism with treason. During their first years in power, arrest and execution were the fate of their real and imagined opponents.

Nearly a century has passed since then, and in that time Turkey has changed beyond recognition. The nation that faced Atatürk when he took power was not only in ruins but truly primitive. Nearly everyone was illiterate. Life expectancy was pitifully short, epidemics were accepted as immutable facts of life and medical care was all but nonexistent. The basic skills of trade, artisanry and engineering were unknown, having vanished with the departed Greeks and Armenians. Almost every citizen was a subsistence farmer. There were only a few short stretches of paved road in a territory that extended more than a thousand miles from Iran to Greece. Most important of all, the Turkish people knew nothing but obedience. They had been taught since time immemorial that authority is something distant and irresistible, and that the role of the individual in society is submission and nothing more.

If Atatürk could return to see what has become of his nation, he undoubtedly would be astonished at how far it has come. Muddy villages have become bustling cities and cow paths have become superhighways. There are universities and public hospitals in even the most remote regions. The economy is booming, and Turkish companies are making profits in every corner of the globe. Thousands of young men and women return home every year from periods of study abroad. People are educated, self-confident and eager to build a nation that embodies the ideals of democracy and human rights. This nation—the Turkey of Turks' dreams—is now, at long last, emerging from long shadows cast by geography and history.

During the last decades of the twentieth century, Turkish society was split by a steadily deepening chasm of culture and ideology—what Marxists might call a "profound contradiction." The entrenched elite, successor to Atatürk's clique of revolutionary officers and technocrats, was accustomed to holding ultimate power and refused to surrender it. But the society it sought to rule was hurtling toward modernity and impatient for democracy.

For years the elite seemed unaware that this brash new nation had come into existence. Military commanders, police chiefs, security officers, prosecutors, judges, university rectors, narrow-minded bureaucrats, lapdog newspaper editors, state governors, nationalist politicians and other soldiers in this superannuated army remained psychologically trapped in the 1920s. They saw threats looming from across every one of Turkey's eight borders and, most dangerously, from within the country itself. In their minds, Turkey was still a nation under siege. To protect it from mortal danger, they insisted on running it themselves. They saw the Turkish people, on whose behalf they claimed to rule, not as the embodiment of the nation but, perversely, as a profound threat to it. Caught in the grip of irrelevant experiences, they fiercely resisted pressure from Turks who wanted their country to break free of its shackles and complete its march toward the democracy that was Atatürk's dream.

As the new millennium dawned, demand for change had spread far beyond intellectual circles in Istanbul and pockets of restive ethnic nationalism. It gripped the psyche of the entire nation. Patriarchs of the old elite, true to form, refused to accommodate it. They had beaten back all other challenges to their permanent government, which Turks call "deep state," and there seemed no reason why they could not crush this one as well. But to the delight of many, the horror of some and the astonishment of almost all, they failed.

Their transcendent failure—or to put it another way, the long-delayed triumph of democracy—has produced nothing less than the re-invention of the Turkish Republic. It portends the doom of a ruling system that may have been appropriate when Turkey and Turks were backward and ignorant, but that became reactionary and repressive as "deep state" failed to change along with the people it sought to rule.

This self-appointed vanguard considers itself modernity's great and indispensable defender. It fears democracy not on principle but because it is convinced that democracy will unleash forces that will drag Turkey back toward ignorance and obscurantism. Allowing Turks to speak, debate and choose freely, it has long believed, would lead the nation to certain catastrophe. To prevent that catastrophe, it devised a ruling system that set the limits of debate and suppressed challenges wherever they appeared. For eighty years it exercised the right to limit freedom as it saw fit.

The most sacred principle of this secular faith—called Kemalism, because it claims to embrace Atatürk's principles—is the abstract idea of "nation." Second is secularism. Democracy comes third—but only as long as it is not seen to conflict with the first two. Since 1923 it has been axiomatic that anytime democracy threatens to erode the state's militantly secular identity, it must be crushed.

For much of Turkey's modern history, state power was directed relentlessly against the very forces in society that most fully represented Atatürk's modernizing vision. Writers, journalists and politicians who criticized the status quo were packed off to prison for what they said and wrote. Calls for religious freedom were considered subversive attacks on the secular state. Expressions of ethnic or cultural identity were banned for fear that they would trigger separatist movements and ultimately rip the country apart. When foreigners reminded Turkey that it could never become a full member of the world community as long as its leaders behaved this way, they were denounced for harboring secret agendas whose ultimate goal was to wipe Turks off the face of history.

Attitudes like these slowly turned Turkey's ruling elite into the enemy of the ideal that gave it life. Originally dedicated to freeing a nation from dogma, it came to defend dogma. Once committed to liberating the mind, it lashed out against those whose minds led them to forbidden places. It became the "sovereign" against whom its spiritual ancestors, the Young Turks, began rebelling in the nineteenth century.

"Our sovereign and our government do not want the light to enter our country," the Young Turk theorist Abdullah Cevdet wrote in 1897. "They want all people to remain in ignorance, on the dunghill of misery and wretchedness; no touch of awakening may blaze in the hearts of our compatriots. What the government wants is for the people to remain like beasts, submissive as sheep, fawning and servile as dogs. Let them hear no word of any honest lofty idea. Instead, let them languish under the whips of ignorant gendarmes, under the aggression of shameless, boorish, oppressive officials."

The Young Turks were members of insurgent groups that defied the absolutism of Ottoman rule during the nineteenth and early twentieth centuries. These groups built a rich tradition of dissent that shaped the intellectual and political life of the late Ottoman period and laid the foundation for Atatürk's revolution. Their principles were admirable, but most of their leaders believed instinctively that the state, not popular will, was the instrument by which social and political change would be achieved. They bequeathed to Atatürk the conviction that Turkish reformers should seize state power and then use it ruthlessly for their own ends, not try to democratize society in ways that would weaken the centralized state.

Turkey's effort to rid itself of this authoritarian mind-set has been difficult and scarred by trauma. Not until 1950 did military commanders, the vanguard of Atatürk's new class, allow free elections. They continued to watch politicians closely, however. Four times—in 1960, 1970, 1980 and 1997—they deposed elected governments. Turks were groping toward democracy, but whenever they tried to establish the primacy of popular will, the military swatted them down.

The 1980 coup, which led to three years of direct military rule, set in motion forces that would define Turkish society for the next two decades. Ruling generals decreed fierce crackdowns, ranging from torture campaigns to the mass firing of university professors. In 1982, before the generals returned to their barracks, they imposed a new constitution designed to assure their permanent power. It guaranteed Turks all civil rights, but then stipulated that the government could suspend any or all rights "with the aim of safeguarding the invisible integrity of the state with its territory and nation, national sovereignty, the Republic, national security, public order, general peace, the public interest, public morals and public health." It allowed judges to ban any political party whose program conflicted with "the democratic and secular order." Most perniciously, it established a new body, the National Security Council, composed of five elected officials (the president, prime minister and ministers of defense, interior and foreign affairs) and five generals (the chief of staff and commanders of the army, navy, air force and gendarmerie), that was to function as the nation's supreme decision-making body, above Parliament and insulated from the people's will. Governments were required to give "priority consideration" to its decisions.

For the next twenty years the National Security Council met once a month. Its deliberations were private, but television reporters were admitted for a few moments to film members as they took their seats. The footage perfectly conveyed the balance of power in Turkey. Government leaders sat on one side of a long table, shifting uncomfortably like guilty schoolboys. Military commanders, ribbon-bedecked and unsmiling, sat opposite, glowering at their charges as they pulled folders from their briefcases and prepared to deliver their decrees. Always they spoke with a single voice, and always it was understood that their will must be done.

"It is a fundamental principle that there is one state," former president and prime minister Süleyman Demirel wryly observed after he retired, "but in our country there are two."

The 1982 constitution and the laws passed to bolster it proved chillingly effective in preventing the flowering of Turkish democracy. It was folly, however, to believe that an essentially anti-democratic system could survive forever in a changing world. In the 1980s and 1990s Turks rebelled against it with steadily growing fervor. By the time the century ended, this conflict had come to dominate Turkish life. On one side was an inbred elite, weaker than it had once been but still accustomed to treating elected leaders like errand boys. Arrayed against it was a large and steadily growing majority of Turks.

Turkey's conundrum during this period was that although most people fervently wished for a new order that would represent their democratic aspirations, no political party or civic movement translated their aspirations into reality. Civilian politicians who claimed to represent the ideologies of left, center and right were in fact all part of the oppressive old consensus. All accepted the bedrock principle that had shaped the Turkish Republic since its birth in 1923: that military commanders and their allies should hold ultimate power because the voting public could not be trusted. The closed political system designed by framers of the 1982 constitution allowed autocratic bosses to dominate political parties, and for years this system effectively prevented the flowering of true democracy.

The 1980 military coup, though, had another, unexpected result. From its wreckage emerged the most dynamic political leader Turkey had seen since Atatürk. Only today, years after his death, is it clear how profoundly he reshaped Turkey.

The towns where Turgut Özal lived while he was growing up—Malatya, Mersin, Mardin and Kayseri—comprise a veritable map of the deep Anatolian heartland. In 1983 he became prime minister despite efforts by departing generals to prevent his election. Shattering taboos wherever he found them, Özal set out to re-revolutionize the Turkish state. "He threw open all the doors and windows in this place," one American ambassador to Turkey told me with evident admiration.

The nation that Özal took over in 1983 was dominated politically by generals and economically by a small class of wealthy, militantly secular and "modern" industrialists based in cosmopolitan Istanbul. The regime pampered this class with subsidies, protected it from competition through high tariffs and anti-competitive regulations and rewarded it for its loyalty with government contracts. In return, the rich backed political parties that were subservient to military power.

Prime Minister Özal undermined the power of this elite by dismantling the subsidy regime, selling off state-owned companies, democratizing access to credit and relentlessly encouraging ordinary Turks to go into business. Millions did. By the 1990s they had come to comprise an entirely new class, eager not only for a more open economy but also for better relations with Europe, where they found lucrative export markets. The rise of this counter-elite was a testament to the unprecedented social mobility that Özal's reforms had brought to the Anatolian masses.

It mounted a heady challenge to the "white Turks" of the old Istanbul establishment, not just economically but also socially and culturally. Finally and inevitably, it turned to politics.

Besides revolutionizing the Turkish economy, Özal also challenged political taboos. When the military chief of staff resigned after disagreeing with him about Turkey's involvement in the 1991 Gulf War, he refused to accept the new candidate the armed forces nominated and chose his own—something no Turkish prime minister had ever dared to do. Once he showed up to review a military parade wearing shorts and a T-shirt; he explained that he had just debarked from a yacht on which he was enjoying a brief vacation, but he was also sending a message that the army must be subservient to political leaders under all circumstances. He was the first modern Turkish leader to admit that Kurds exist in Turkey and constitute a distinct ethnic group, and he even announced that he himself was partly Kurdish. He openly embraced a Sufi order, the Nakşibendi, that was among those Atatürk had banned in the 1920s. Once while musing about how to improve Turkey's relations with Armenia, he asked, "What if we recognize the genocide?"

Özal challenged the old elite in such fundamental ways that when he died of a heart attack in 1993 at the age of sixty-five, more than a few Turks suspected foul play. Some still believe that, as one of the country's most powerful politicians told me over dinner one night, "they killed him."

Natural or not, Özal's death removed from national life the greatest threat that the ruling system had faced since the founding of the Republic. Momentum for change quickly dissipated. For a time it seemed that Özal's outsize dreams had died with him and that Turkey would settle back into torpor and frustration.

The 1990s were lost years for Turkey. Small-minded politicians devoted their energies to bickering and stealing money while the country drifted toward social and political fragmentation. Governments were weak, divided and short-lived. The military, through its National Security Council, filled the power vacuum, blocking democratization and pursuing a brutal war against Kurdish rebels. Inflation raced out of control, and the economy careened wildly from crisis to crisis. Prosecutors relentlessly indicted dissenters and freethinkers.

One of those who were imprisoned during this period was no less a figure than the mayor of Istanbul, Recep Tayyip Erdoğan (pronounced AIR-doe-wan). His offense, like that of others jailed in the 1990s, was to have spoken words in public that the old elite found treasonous. They were based on the text of a century-old poem:

> The mosques are our barracks, their domes are our helmets,
> Minarets are our spears, the faithful are our army.

This poem was not, however, the real reason Mayor Erdoğan was indicted. His true crime was establishing a political movement that openly embraced Islam and persuading millions of Turks to support it. The old elite recognized him as a potent threat and set out to crush him.

Erdoğan is a product not of Istanbul's high society but of its rough-and-tumble Kasimpaşa district, where he developed a reputation as a street fighter and fine soccer player. For several years he worked as a salesman for the Ülker candy company, and his work helped him develop a winning manner that led him naturally into politics. Because he prayed every day, did not smoke or drink, fasted during Ramadan and was married to a woman who wore a head scarf, he joined a religious-oriented party.

Here, then, was the second outsider to challenge the Turkish establishment in the space of two decades. Like Özal, he was an observant Muslim shaped by conservative rural values, not by Istanbul's chic modernity. His crime was helping to build a political movement rooted in Islamic values, something the elite found terrifying and intolerable.

For a while I, like others in Turkey, found it difficult to imagine that "deep state" would take such a drastic step as to imprison the mayor of the country's largest city. That, however, was exactly what happened. Mayor Erdoğan was found guilty of inciting "religious hatred," sentenced to ten months in jail and banned from public office.

Many Turks were outraged by this verdict. It was yet another sign, more vivid than most, of how fiercely the old establishment was clinging to rigid dogmas of the past while society rocketed toward the future. All over Istanbul, walls sprouted posters bearing the mayor's portrait and the vow he had made outside the courtroom after being convicted: "This

Song Is Not Over Yet!" No one could imagine how true that would turn out to be.

A few days after the verdict, I visited Mayor Erdoğan at his city hall office. On the plaza outside, supporters sat behind tables gathering signatures on a petition of protest. From one table hung a banner proclaiming, POETRY-READING MAN, YOU DESERVE A MEDAL! A young woman wearing a head scarf sat behind it. "Everyone is crying over what happened," she told me. "We are very angry. His only crime was to work for God."

Inside I found Erdoğan, who was then forty-four years old, reflective but unrepentant. We agreed that the poetry-reading charge against him was a pretext, and I asked him what he thought was the real reason he was being punished.

"My prosecution was aimed at blocking me or turning people against me," he said. Then, after a pause, he added what sounded like a warning: "No politician can be artificially removed from the scene. The nation raises politicians up, and only the nation can bring them down." I tried to goad him into saying more, but he demurred. "I have to be very careful about what words I use," he explained. "It is a very strange position to be in."

Like other outsiders who came to know Erdoğan during his term as mayor, I admired his achievements but doubted he could become an effective national leader. Some didn't like his religious impulses, which he expressed in policies like a ban on the sale of alcohol at city-owned cafés, but what bothered me was that in our interviews he seemed out of his depth whenever we talked about world affairs. He had troubling, ill-defined notions about the power of Islamic politics and the shortcomings of democracy. Several times he suggested to me that Turkey might be wise to throw in its lot with its Middle Eastern neighbors rather than with faraway Europe. Once he famously compared democracy to a streetcar: you ride it until you reach your destination, then you step off.

This lack of sophistication suggested to me that Erdoğan would never emerge as a serious national leader and certainly not as a figure of Özal's stature. Their backgrounds were starkly different. Özal was an engineer who had run a business, worked for the World Bank, served in demanding government posts, learned foreign languages and traveled widely. Erdoğan, a former candy salesman who had never held public office before being elected mayor, was a bumpkin by comparison. When he was packed off to jail—his sentence was reduced on appeal to 120 days—I thought his political career might be over.

On the morning of March 21, 1999, a caravan of two thousand automobiles followed Erdoğan as he was driven along the 170-mile route from Istanbul to Kırklareli, near the Bulgarian border, where he was to serve his sentence. Supporters had paid to paint and carpet his jail cell, install a television and arrange for meals from outside to be brought in. His wife rented a house nearby. Before he reported to the warden, friends sacrificed a sheep in his honor. "I am not saying goodbye!" he promised the emotional crowd. "This is just a pause."

After serving his four-month term, Erdoğan was released and returned to his home in Istanbul. Soon afterward friends of his began telling me that he seemed deeply changed. They were right. His imprisonment decisively reshaped his worldview.

Mayor Erdoğan had entered prison believing, as did many other pious Turks, that the country's great failing was its refusal to respect religious belief. He also shared the classically Islamist view of the West, a one-dimensional, cartoon-like vision of a hostile and sinful place. By the time he was released, he had greatly broadened his perspective. The essential weakness of the Turkish state, he came to realize, was not its extreme secularism but something more profound: its abiding fear of free discourse. This realization, in turn, led him from contempt for the West to admiration for its pluralistic ethos.

Erdoğan's jailhouse conversion formed the basis for a political movement unlike any Turkey had ever seen. He shaped it to reflect what had become his central conviction, one that directly challenged fundamental Kemalist principles. Democracy and Islamic belief were not incompatible, he began insisting. In fact, he told his comrades, the most fervent desire of most Turks was to enjoy both.

Once out of jail, Erdoğan plunged into the task of building a political movement that embraced both Turkey's Muslim identity and its intensifying desire for democracy. He appealed for support from the Anatolian counter-elite that Turgut Özal had brought to life in the 1980s. Having established its economic power, this new class was looking for a political leader. It found him in Erdoğan.

By the time the national election of 2002 approached, Erdoğan's Justice and Development Party, known in Turkish as Adalet ve Kalkınma Partisi, or AKP, had become a potent force. It turned the campaign into a confrontation sharper than any that Turkish voters had ever faced. On one side, as always, was the old elite. It insisted on its vision of an all-powerful state before which citizens were supposed to cringe; preached a rigid nationalism that denied Turkey's rich ethnic, religious and cultural diversity; insisted on a form of secularism so militant and intrusive that it became a religion in itself; and saw demands for change and social evolution not as welcome signs of a vibrant society but as germs of a frightful epidemic to be suppressed at all costs. This elite saw Erdoğan as the incarnation of its most terrifying nightmare. Some of its leading figures were convinced that his ascent to power would signal nothing less than the death of the Turkish Republic.

During the 2002 campaign Erdoğan preached coexistence and mutual respect among Turkey's many groups rather than pretending that they did not exist. He called for a "normalization" of politics, which in Turkey is a radical idea because it means that election results must always be respected, elected leaders must have full authority and generals must stop trying to run the country. Yet he insisted he was no ideologue. As mayor of Istanbul he had shown a diligence and honesty that were rare in Turkish politics. Streets were paved, garbage was picked up and water mains were repaired more quickly and efficiently than ever before. The AKP, its leaders said time and again, was devoted to providing services, not imposing ideology.

"My story is the story of this nation!" Erdoğan proclaimed in one of his final campaign speeches. "Either this nation is going to win and come to power, or the arrogant and oppressive minority group, which looks at Anatolia with contempt and rejects Anatolian realities, will continue to remain in power. The nation has the power to decide. Enough! Sovereignty belongs to the nation!"

As I listened to Erdoğan's campaign rhetoric, I sensed that he had truly transcended his background in Islamic politics. He ran on three pledges: to energize Turkey's economy, to consolidate its democracy and to bring it into the European Union. When asked to define his political orientation, he said he was a "conservative democrat." Others called him "post-Islamist."

But was he really?

Millions of modern, worldly Turks had been losing hope that they would ever find a political leader who combined national popularity with democratic principles. When Erdoğan emerged, they embraced him. Some in the intellectual class, however, were more hesitant, even to the point of hostility. They wanted Turkey to go where Erdoğan promised to take it, but because of his Islamist background, they deeply mistrusted him.

In Turkey, as elsewhere, it has long been a truism that Islamic-oriented politicians scorn democracy and secular ones defend it. By the time of the 2002 election, though, these roles had been reversed in a deliciously subversive way. One candidate was an Islamic-oriented democrat; the others were secularists who feared democracy.

All during the 1990s, democrats in Turkey had looked eagerly for a secular leader who would adopt their agenda. To their intense frustration, every leading secular politician of that era had turned out to be venal, corrupt or a willing servant of "deep state." In desperation they turned to Erdoğan. He was not the horse they had hoped to ride toward liberation, but he was the only one galloping in the right direction, so they bet on him.

At every stop on the campaign trail, Erdoğan insisted that he was as much a democrat as he was a Muslim. Not true and a dangerous lie, howled his opponents. Beneath Erdoğan's democratic rhetoric they saw a sinister plot to use democracy as a way to roll back Atatürk's reforms and transform Turkey into an Islamic state. But these warnings did not scare voters. In the most pivotal election ever held in Turkey, they gave the AKP a historic victory. It won only 34 percent of the vote, but because of divisions among other parties and quirks of the Turkish electoral system, that was sufficient for a majority of seats in Parliament and allowed it to establish a one-party government—the first Turkey had known in nearly twenty years.

Erdoğan could not become prime minister immediately because of the political ban that had been imposed on him, but in short order

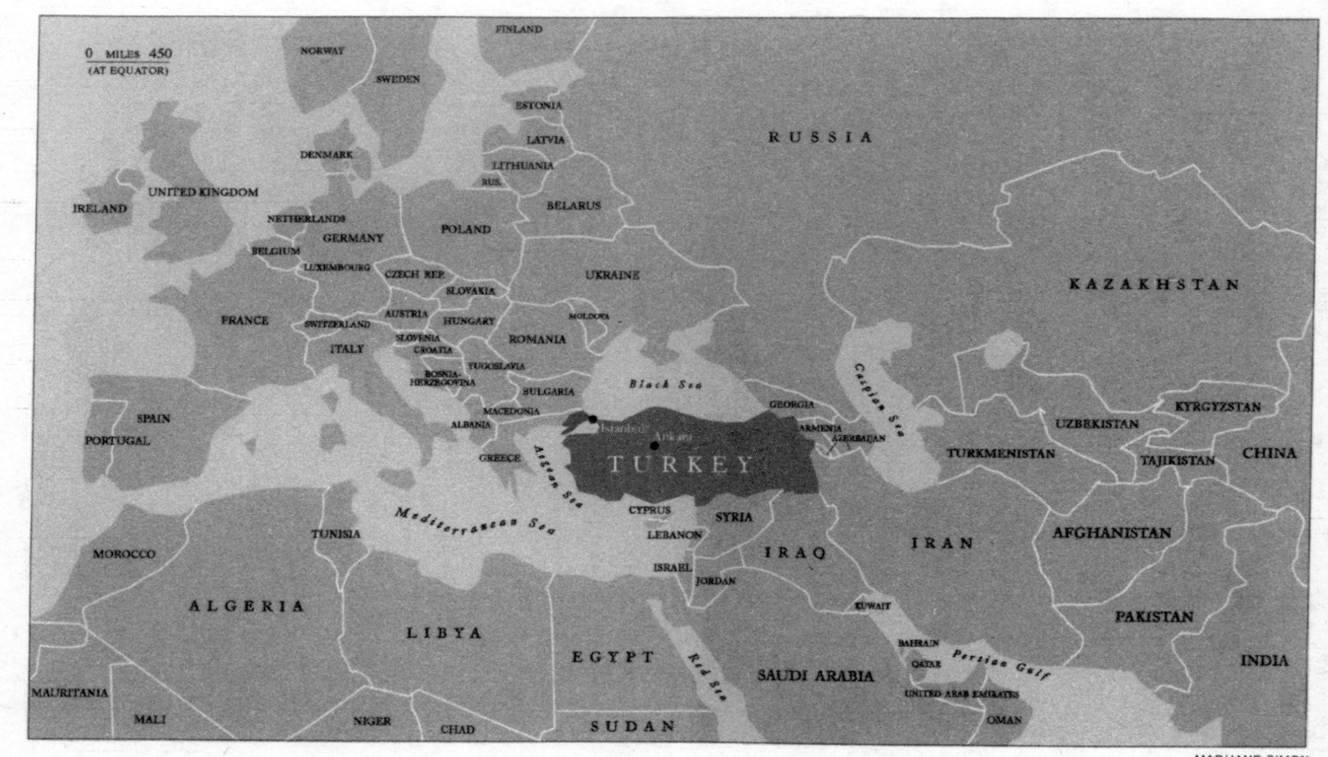

MAP/JANE SIMON

Parliament lifted it and he was able to claim his prize. The day of his inauguration marked a decisive defeat for the old Kemalist elite and a breathtaking victory for the emerging counter-elite, with its new-found belief in Islamic democracy or democratic Islam. In modern Turkish history, only Atatürk's seizure of power in 1923 was a more profound turning point. Erdoğan won by attracting two great voting blocs that had traditionally considered each other enemies: religious believers and democrats. In a larger sense, he succeeded because he was expressing a new Turkey that had been taking shape for years. Since 1923 the country had been ruled by a self-perpetuating elite shaped above all by paralyzing fear of the people. Now it is ruled by elected leaders.

Liberating as this breakthrough is, however, it carries within itself a great uncertainty. The new regime's commitment to democracy was boundlessly admirable in its rhetoric but less so in its concrete actions. It did not move decisively to wipe away the crippling restrictions on free speech that have defined the Turkish Republic since its founding. Its efforts to resolve the festering Kurdish challenge were weak and tentative, and despite its insistence that it would forever respect the rights of secular Turks, many remained profoundly worried about whether that was true.

Women were especially concerned. The Muslim head scarf became more visible in Turkey, including on the streets of Istanbul and other big cities, than ever in modern history. If this is simply a sign that devout Muslim women are taking the chance offered to them by flowering democracy and finally living as they choose, that is fine. More than a few Turks, however, fear that it is the beginning of a wave of social pressure that will roll back the spectacular progress Turkish women have made since the time of Atatürk.

All these concerns relate directly or indirectly to the rise in militant ethno-nationalism that has been the most disturbing aspect of Turkish life in the years after the new regime came to power in 2002. The principal targets of this increasingly violent movement have been those who defended the rights of Kurds, Christians and other minorities. Fomented by supremely irresponsible politicians and journalists, fueled by an undeveloped educational system that turned out narrow-minded chauvinists, and encouraged by the authorities' failure to find or prosecute the true authors of nationalist crimes, it has spread a disturbing shadow over a land that was once a world center of tolerance. "Nationalist obsession mixed with religious intolerance may be the greatest problem this country has ever faced," the newspaper columnist Yusuf Kanlı wrote after a young man stabbed a Catholic priest in the Aegean city of Izmir at the end of 2007. "If our security forces and judicial system are satisfied with arresting and prosecuting the teenagers involved in these crimes, if they do not pursue the masterminds behind them, and if they fail to bring to justice elements in the police and gendarmerie that are apparently involved in this mess, the country will be forced to live through new episodes of the same tragedy every couple of months."

Turkey has entered a period of unprecedented change. The new regime's central challenge is to democratize the country without releasing atavistic forces that will pull it away from the traditions that have brought it so much success.

For generations Turkish leaders sought to bind their people together by creating a concept called *devlet*. Over the years this became my least favorite Turkish word. The dictionary says it means "state," but it also means something uglier. *Devlet* is an omnipresent entity that for decades stood above every citizen and every institution. Loyalty to it was held to be the Turk's supreme obligation, and questioning it was considered treasonous. No one ever defined what it meant, but everyone was supposed to know. In the mind of the country's self-perpetuating elite, serving *devlet* was a responsibility so transcendent and sublime that not even law was allowed to obstruct it. *Devlet*, much more than an abstract concept and much more than a focal point for national unity, was Turkey's apocalyptic swordsman, the repressive mentality that overwhelmed, constricted and suffocated the citizenry.

No two words in Turkish are as fundamentally contradictory as *istiklal* and *devlet*. The first stands not just for national independence but for the freedom and progress that independent thought brings to any society that encourages it. The second is a reactionary force that represents fear, mistrust and arrogance, a force that long kept Turkey in chains.

The hurricane of political, social, economic and cultural change that

The first friends I made in Turkey told me that if I really wanted to understand their country, I would have to drink a lot of rakı. *These were wise people, so I took their advice. Every year the annual level of* rakı *consumption in Turkey rises by slightly more than one million liters, and my contribution to the increase has not been inconsiderable.*

In the bottle rakı *is absolutely clear, but it is rarely consumed that way. Instead it is mixed with water, which turns it translucent. Drinking it has the same effect on one's perception of Turkey. After a glass or two, what at first seemed clear becomes obscure. By the time the bottle is empty, everything appears murky and confused. Yet through this evocative haze, truths about Turkey may be most profoundly understood.*

Many countries have national drinks, but rakı *is much more than that because it embodies the very concept of Turkey. The mere fact that a Muslim land would fall under the spell of a powerful distilled drink is enough to suggest this nation's unexpected and tantalizing appeal. Do not speak to a Turk about ouzo or other anise-based drinks supposed to reflect the characters of other lands. The careful mix of natural ingredients in* rakı *and the loving process by which it is distilled, they believe, make it gloriously unique.*

History books say that Mustafa Kemal Atatürk died from the effects of overindulgence in rakı. *That is only partly true. In fact he died from an overdose of Turkey. His involvement with Turkey, like his involvement with* rakı, *was so passionate and so intense that it ultimately consumed him.*

The same almost happened to me. I had admired Turkey from afar, but it was only after long nights drinking rakı *with friends that I came to understand the true audacity of the Turkish idea. Its grandeur and beauty filled me with awe. My excitement rose with each glass as I realized how much Turkey has to share with the world, to give the world, to teach the world.*

I should have stopped there, but you never do with rakı. *That is its blessing and its curse. As months and years passed,* rakı *began to work subtly on my mind. Slowly the delight I had found in discovering Turkey became mixed with other, more ambiguous emotions. No longer did my evenings end with the exhilarating sensation that I had found a jewel of a country poised on the brink of greatness.* Rakı *led me inexorably toward frustration and doubt. It never shook my conviction that Turkey is a nation of unlimited potential, but it did lead me to wonder why so much of its potential remains unrealized. Turkey is undoubtedly the country of the future, but will it always be? Can it ever become what it hopes to be, or is it condemned to remain an unfulfilled dream, an exquisite fantasy that contains within it the seeds of its own failure?*

There are as yet no answers to those questions, and therein lies the Turkish conundrum. This nation is still very much a work in progress, a dazzling kaleidoscope of competing images and ideas. Born of trauma and upheaval, it remains deeply insecure, shrouded in old fears and uncertain which direction it should take.

This identity crisis led to a near-collapse of the rakı *tradition in the 1960s and 1970s. Turkey was opening itself to the world, and a class of educated and sophisticated Turks was emerging. These people considered* rakı *anathema because it symbolized the primitive mentality of rural peasants. If illiterate hillbillies wanted to drink it in their broken-down shacks, that was one thing, but no modern Turk would do so; much better to sip wine, cognac or some other drink with a European pedigree.*

Fortunately, those days are past. Turks no longer feel embarrassed to embrace their heritage and identity. Drinking rakı is an ideal way to do so while at the same time enjoying a sublime pleasure.

Rakı is the key to Turkey, not because of the drink itself but because of the circumstances in which one consumes it. This is not a drink like whiskey, useful for solitary reflection; not like beer, good for drinking in a noisy bar while munching on pretzels; and not like gin or vodka, lubricants for cocktail-party chatter. Bars and cocktail parties are, in fact, mortal enemies of the Turkish drinking tradition. Resistance to these pernicious influences is centered around the meyhane, a sort of bistro created especially for rakı drinking. The meyhane is a temple of Turkish cuisine, but it is also a place where people meet, talk, debate, embrace and lament. Turkey's diversity is most tangible at the meyhane because it is spread out on tables for all to see.

An evening at a meyhane is centered around rakı, but rakı never stands alone. It is only one component, albeit the essential one, of a highly stylized ritual. With rakı always come meze, small plates of food that appear stealthily, a few at a time. Theoretically, meze are appetizers leading to a main course, but often the main course, like Turkey's supposedly great destiny, never materializes. No one complains about that because eating meze while sipping rakı is such a supreme pleasure in itself. The path is so blissful that the idea of a destination seems somehow sacrilegious.

Meze usually come in waves. The first will include salad, thick slabs of white cheese, smoked eggplant purée and honeydew melon. What comes next depends on the chef's whim. There might be a selection of cooked, cooled vegetables in olive oil, each presented on its own miniature platter, or small dolma, which are peppers stuffed with rice, currants and pine nuts, and their close cousins, sarma, made from grape or cabbage leaves. After the next pause might come spicy red lentil balls, mussels on the half shell, mashed beans with lemon sauce, puréed fish roe, yogurt seasoned with garlic and dill, raw tuna fillets, poached mackerel with hazelnut paste or an explosively flavorful dish made of baby eggplants stuffed with garlic cloves, tomatoes, sliced onion and parsley. This last is called Imam Bayıldı, meaning "the Imam fainted."

After these come piping-hot börek, delicate pastries filled with feta cheese and sometimes also spinach, diced chicken, ground lamb or veal, pistachios, walnuts or whatever else is lying around the kitchen. Some are layered, others triangular and still others cylindrical or crescent-shaped. Often they are served with squid rings fried in a light batter, which are to be dipped in a white sauce made from wine vinegar, olive oil and garlic.

Turkey's ethnic vitality shines through as the evening proceeds. Kebabs and other meze made from meat recall the Central Asian steppes from which nomadic Turkic tribes migrated to Asia Minor, now called Anatolia, a thousand years ago. With them come hummus from Arabia, shredded chicken with walnuts from the Caucasus, diced liver from Albania and cooked cheese thickened with corn flour from coastal villages along the Black Sea. Then comes the crowning glory, the seafood, a gift from the Greeks, who for millennia did all the cooking along what is now Turkey's Aegean coast. Rakı sharpens the taste of all food, but its magic works best with fish. An old proverb calls rakı the pimp that brings fish and men together for acts of love.

The variety of fish in Turkey seems endless. It changes according to what body of water is nearest and also according to the season. Always the fish is very fresh, and always it is prepared very simply, grilled or pan-fried and served with no sauce, only a lemon wedge and perhaps a slice of onion or sprig of parsley.

Such a meal is a microcosm of Turkey. It is an astonishingly rich experience but yields its secrets slowly. Patrons at a meyhane, like all Turks, confront an ever-changing mosaic, endless variations on a theme. Each meze tastes different, has its own color, aroma, texture and character. The full effect is comparable to that of a symphony, complete with melodies, different rhythms, pacing and flashes of virtuosity, all contained within an overarching structure.

Meze make a feast, but drinking rakı with them raises the experience to a truly transcendent level. "All the senses are involved," my friend Aydın Boysan, an architect and bon vivant who had been drinking rakı for more than sixty years when I met him, told me during a long night we spent at a meyhane overlooking the Bosphorus. "First you watch the water being poured into the glass and mixing with the rakı. Then you pick up the glass and inhale the aroma. When you drink it, you take a small sip, feel the pleasure of it flowing down your throat, take another small sip, then put the glass down."

Aydın demonstrated this ritual to me, seeming to enjoy it every bit as much as he might have half a century earlier, and then closed his eyes for a moment. "The best part is feeling it go down your throat," he said lovingly. "A giraffe—that's an animal ideally made to appreciate rakı.*"*

The meyhane *culture tells a great deal about Turkey. Like the country, it offers almost infinite possibilities because it blends the heritage of so many different peoples. It encourages discourse and deepens friendship, but because the food is brought unbidden by a waiter instead of ordered from a menu, it does not require any action, any decision, any act of choice other than turning away dishes that do not strike one's fancy.* Rakı *can evoke either determination or resignation, a desire to rebel or an acceptance of the inevitability of submission.*

At a meyhane, *the world can be either invited in or shut out. Turks have not yet decided which is the wisest path. By the time they drain their final glasses and step out into the darkness, they have often concluded that their country is either the "golden nation" destined to shape world history or a hopeless mess certain to remain mired in wretched mediocrity.*

• TWO •

THE HERO

One of my Turkish friends is a proud father who has saved the first essay his son ever wrote. The boy was a third-grader when his teacher explained to the class what an essay is, read a few simple ones aloud and then assigned her pupils the topic "love" for their first try. His essay began like this: "Love means love for Atatürk. Love means love for Atatürk's mother, Zübeyde Hanim. Love means love for Atatürk's father, Ali Rıza Bey."

By instinctively associating the deepest human emotion with the person of Mustafa Kemal Atatürk, this young boy showed how fully he had already absorbed the holy creed of the Turks. According to its constitution, Turkey is a secular state with no official religion. But the truth is that Turks profess, and must profess, a highly developed faith enveloping and defining every aspect of their lives. It is the cult of Atatürk, founder of the Turkish Republic and now a virtual deity.

The Atatürk faith, known as Kemalism, has its churches, dozens of houses and rooms around the country where the Great Man slept, spoke or ate; its holy writ, scores of adoring books, poems and films in which his exploits are recounted; its icons, countless portraits, busts, plaques and statues that are to be seen even in the remotest corners of the country; and its clergy, the military and political elite, faithful beyond measure and ceaselessly on the watch for apostates. It also has its holy center, its Vatican, its Mecca. On a hillside near the center of Ankara, imposing and lugubrious behind a wall of forbidding quadrangular columns, stands a combination mausoleum, museum and cathedral beneath whose marble floor Atatürk's body lies interred. On national holidays, the gravest of which is November 10, the day on which he departed this world, huge throngs gather to pay tearful homage to his memory and pledge eternal fidelity to his cause. Visiting heads of state are expected to lay wreaths upon the tomb before they begin their official business. Generals come regularly to rededicate themselves to their role as Kemalism's high priests. Politicians and others who fall under suspicion of heresy unfailingly turn up as a way of proving that they do, in fact, embrace the true faith.

"In this country it is allowed to say bad things about God," one young man told me confidentially soon after I arrived in Turkey, "but it is not allowed to say bad things about Atatürk."

There is much to justify Turkey's reverence for Atatürk. He is the force that allowed Turkey to rise from the ashes of defeat and emerge as a vibrant new nation. Without Atatürk's vision, without his ambition and energy, without his astonishing boldness in sweeping away traditions accumulated over centuries, today's Turkey would not exist and the world would be much poorer.

Kemalism emerged at a time when new ideologies were being born from the rubble of a world laid to waste by the Great War of 1914–18. Fascism, national socialism and bolshevism have been swept away by history, leaving behind a heritage of immeasurable suffering and pain, but Kemalism remains triumphant, modern Turkey its crowning glory. Trying to understand Turkey without understanding Atatürk would be like studying European history without considering Christianity.

Yet a century after Atatürk began his rise to power, the Kemalist faith is in crisis. Its promise of liberation, so vividly fulfilled at the beginning, is fading. Once it embodied reason and progress, the purest principles of the Enlightenment. "For everything in the world—for civilization, for life, for success—the truest guide is knowledge and science," Atatürk declared in one famous speech. But today, many Turks who seek knowledge find themselves victims of Kemalism rather than its paragons.

The man around whom this passionate faith was built remains largely unknown outside his homeland. Perhaps that is because upon assuming power, he concentrated his efforts on building his own nation rather than on conquest. Perhaps it is simply because Turkey has remained for so long on the fringes of the world's consciousness. Whatever the reason, Atatürk's obscurity is unfortunate. He deserves to be recognized and celebrated as one of the twentieth century's most successful revolutionaries. The story of his life and the story of what has become of his legacy embody both Turkey's greatest glories and its most daunting challenges.

This titanic figure was born in 1880 or 1881 to a humble family in Salonika, now the Greek city of Thessaloniki, a thriving port on the outer edge of the crumbling Ottoman Empire. His father was a minor clerk in government service who died young and unhappy. His mother was the family's guiding force, and like many Turkish mothers, Zübeyde Hanim doted on her son. At first he seemed a difficult case, truculent and rebellious, often in trouble at school. Zübeyde, a traditional Muslim woman who spent most of her time at home and was never seen without her head scarf, hoped that he would become a religious teacher or Koran reader. Young Mustafa never showed the slightest interest in following that path. An uncle suggested that he pursue a military career, and with the help of a retired officer who had been a friend of his father's, he arranged to take the entrance examination that led to his admission into the local academy. There he took a surname, Kemal, supposedly after the radical nineteenth-century poet Namık Kemal, one of whose couplets was later to spur him into action:

> The enemy has pressed his dagger to the breast of the motherland.
> Will no one arise to save his mother from her black fate?

As Mustafa Kemal rose rapidly through military ranks, the decadent Ottoman monarchy was in its death throes. The reigning sultan, Abdülhamid II, was an intolerant and narrow-minded tyrant who countenanced no talk of reform. His empire was shrinking steadily, and in 1912 Kemal himself had the chance to watch Balkan rebels win their independence after easily defeating a demoralized Turkish force twice their size. Even the city of his birth fell to advancing Greek patriots shouting "Christ is risen!"

During postings in Istanbul, Tripoli, Cairo, Damascus and Sofia, and in trips to Germany and Austria, Kemal became aware of the wider world and the currents that were surging through it. He learned French and devoured the works of Voltaire and Rousseau, together with translations of Thomas Hobbes and John Stuart Mill. They helped him grasp the great challenge that was to shape his life. "The Turkish nation has fallen far behind the West," he told a German officer he met in the Balkans. "The main aim should be to lead it to modern civilization."

While still a young officer, Kemal became a clandestine operative for a subversive group founded in the 1890s and known as the Committee of Union and Progress; the world called its members Young Turks. In 1913 the committee managed to seize key posts in the Ottoman regime, but war broke out before its work could begin in earnest. Some Young Turks believed that if their country allied itself with Germany, the two powers could ride a wave of re-colonization that would allow both to pursue their imperial dreams. One of them, Minister of Defense Enver Pasha, whose irredentist passion was later to lead the Ottoman Empire to its end and himself to ignominious death while fighting to reclaim Central Asia for the Turks, met secretly with German envoys in a mansion on the shore of the Bosphorus and signed a pact of alliance.

Turkey's experience as an ally of Kaiser Wilhelm's Germany was disastrous, with one shining exception. To the astonishment of Europe and the world, in 1915 a Turkish force managed to resist and then repel British-led invaders whose battle plan had been drawn up by no less a personage than First Lord of the Admiralty Winston Churchill. The battle was fought on the Gallipoli Peninsula overlooking the crucial Dardanelles strait, which the Allies needed to capture if they hoped to control Istanbul and the Black Sea beyond. In fierce fighting that lasted eight months and cost tens of thousands of lives, Turkish soldiers managed to hold their peninsula, keep their strait and ultimately overwhelm the Allied expeditionary force. The commander who achieved this, thereby winning the only important Turkish victory of the war, was Mustafa Kemal. Alone among Turkish officers, he emerged from the Great War as a hero.

With the war ending in defeat for the Germans and their Turkish allies, the German imperial monarchy was overthrown and the once-glorious Ottoman Empire lay prostrate. Triumphant Allied leaders presumed they had won the right to carve up its rich carcass, a huge tract of land stretching from southeastern Europe to the frosty Caucasus and parched Arabian deserts. Under the guidance of Prime Minister David Lloyd George of Great Britain, they decreed that all Turkish territory in Europe, together with most of the lush Aegean coast, where Hellenic civilization had flourished for millennia, would be given to Greece. Armenians and Kurds would be given the chance to form new states in the east. France was awarded a vast "zone of influence" in the south, abutting its territory in what is now Syria. Italy won an even larger zone that encompassed the entire Mediterranean coast and thousands of square miles inland. Istanbul, along with the Bosphorus and the Dardanelles, for which Kemal had fought so brilliantly, was to be placed under international control. All that remained for the Turks themselves was a swath of central Anatolia, much of it mountainous and inhospitable. This was a settlement even more punishing than the one imposed on Germany at Versailles. Three emissaries from the sultan signed it without protest at a ceremony in the Paris suburb of Sèvres on August 10, 1920.

There seemed no way the Turks could resist. Their army was defeated and leaderless, their sultan dispirited and willing to accept the victorious Allies' every dictate. Foreign troops occupied their most historic cities. A French commander had ridden into Istanbul on a white horse, just as Sultan Mehmet the Conqueror had when his Ottoman army captured the city nearly five centuries earlier. Italian forces had landed at Antalya, gateway to the Turkish Mediterranean, and the Greek army had occupied Smyrna, the jewel of Turkey's Aegean coast, and begun annexing the land around it.

As the only Turkish commander with a major battlefield victory to his credit, and a magnificent one at that, Mustafa Kemal was the logical figure around whom this defeated nation could rally. He eagerly embraced the savior's role, winning the loyalty of disaffected officers and denouncing the dying regime in terms so contemptuous that its courts sentenced him to death in absentia. "Cowards, criminals! You are engaged in treasonable conspiracies with the enemy against the nation," he wrote in one telegram to the Ottoman interior minister. "I did not doubt that you would be incapable of appreciating the strength and will of the nation; but I did not want to believe that you would act in this traitorous and murderous way against the fatherland and the nation."

Seeing their homeland on the brink of dismemberment, Turks by the thousands flocked to Kemal's side. He established a National Assembly and shadow government of his own, built an army of eager volunteers and declared war on the foreign powers occupying Anatolia. A chastened Winston Churchill later wrote:

> Loaded with follies, stained with crimes, rotted with misgovernment, shattered by battle, worn down by long disastrous wars, his Empire falling to pieces around him, the Turk was still alive. In his breast was beating the heart of a race that had challenged the world, and for centuries had contended victoriously against all comers. In his hands was once again the equipment of a modern army, and at his head a Captain, who with all that is learned of him, ranks with the four or five great figures of the cataclysm. In the tapestried and gilded chambers of Paris were assembled the law-givers of the world. In Constantinople, under the guns of the Allied Fleets there functioned a puppet Government of Turkey. But among the stern hills and valleys of "the Turkish homeland" in Anatolia, there dwelt that company of poor men . . . who would not see it settled so; and at their bivouac fires at this moment sat in the rags of a refugee the august Spirit of Fair Play.

Kemal's first assaults on positions held by his main adversaries, the Greeks, did not go well. Later he and his growing force returned, better armed and organized, and won several important victories. Finally, in the summer of 1922, the tide turned decisively in their favor. Whipped into a patriotic frenzy by their gifted commander, Turkish troops stormed from their Anatolian heartland toward the Aegean, driving the Greek force before them in frantic retreat and finally pushing it into the sea. Allied contingents posted at the Dardanelles withdrew rather than face this newly self-confident army. French and Italian units along the Mediterranean wisely followed suit. In one of the most astonishing military reversals of modern history, Kemal had turned utter defeat into brilliant triumph, ripping to shreds the Sèvres treaty under which modern Turkey was to have been aborted before it could be born.

A new treaty recognizing new realities now had to be negotiated to replace the one that had been imposed at Sèvres. Its signing in 1922 at Lausanne signaled the arrival on the world scene of two powerful new phenomena: the Republic of Turkey and Mustafa Kemal. Turkey emerged with all the land that the Sèvres treaty had awarded to Greece, Italy, the Kurds and the Armenians, along with most of what had been the French zone. Kemal did not insist on taking Greek islands, many of which are far from Greece and within sight of the Turkish mainland, but he did win a good-size chunk of land on the western side of the Bosphorus, giving the new nation a firm foothold in Europe, where the Ottoman Empire had once controlled much territory. The country he took over was in ruins, devastated not only by war but by the horrible consequences of a "population exchange" agreed upon by Greek and Turkish leaders, in which hundreds of thousands of ethnic Greeks were forced to leave their homes in Turkey, taking their skills with them. Nonetheless, after Lausanne Turks had a homeland where they could work, build and begin to rise again.

With this amazing victory, Kemal had summoned his nation out of the coffin in which it was about to be buried. That alone would have been enough to earn him a secure place in history. But after emerging as Turkey's liberator, he went on to even more extraordinary achievements. The first of them was not something he did, but something he chose not to do: build on his triumph in Anatolia to push farther. He might well have sought to retake European parts of the old empire, at least seizing the city of his birth back from the exhausted Greeks. Or he might have turned eastward, joining with Muslims in Central Asia who were resisting assimilation into the nascent Soviet Union. Instead he renounced pan-Islamic and pan-Turkic ideologies, resisted the expansionist temptation that has brought down so many leaders and took off his military uniform once and forever. Looking about him, he saw a backward nation of twelve million people mired in poverty and ignorance. "The civilized world is far ahead of us," he proclaimed, echoing the view he had first expressed as a cadet. "We have no choice but to catch up."

Perhaps alone in Turkey and even the world, Mustafa Kemal believed that Turks could become everything they had never been: modern, secular, prosperous and, above all, truly European. He became a one-man revolution, pushing and dragging a baffled and sometimes resistant nation toward the radical vision that blazed in his imagination. Earthquake, bomb, whirlwind, cyclone, tornado, tidal wave—none of these metaphors can capture the force of Kemal's impact on his nation.

With no official power, using only the moral authority he had won on the battlefield, Kemal in 1922 ordered his rubber-stamp National Assembly to abolish the Ottoman monarchy. Not even his closest comrades had ever contemplated such a step. "It was by force that the sons of Osman seized the sovereignty and sultanate of the Turkish nation," he told the astonished Assembly. "They have maintained this usurpation for six centuries. Now the Turkish nation has rebelled, has put a stop to these usurpers, and has effectively taken sovereignty and sultanate into its own hands."

On October 29, 1923, the Assembly proclaimed the Turkish Republic and unanimously elected Kemal as its first president. He was forty-two years old, a dashing figure with fair hair and piercing blue eyes, always dressed impeccably from his dandy cravat down to his imported French underwear. His pleasures, like his politics, were Western: dancing, drinking, smoking cigarettes, visiting restaurants and nightclubs, swimming, yachting and seducing women. Since childhood he had been absolutely convinced that he was destined for greatness. "History has proven incontrovertibly," he asserted after taking power, "that success in great enterprises requires the presence of a leader of unshakable capacity and power."

Having abolished the Ottoman regime with the stroke of a pen, Kemal set his sights on an even more sacred institution, the Islamic caliphate. For centuries the caliph had been revered by Muslims everywhere as "God's shadow on earth," and had used his power for political as well as religious ends. For many years the sultan had served simultaneously as caliph, embodying the Ottoman theocracy and ruling with divine as well as earthly authority. But late on the night of March 3, 1924, only sixteen months after the last sultan, Mehmet VI Vahidettin, had fled Istanbul on a British warship, his cousin Abdülmecid, who had been

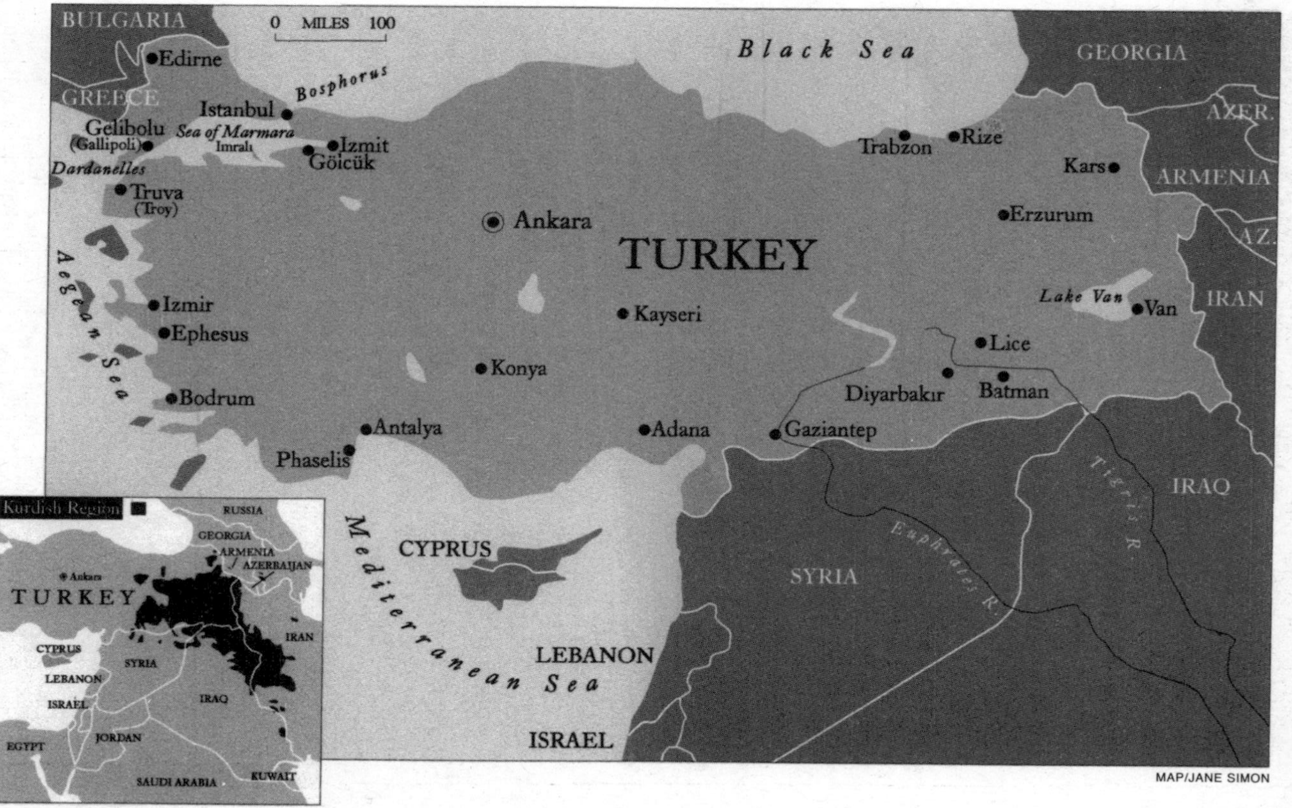

MAP/JANE SIMON

chosen to succeed him as caliph, was visited by an emissary from Atatürk, told that the National Assembly had voted to abolish the caliphate, put aboard a train and packed into exile. This crushing blow to religious power was quickly followed by the dissolution of Islamic courts and a ban on religious brotherhoods. With the same reckless daring he had shown on the battlefield, Kemal had torn down the central pillars of Ottoman political and religious tradition.

After moving his new government to Ankara, a small Anatolian town far from the pleasure domes of Istanbul and infinitely closer to the masses in whose name he was ruling, Kemal continued his demolition work. His next target was the fez, the crimson headgear with a flat top designed to resemble a prayer mat and a tassel meant to symbolize the prospect of escape to Heaven. The fez had been a symbol of Muslim identity in the Ottoman world, but to Kemal it was "an emblem of ignorance, negligence, fanaticism, and hatred of progress and civilization." His will, as ever, was quickly translated into law, and in November 1925 the fez was banned.

"A civilized, international dress is worthy and appropriate for our nation, and we will wear it," Kemal declared. "Boots or shoes on our feet, trousers on our legs, shirt and tie, jacket and waistcoat—and, of course, to complete these, a cover with a brim on our heads. I want to make this clear. This head-covering is called 'hat.' "

Shock waves from this act spread across Turkey and beyond. The chief mufti of Egypt, who since the abolition of the caliphate had become a leading voice of orthodox Islam, proclaimed that any Muslim who wore a hat was an infidel and a sinner, and asserted that the wearing of hats would lead to "the annihilation of our own identity." Such challenges only stirred Kemal to new vigor. Why stop with banning the garb that Islamic men had worn for centuries? The veil must also go, and with it the subservience of women.

"In some places I have seen women who put a piece of cloth or a towel or something like it over their heads to hide their faces, and who turn their backs or huddle themselves on the ground when a man passes by," Kemal said in one speech. "What are the meaning and sense of this behavior? Gentlemen, can the mothers and daughters of a civilized nation adopt this strange manner, this barbarous posture? It is a spectacle that makes the nation an object of ridicule. It must be remedied at once."

Although the veil was not officially banned for several more years, by attacking it Kemal had made clear that he considered nothing sacred simply because it was long-established. Indeed, the opposite seemed to be true. At the end of 1925 he decreed that the Muslim calendar should be replaced with the European one, which dates years from the birth of Christ. The next year he imposed a version of the Swiss civil code that banned polygamy, permitted the marriage of Muslim women to non-Muslim men, gave all adults the right to change their religion and replaced the Muslim practice of "repudiation" with civil divorce (though not before he took advantage of it to "repudiate" his own wife). Later he shifted the weekly day of rest from Friday to Sunday. Finally, in case the point was lost on anyone, his Assembly repealed the constitutional clause stipulating that "the religion of the Turkish state is Islam."

One of the last tangible links connecting Turkey to its Ottoman past and to the rest of the Muslim world, while at the same time separating it from the West, was Arabic script. Turks had always had their own language, but for many centuries had written it with Arabic characters. Breaking with that tradition would mean cutting Turks off from the rich cultural heritage of their ancestors, making it impossible for them to read the words of their own poets, scientists and philosophers. This disturbed Kemal not a whit. He convened a group of specialists to transliterate the Turkish language into Latin letters, and introduced the new alphabet himself at a gala party to which he invited the country's leading figures.

"We must free ourselves from these incomprehensible signs which for centuries have held our minds in an iron vise," he told them. "Our nation will show, with its script and with its mind, that its place is with the civilized world."

Kemal took fewer years to wipe away the defining traditions of Turkish life than centuries had been spent building them. Some of the steps he took were relatively innocuous, such as introducing the metric system and opening a conservatory under the direction of the German composer Paul Hindemith. Others were momentous but grudgingly accepted, such as giving women the rights to vote and hold office. A few were so bitterly resisted that they were ultimately repealed, including a ban on the broadcast of Oriental music and a decree that the *ezan*, the Muslim call to prayer, must be chanted in Turkish rather than Arabic. None of them, however, could have been imposed if Turkey had been a democracy. Great as Kemal's personal prestige was, it alone could not have made his revolution possible. Demolishing the legacy of an ancient nation so suddenly, and imposing such a completely new order on the rubble, required the use of much raw power. Kemal did not shrink from using it.

During the War of Liberation, as Kemal's uprising against the Sèvres treaty came to be known, everyone who wanted to fight against foreign occupiers was welcomed into the revolutionary army. After the war was won, however, Kemal did not hesitate to crush former allies who opposed his radical program. The first challenge came in 1925 from Kurdish tribesmen in the east, who rose up in the name of Islam and called upon God to help them chase the infidels from Ankara. Immediately a "law for the maintenance of order" was pushed through the National Assembly, giving Kemal's government dictatorial powers and establishing "independence courts" with powers of summary execution. Among the first victims were leaders of the Kurdish rebellion; forty-seven were captured, tried and hanged at Diyarbakır, the main Kurdish city. A year later, plotters who sought to assassinate Kemal in the Aegean port of Izmir, formerly known as Smyrna, were sentenced and executed in the same manner. Later the web spread to more peaceful opponents. In all, the "independence courts" dispatched several hundred enemies and critics of the regime. Some victims did not even enjoy its dubious justice. Eighteen leaders of the Turkish Communist Party were put aboard a ship in Trabzon for deportation across the Black Sea to the Soviet Union, but they disappeared somewhere along the way. By 1927 all opposition to Kemalism had been crushed.

Twice Kemal arranged for friends of his to form opposition parties, but both times the parties disappointed him by trying to behave like true opponents. Convinced that his reforms were too important to be debated and delayed, and probably realizing that they horrified many Turks, he banned these parties before they could build popular bases.

With the same conflicting impulses, he praised freedom of the press as a cornerstone of liberty but did not hesitate to silence critical journalists and close their newspapers. "His dictatorship—a benevolent, educating, guiding dictatorship—was the only form of government possible at the moment," concluded one of his first biographers, the British historian H. C. Armstrong. A later historian, Bernard Lewis, elaborated the same conclusion:

> An autocrat by personal and professional bias, dominating and imperious by temperament, he yet showed a respect for decency and legality, for human and political standards, that is in astonishing contrast with the behavior of lesser and more pretentious men. His was a dictatorship without the uneasy over-the-shoulder glance, the terror of the door-bell, the dark menace of the concentration camp. Force and repression were certainly used to establish and maintain the Republic during the period of revolutionary changes, but no longer; and after the executions of 1926 there was little danger to life and personal liberty . . . At the darkest moment in their history, the Kemalist revolution brought new life and hope to the Turkish people, restored their energies and self-respect, and set them firmly on the road not only to independence, but to that rarer and more precious thing that is freedom.

Toward the end of his life, Kemal recognized one more element of Turkish life that reminded him of the hated past. Since time immemorial, Turkish life had been centered on villages and clans small enough that in each there was likely to be only one Abdullah, one Hikmet and one Fatma. Those days were gone, and as a logical result of his Westernizing impulse, Kemal decreed that each citizen must have a last name. The head of every family was ordered to choose one. Some thought first of their fathers, so today there are names like Berberoğlu (barber's son), Karamehmetoğlu (Black Mehmet's son) and even Yarımbıyıkoğlu (son of the man with the half-mustache). Others took martial names like Eraslan (brave lion) or Demirel (iron hand). For those who had trouble choosing, books of names were sent to every town hall. Many people selected lyrical ones like Sarıgül (yellow rose) or Akyıldız (pale star). Only one name was forbidden: Atatürk (Father of the Turks). That was the name Kemal chose for himself. He embraced it, even dropping his first name, Mustafa, which he considered too Arab-sounding. From then until his death of cirrhosis in 1938, he called himself Kemal Atatürk. Under that name, for good and ill, he has become the overwhelming presence in every aspect of Turkish life.

After Atatürk's premature death at the age of fifty-eight, his successors had to make a difficult choice: whether to cling to his program as sacred dogma or adjust it to meet the demands of new times and new generations. That the Hero laid down clear principles and fought for them all his life is indisputable. Yet his central belief was in reason and progress. Certainly he hoped that his successors would march in the vanguard of humanity rather than fight endless rear-guard actions to keep Turks in the political straitjacket into which they had been bound during the 1920s and 1930s.

When Atatürk's successors introduced multiparty democracy in 1950, they gave Turks the right to elect a parliament and by extension a prime minister, as well as mayors and city councils (although not state governors, who to this day are appointed from Ankara). With this step, the country began to embrace the political creed of the Western world to which Atatürk so passionately wanted Turkey to belong. Human rights, free speech and unity in diversity are its pillars.

Not all of today's Kemalists, however, believe in those principles. In the late 1990s one fervent member of this secular priesthood, General Doğu Silahcıoğlu, attended a meeting in the Black Sea town of Samsun at which local officials were making plans for a patriotic celebration. A city councilor ventured the opinion that since Samsun is home to people from various ethnic groups and Muslims of various persuasions, the celebration should emphasize the value of tolerance. That suggestion touched the general's rawest nerve. "Tolerance!" he shouted. "Tolerance is the password of those people with a certain ideology. You cannot use that word here!"

This narrow-mindedness, expressed in a thousand different ways, led many Turks to conclude that Kemalism had lost touch with its revolutionary roots, which is why they supported the civic revolution of 2002. Yet guardians of the old order could honestly say that in their elitism, in their insistence that an "enlightened" vanguard should rule on behalf of the ignorant masses, they were in fact embracing an essential feature of Atatürk's ideology. He had, after all, given his political party the slogan "For the People, In Spite of the People." Popular opinion meant nothing to him, and for generations his successors scorned it as well. They believed that if Turks were allowed to choose the course of their nation, they would make terrible mistakes that would drag it back to the pre-Kemalist era and turn it into a fundamentalist theocracy. This was the fear that gripped them when Tayyip Erdoğan began his rise to power, and this is why they tried so hard to block him.

The Kemalist elite's historic miscalculation lay not in its embrace of Atatürk's ideology but in its refusal to allow that ideology to evolve as Turkey evolved. The winds of freedom that swept across the world in the post-colonial era, and that blew even more powerfully as the Berlin Wall fell and Communism collapsed, brought Turks a vibrant civic consciousness. They became eager to shape their own destiny and unwilling to continue accepting guidance from above. The old elite should have recognized this profound change in national consciousness, accepted it as an embodiment of Atatürk's rebellious spirit and begun stepping back from power. Instead, moved by fear, self-interest and an extraordinary lack of political judgment, it insisted on ruling as it always had. That historic miscalculation turned Kemalism into the enemy of the ideals that gave it birth.

It is one of the great ironies of modern Turkish life that the name of the heroic figure who devoted his life to destroying taboos was used for years to enforce taboos. The authority of the great Westernizer was invoked to justify acts that kept Turkey isolated from the West. Atatürk's obsession was to bring his country into the world's mainstream, but some of his self-appointed heirs worked ceaselessly to prevent this dream from becoming real. In doing so they rejected Atatürk's own passionate belief in progress and ignored one of his last pleas.

"I am leaving no sermon, no dogma, nor am I leaving as my legacy any commandment that is frozen in time or cast in stone," he said shortly before his death. "Concepts of well-being for countries, for peoples and for individuals are changing. In such a world, to argue for rules that never change would be to deny the reality found in scientific knowledge and reasoned judgment."

Half a century after Atatürk's death, Turkey is governed by observant Muslims who abstain from alcohol, pray regularly and observe the Ramadan fast. How would he react to that? Many of his most faithful followers assume he would be horrified. I doubt it. I prefer to believe he would be thrilled to see the country he created breaking out of its autocratic shell and claiming the right to self-government. Rather than be outraged at the emergence of a government that embraces Islam as well as democracy, he might be angry at those who have used his name in a campaign to keep Turkey trapped in the past.

The hero-worship that raised Atatürk to secular sainthood began during his own lifetime and with his blessing. During his early years in power, he approved the erection of monuments to independence that were actually monuments to him. By the end of the 1920s, statues depicting him on horseback or in other martial poses had assumed commanding positions in Ankara, Istanbul, Izmir, Konya and Samsun. In later years, and especially after his death, they became such a common feature of the Turkish landscape that today they are hardly noticed. No town or village or neighborhood is without one. At every school in the country, every day begins with pupils assembling before one of these icons and pledging eternal loyalty to Kemalism. The cult has even come to embrace Atatürk's mother, who by the act of giving birth to him is now held up as the ideal of Turkish womanhood.

The sanctity of Atatürk's person is protected not just by tradition and social pressure but also by law. Statute 5816 establishes the crime of "cursing Atatürk's memory," punishable by up to three years in jail, and that of damaging or destroying statues or busts of him, punishable by up to five years at hard labor. In many communities the police also enforce regulations, especially odd in light of Atatürk's own habits, that ban the serving of alcohol anywhere near monuments dedicated to him.

Trying to count the images of Atatürk in Turkey would be akin to counting the stars in the sky. His gaze is quite literally inescapable. It stares sternly from every coin and banknote and from the wall of virtually every shop, office, restaurant, *meyhane*, hotel lobby, bank, cinema and tea house. Judges, prosecutors, provincial bureaucrats, military commanders, school principals and others who consider themselves part of the Kemalist vanguard often display five or ten or more, not just photographs but also paintings, etchings, busts, engraved paperweights, ceramic plates and whatever else they can find. No form of veneration is considered too extreme or too vulgar. In Kars, near the Armenian border, an enormous silhouette of Atatürk dominates the ruins of a twelfth-century citadel. Another is painted in white on the side of a mountain near the Anatolian city of Erzurum. In Gaziantep, a provincial capital in the south, the governor's conference room is decorated with no less than fifty images, truly a blinding spectacle.

There is a ludicrous quality to this excess, and a dark side too, since anyone who does not join the ostentation is immediately suspected of insufficient patriotism or worse. But pressure to conform to the official ideology is not the only reason Turks surround themselves with these graven images. Respect and grateful admiration for Atatürk, and even a mystical attachment to him that resembles love, are widespread and genuine.

I too succumbed to these feelings, and although I came to question some tenets of the Kemalist faith, I kept two pictures of the old man on my office wall. They are not the usual portraits, most of which show him frowning like a harsh schoolmaster. In one he is on a swing, dressed in a natty three-piece suit but with what looks like a mischievous smile on his face, his legs extended in front of him. The other is even more subversive, showing him as a young man at a costume ball. For the occasion he chose to dress as a member of the Janissary corps, the elite guard that had protected Ottoman sultans, with an elaborate headdress and two richly embroidered vests. In his right hand he holds the hilt of a sword that he seems ready to pull from its scabbard at the slightest provocation.

Both of these images depict the Atatürk I like to imagine: the transgressor, the adventurer, the lover of life. Unlike many of those who today claim his mantle, Atatürk eagerly grasped the opportunities presented by a rapidly changing world. He understood that Turkey can become modern only by embracing modern values. It is in his true image, not in the distorted one promoted by the modern Kemalist elite, that the new Turkey is being shaped.

A charge of emotion surged through my body as I placed my hand against a crumbling wall on a field near Turkey's Aegean shore. Poseidon claimed to have built it: "Indeed I built a wall around their city for the Trojans, a broad and very beautiful wall to make the place impregnable." It was below this wall that the enraged Achilles chased Hector "three times around the city of Priam" before overtaking and killing him. Afterward he tied Hector's body to his chariot and dragged it around the citadel while Priam and other Trojan heroes watched in horror. Within sight of this wall, events unfolded that serve as the wellspring of Western civilization. On the day I stood beside it there was not a soul in sight on Homer's "vast, untilled and mountain-shirted plain." It was several minutes before I could bring myself to pull back my hand.

Skeptics have long argued that Homer's epics were fiction. In 1796 a professor at Cambridge University published "A Dissertation Concerning the War of Troy and the Expedition of the Grecians as described by Homer, showing that no such expedition was ever taken and that no such city of Phrygia existed." Slowly, however, as the science of archaeology began to develop, curious seekers combed Homer's epics for clues and compared what they found to the topography of what is now Turkey's northwest coast. In the 1870s a German businessman named Heinrich

Schliemann, an amateur archaeologist whose main experience with digging had been during the California gold rush, found what he believed was the true site. He even discovered a hoard of jewelry and other artifacts that he quickly announced was "Priam's Treasure." Much of what Schliemann found, including the treasure, turned out not to have been what he believed it to be, but he had indeed found Troy.

Several later expeditions built on Schliemann's work, and in 1988 American and German archaeologists launched an intensive new excavation project at the site. On my visits to their dig I found them reluctant to answer my questions about the historical accuracy of Homer's epics. They are, after all, scientists whose business is uncovering verifiable secrets of the past, not speculating on the relationship between literature and truth. Nonetheless, they cannot help being acutely aware that they are not digging at the site of just another ancient settlement. Their work and that of their predecessors has proven conclusively that there was a Troy and that they have found it. It also strongly suggests that a great battle was fought there around 1250 B.C.*, exactly the period of Homer's Trojan War. Since I allow myself to draw conclusions that go slightly beyond what scientists might accept, and since, like so many people over the eons, I have been thrilled by the Homeric epics, these findings persuade me that Achilles, Odysseus, Agamemnon and their noble comrades all gazed upon the very wall I touched.*

Ever since Homer composed his epics twenty-seven centuries ago, an unbroken though not unchallenged tradition has held that his "meadow of Asia" was at the edge of a cape overlooking the southern entrance to the Dardanelles, the strait then known as the Hellespont, and that his "well-walled city of Troy" stood on a floodplain near the coast. Both Herodotus and Thucydides wrote of the city and of a great war fought there. Although no one knew the city's exact location, it has long been presumed not only that the Trojan War was a historical event but that it crystallized the age-old conflict between Asia and Europe.

Before Xerxes led his Persian army against Greece in 480 B.C.*, he stopped at the peninsula where Troy had stood and sacrificed a thousand oxen to Athena in the hope that she would bless his campaign. When Alexander the Great, who supposedly carried a copy of* The Iliad *with him on campaigns, set off from Macedonia to reverse the tide of*

Persian conquest in 334 B.C., he visited the same site to pray to the spirit of Achilles, his greatest hero and role model. Julius Caesar considered moving his capital there from Rome, but the move was aborted by his assassination. Constantine also thought of making it the capital of his empire before choosing Byzantium, which he renamed Constantinople in his own honor.

Crusaders later justified their wars partly on their desire to bring Troy, or at least the land on which it had stood, back under European control. "Troy belonged to our ancestors, and they escaped and went to live in the land from whence we have come; and it is because they were our ancestors that we have come hither to conquer their land," the crusader Peter of Bracheaux told an opposing commander during the Fourth Crusade, which lasted from 1202 to 1204. Two and a half centuries later, after taking Constantinople for the Turks in 1453, Sultan Mehmet the Conqueror traveled to the plain and declared that his triumph was Asia's long-delayed vengeance for Greece's defeat of the Trojans.

Archaeologists have identified nine distinct cities that existed on these "proud heights" over a period of more than three thousand years. The one they call Troy VI is probably the one that existed when the Trojan War was supposedly fought. As early as 1902 the archaeologist Wilhelm Dörpfeld, who spent years excavating Troy VI, had found enough evidence to convince him that it "was thoroughly destroyed by enemy action." Discoveries since then have lent much support to his view. The wall of Troy VI, which was excavated in 1995, was the one on which I laid my hand.

Some have suggested that the Trojan War may have been nothing more than a minor pirate raid, or that Homer drew on accounts of various conflicts to invent a single great one. I choose not to believe that, though admittedly my reasons are emotional rather than scientific. Like most romantics, I want there to have been a Trojan War and am overjoyed that so much evidence has emerged to suggest that there was. I hope the archaeologists who guided me on my visits to the site, or perhaps their successors, will find what even they can accept as conclusive proof.

Compared with other ancient sites that have been uncovered in

Turkey, Troy is only modestly impressive. Without the timeless aura that Homer gave it, it might not even rank among the hundred most interesting ones. But there is something quite extraordinary about the entrance to the Dardanelles that would make the place fascinating even if Homer had never written about it. This strait, together with the Bosphorus to the north, is the greatest strategic prize in a region over which nations have fought for ages. In ancient times sailors had to put ashore at the southern entrance to the Dardanelles to wait for favorable winds. Troy was then on the coast rather than two and a half miles inland, as it is today, and those who controlled it could extort whatever tribute they wanted in exchange for allowing these sailors free passage toward the Black Sea. Simple geography explains why so many battles have been fought for control of the Dardanelles. The Trojan War was probably one of them.

Each time I visit Troy I take time to stop at a spot on the other side of the strait that is equally pregnant with memories of war, death and heroism. It is Gallipoli, the place where rivers of blood were spilled during one of the fiercest battles of World War I. Since most of the fighting there took place in an area of only two or three square miles, everywhere a visitor treads is likely to be a soldier's grave. There are thirty-one cemeteries on this narrow spit of land, fields of gravestones with inscriptions like this one: "Trooper G. R. Seager. 7 August 1915. Age 17. He Died a Man & Closed His Life's Brief Day Ere It Had Scarce Begun."

When Winston Churchill planned the Allied assault on Gallipoli, he had every reason to be confident of victory. Britain was at the peak of its imperial might, and the ragged Turks who held the peninsula were the last gasp of dying Ottoman power. But the invading force, which included many soldiers from Australia and New Zealand, found Turkish defenders astonishingly tenacious and willing to take staggering casualties. For most of 1915 the two armies fought from trenches that were often less than ten yards apart. Finally the invaders were forced to withdraw in defeat, many of them recording in letters and diaries their newfound respect for Turkish fighting men.

Today many Australians and New Zealanders consider Gallipoli to have been a crucible in which the identities of their young nations were forged. Hardly a day passes without visitors from one country or the other walking somberly over its gentle hills, and each year on April 25, the anniversary of the Allied landing, diplomats from Australia, New Zealand, Britain and Turkey gather there for solemn memorial services. But perhaps the most significant result of the campaign was the emergence of Mustafa Kemal, the victorious commander who went on to become President Kemal Atatürk.

In 1934 Atatürk learned that a ship carrying relatives of fallen Allied soldiers had docked near Gallipoli and that its passengers were mourning at the site. He sent them a moving message that is now chiseled, in English translation, into a memorial stone there. "Those heroes that shed their blood and lost their lives," he wrote, "you are now lying in the soil of a friendly country. Therefore rest in peace. There is no difference between the Johnnies and the Mehmets to us, where they lie side by side in this country of ours . . . You, the mothers who sent their sons from faraway countries, wipe away your tears. Your sons are now lying in our bosom and are in peace. After having lost their lives on this land, they have become our sons as well."

The Trojan War and the Battle of Gallipoli were fought on fields almost within sight of each other. Churchill wanted the Dardanelles so that Britain could send Allied warships through to supply Russia's Black Sea ports, perhaps giving Russia enough power to attack Austria-Hungary from the east. Greeks attacked Troy, I believe, not to avenge the kidnapping of a Spartan queen but for the same reason Churchill did: to win control of the strait. These campaigns, fought more than three thousand years apart, reflect the patterns, symmetries and repetitions in which history delights. Nowhere does history delight in them as fully as in the land now called Turkey.

· THREE ·

CALL TO PRAYER

One of my Turkish friends is a famous journalist whose name and face are familiar to almost everyone in the country. He has traveled the world, written insightful books and interviewed dozens of world leaders. Educated, urbane, charming and articulate in several languages, he is a paragon of the modern Turk.

Part of what qualifies my friend for membership in the Turkish elite is that he comes from a rigorously secular background. He has never said a prayer and readily—almost proudly—admits that he cares little and knows less about Islam.

"Take me into a mosque and I would have no idea what to do," he once told me. "I don't know how to pray. No one ever taught me, and I was never interested in learning. Religion is like an alien planet to me."

One of the glories of modern Turkey is that it has produced a class of people who feel comfortable expressing their lack of religious belief. That glory is incomplete, however, because the state has not shown equal tolerance to believers. Its equation is simple. A Turk who is modern and embraces correct principles is one in whose life religion plays a marginal role or none at all. Believers, on the other hand, are backward provincials who are caught in the grip of primitive superstition and fail or refuse to embrace the modernizing ethos that is supposed to be the foundation of Turkish life.

Over the course of the twentieth century, this attitude alienated the Turkish state from much of the society it was supposed to reflect and serve. In any country, political movements succeed only when they address people's cultural as well as ideological longings. Many, perhaps most, Turks are pious Muslims, and my agnostic friend in Istanbul does not represent them. Nor does the Kemalist elite. Its radical form of secularism, which views religious belief and religious believers as threats to the state, never penetrated the hearts of most Turks. It offered a political program that not only lacked a spiritual component but seemed to reject as retrograde the very idea that people thirst for spiritual solace. That cut the link that was supposed to bind government to the governed. It also set the stage for the emergence of a movement that claimed to be based on the two principles most anathema to the old elite: true democracy and true religious tolerance.

The zealous officers who conceived and built the Turkish Republic believed that religion could be domesticated by fiat. Their official history asserts that Turks "adopted and rapidly assimilated" Atatürk's sweeping secular reforms. Today, however, that conclusion looks dubious. In much of the country's heartland, religious belief remains strong. Mosques are full, women wear head scarves and imams command great moral authority.

In other countries where Muslim believers rise up to challenge secular regimes, deep polarization threatens to upset stable societies as growing majorities reject suffocating state control. That has not happened in Turkey. On the contrary, the emergence of Tayyip Erdoğan's new regime may be seen as a profoundly stabilizing development. It gives pious Turks, who for generations were unwelcome in public life, a sense that they are a valuable and integral part of their nation. The new class from which they spring is not confrontational. It seeks not revenge on the old elite but a society in which Muslims can worship as they wish.

No fear at all, not even the fear of their country being torn apart by foreign enemies or ethnic separatists, defined the old ruling elite so profoundly as the fear of Islamic fundamentalism. This is not hard to understand. Turks lived under a form of religious rule for centuries and did not emerge from it until Atatürk's revolution in the 1920s. One of their neighbors, Iran, is ruled by repressive mullahs, and the sheiks who run the nearby Persian Gulf states are in some ways even more radically Islamic. Afghanistan is farther away geographically, but not far enough. Powerful figures in these countries consider Turkey a heretical state that has betrayed its Islamic roots and must somehow be brought back into the fold. So it is reasonable and indeed essential that Turkey be on guard against fundamentalism.

For eight decades the state maintained this vigilance. No mosque could be built without the permission of a powerful and well-financed state agency called the Religious Affairs Directorate. This same agency paid the salaries of most imams, closely monitored what they said in their sermons and often even sent them texts that they were required to read to their congregations. It worked closely with the ministry of education, which regulated religious schools and provided all texts from which religion was taught; it was a crime to publish others. If a dozen friends began meeting regularly to discuss religious topics, they could expect a police raid and prosecution for operating an "illegal Koran school." Prosecutors also jumped to indict anyone who publicly suggested that religion should play a greater role in national life. When Muslims slaughtered sheep during the annual Feast of Sacrifice and followed tradition by donating the sheepskins to charity, they were required to donate every skin to a specific government-sponsored charity. Otherwise, it was feared, they would give the skins to religious groups that would sell them to raise money for suspicious projects.

These practices violated modern concepts of free choice and the privacy of religious belief. They also led many Turks to view the state as an enemy. In other Muslim countries, such disaffected citizens might have isolated themselves in religious communities, turned to fundamentalism and plotted God's vengeance. Because Turkey offered genuine democratic opportunities, however, they turned outward instead of inward.

In every culture that has existed over the entire course of human history, people have sought answers to the great mysteries of existence. Invariably they turn to religion. Governments often seek ways to separate religion from state policy, but they cannot hope to crush it. Wise leaders, even the most atheistic among them, know they must balance the sacred and secular impulses in their societies. Those who governed the Turkish Republic for the first eighty years of its existence were unable or unwilling to strike that balance. This led many Muslims to conclude that they had to choose between their religious faith and allegiance to the state. No state has ever prevailed in such a confrontation.

Atatürk's scorched-earth campaign against religious power set the stage for this conflict. He had bitter memories of his years at a Muslim primary school, where pupils were made to memorize long passages from the Koran and robed imams cudgeled those who faltered. Many of the European writers he discovered in his teenage years were militantly anti-clerical, as were the positivist Turkish thinkers whose works he devoured. The Young Turk circles to which he gravitated as a cadet included some who drank alcohol and ate ham to show their modernity.

The sultan's meek subservience to foreign powers after World War I, not to mention his proclamation that independence fighters were apostates and that killing them was a religious duty of all true Muslims, led Atatürk to conclude that traditional Islam was the enemy of both reason and national dignity. "Can a civilized nation tolerate a crowd of people who let themselves be led by the nose by sheiks, dervishes and the like," he demanded, "and who entrust their faith and their lives to fortune-tellers, magicians, witch doctors and amulet-makers?"

When Atatürk declared soon after taking power that he intended to lead Turkey along "the path of civilization," he certainly wanted that path to lead away from state-sponsored religion. He was not reckless or foolish enough to break publicly with Islam, and during the War of Liberation he was even photographed praying in public. But as president he banned mystic religious sects, forbade the wearing of religious garb and denounced "superstitions dwelling in people's minds." In an assault on religious authority comparable to Luther's, he ordered the Koran translated into Turkish so that ordinary people could read it for themselves rather than relying on the interpretations of Islamic teachers. When a British correspondent asked him about his own beliefs, he replied: "I have no religion, and at times I wish all religions at the bottom of the sea."

As Turkey moved toward democracy in the years after Atatürk's death, it was inevitable that some of his draconian sanctions on organized religion would be eased. Leaders of his own Republican People's Party began the process by authorizing Koran courses, opening schools for training imams and establishing a theology department at Ankara

University. The process accelerated after the party suffered a crushing defeat in Turkey's first free election in 1950. Adnan Menderes, who was elected prime minister in that year, was a secularist, but he did not detest or fear religious practice, as many Kemalists did. Soon after his election, religious schools and academies were opened in many cities. Islamic books and periodicals began appearing. The law requiring that the Muslim call to prayer be chanted in Turkish was repealed, and mosques were equipped with loudspeakers so that everyone could hear it in the original Arabic. Throngs turned out to protest whenever religious figures were brought to trial for violating one or another restriction on their practice. The number of people making pilgrimages to Mecca grew steadily.

Within a few years the new regime began to lose popularity, and sought to regain it by identifying even more fully with Islam. To a certain degree it succeeded, especially in rural areas, where the pull of tradition remained strong. But military commanders, disturbed by growing political and economic troubles as well as by what they saw as the regime's infidelity to Kemalist principles, grew increasingly unhappy. In 1960 they staged a coup, overthrew Menderes and imposed a regime of young officers. There was jubilation in the streets, but joy turned to horror when Menderes and two of the cabinet ministers ousted with him were arrested, hauled before a military tribunal, convicted of treason and hanged. Some Turks considered them martyrs to their faith.

Menderes's success at mobilizing pious Muslims made it inevitable that budding politicians would now recognize Islam as a powerful political force. One of the first to do so was a young engineer named Necmettin Erbakan. The son of an enthusiastically Kemalist judge, Erbakan had been educated in Germany, and after returning home had sought unsuccessfully to be named as a parliamentary candidate by an established center-right party. Stung by his rejection, he established his own party, National Order, in 1970. Soon he was barnstorming across Turkey, rousing the faithful with calls for a return to religious values. When the army staged a second coup in 1971, Erbakan and other National Order leaders were not arrested, as were leaders of leftist parties. A court later banned the party for fomenting fundamentalism, however, and Erbakan moved temporarily to Switzerland.

After a while, Erbakan received word from Ankara that conservative politicians and perhaps even some military officers wanted him back. The student unrest that had already shaken America, Mexico and Europe had arrived in Turkey. Marxist ideologies were spreading. Generals feared that the election they had called for 1973 would not turn out as they wished, and they hoped that Erbakan would pull votes away from Süleyman Demirel, whom they mistrusted, and would possibly attract voters who might otherwise lean toward populist parties.

By cooperating with Erbakan, Kemalists were not only deciding to embrace religious politics but quite consciously choosing Sunni Islam, the branch to which most Turks belong and of which Erbakan was a leading symbol, over the more tolerant, heterodox Alevi tradition. They decreed that all religious education was to be in the Sunni doctrine, as it remains to this day, and in a variety of ways made clear that they favored Sunnis over Alevis. This angered and still angers the Alevis, who make up about one-fourth of the Turkish population, because they consider themselves Turkey's true democrats. Their tolerance of alcohol, their belief that Muslims need not pray in mosques, their refusal to fast during Ramadan, their conviction that pilgrimages to Mecca are less important than the pilgrimage into one's own heart—all of these are beliefs that Atatürk certainly would have favored over those of the Sunnis. In fact, Alevis suffered for centuries because of their resistance to the sultans, and they rallied enthusiastically to Atatürk's side when he rose in rebellion. Today's Kemalists are not sure what to make of them. They see Alevis as guarantors of the secular state but fear them because many of them resist authority and are by nature skeptics, individualists and freethinkers.

As part of their blind refusal to recognize that their country is made up of communities with coherent identities, Turkish leaders have for decades sought to deny the Alevi reality. That has pushed Alevis steadily away from the political mainstream and toward leftist political movements. It has also led Sunnis to attack them, sometimes with terrible violence. Many of the massacres during the late 1970s that were officially portrayed as clashes between rightists and leftists were actually cases of Sunnis massacring Alevis, most horribly during a spasm of violence in 1978 around Kahramanmaraş in southern Turkey, where scores were killed. In 1993 a mob of Sunni fundamentalists set fire to a hotel in Sivas where pro-Alevi intellectuals were holding a conference, killing thirty-five of those inside as police officers stood by.

Necmettin Erbakan, the politician who Kemalists once hoped would seduce Turks away from leftism, was an orthodox Sunni. His more than thirty years in public life established him as a truly historic figure, and the story of religious politics in Turkey is also his story. Fate and his own hard work gave him a historic chance to reshape Turkey by forging a synthesis between modernity and conservative religious values. He failed miserably, and his country is still paying the price.

After his return from exile in Switzerland, Erbakan became increasingly popular. His new party, called National Salvation, never won broad support but was successful enough at the polls to make him a kingmaker. During the 1970s he joined two coalition governments as deputy prime minister. In a remarkably short time he had risen from a position as an outsider and virtual fugitive to the citadel of state power.

Over the years that followed, National Salvation grew steadily more radical. The 1979 Islamic revolution in Iran inspired its members, and at rallies they began chanting "Khoumeni in Iran, in Turkey Erbakan!" In September 1980, one of its rallies in Konya degenerated into violence as militants smashed the windows of tourist hotels and ransacked shops where alcohol was being sold. They shouted slogans calling for Islamic law, and when a band struck up the national anthem, they drowned it out with chants of "We want the Koran!"

That was too much for the authorities. Several dozen of the rioters were arrested, and Erbakan was warned to curb his rhetoric. But the episode was quickly overshadowed by a much more profound event, the military coup of September 12, 1980, whose leaders soon issued a decree dissolving all political parties. By then, however, Erbakan had become the unchallenged leader of the Islamic political movement. He knew that whatever else happened in Turkey, an army of believers was awaiting his command.

The dour generals who seized power in September 1980 hoped to use Islam as a counterweight to liberal and radical ideologies that were gaining strength in Turkey. They authorized the training of more imams and opened scores of religiously oriented high schools called *imam hatip*. Apparently they never imagined that these schools would produce a class of Turks who rejected not only socialism but also Kemalism. Among their thousands of graduates was Tayyip Erdoğan.

The military officers who held power until 1983, and then organized an election from which, much to their dismay, Turgut Özal emerged as prime minister, also issued an extraordinary decree permanently banning most of the country's precoup political leaders from public life. That struck Özal as undemocratic, and in 1987 he called a national referendum on the question of whether to lift the ban. On the night of the vote, one of my friends was with Özal as he awaited the results.

"Around midnight, an aide came in and reported, 'The voting is very close. It could go either way,' " he told me. "Özal looked up and said, 'As far as I'm concerned, I hope it passes. Any politician who's popular enough to win votes should be allowed to compete.' The aide looked at him for a second, then nodded his head and left. A couple of hours later he showed up again and told us, 'Good news! It passed.' "

Among those who were now free to return to the political arena was Erbakan. He took back the reins of his Welfare Party, and Muslims who had come to view him as a religious warrior jumped fervently back into the fray. Soon Welfare was electing mayors around the country, capping its campaign with Erdoğan's astonishing victory in Istanbul. Most Welfare mayors performed exceptionally well, setting new standards for honesty and seriously addressing chronic problems like sewage treatment, public transit and others that confront cities around the world.

Welfare also became the first party in Turkey to emphasize grassroots political organizing. Passionately committed party volunteers, many of them women, did not simply arrive on doorsteps to ask for votes at election time. They made it their business to know the needs of their neighbors all year long, and to ensure that no one who sought the party's aid went unsatisfied. Through their efforts thousands of hungry Turks were fed, the homeless sheltered and the sick given medicine. In big cities, party workers waited at bus stations to greet migrants who had abandoned their bleak lives in rural provinces to search for work and prosperity. Many arrived without a clue of how to begin, so Welfare found them places to sleep and, in many cases, jobs at factories owned by pious businessmen. Naturally, their gratitude was limitless; many became not simply Welfare voters but enthusiastic organizers.

Erbakan brought to Turkey the same campaign techniques that have worked for political bosses from the Peróns in Argentina to the Daleys in Chicago. He also alarmed the establishment by showing how effectively he could turn the religious zeal of his followers into victory at the polls. The core of his support remained among political Muslims, but by most estimates these Islamists comprised only 7 or 8 percent of the Turkish electorate. Erbakan's party was winning far more votes than that. Obviously he was attracting voters who were not especially religious. All they shared was disgust for the self-serving political establishment.

In the campaign leading up to the 1995 national election, Erbakan emerged as a potent force. He was then sixty-nine years old and master of an avuncular, didactic political style that resembled that of a religious teacher. In fact, he was universally known as "Hoca," a title usually reserved for such teachers.

One day during this campaign, I stopped into a small antiques store in Ankara, and while bargaining for a silver-framed mirror that struck my fancy I learned a little about the proprietor. He was in his mid-twenties, full of ambition and obviously bright. His girlfriend was Austrian, and he flew to Vienna to see her whenever he could scrape together the plane fare. Other than dreaming of her, his favorite pastimes were drinking *rakı* and dancing in discos until the wee hours. When I asked him which party he was voting for, he immediately replied, "Welfare."

I was astonished and told him so. Here was a budding capitalist with a Christian girlfriend who spent his free time drinking and dancing. He was about to cast his ballot for a party that preached religious chauvinism, considered alcohol a tool of the devil and wanted to turn Turkey away from the West and toward a new brotherhood of Islamic states. How could this be? The answer came in a tirade that shocked me with its intensity.

"Politics in this country is totally corrupt," my new friend began, shaking his finger in my face. "Politicians only care about their privileges and keeping themselves in power. Everyone knows the problems this country faces, but no one does anything to solve them because that would mean shaking up the power structure. I tried to start a shop in my village, but so many people wanted bribes that I finally had to give up.

No one expects this place to run like Switzerland, but things have gone too far. I've had it! Welfare is the only honest party. They aren't in politics for what they can steal. They really want to serve. I'm ready for them."

Many Turks shared these views. Thoroughly disgusted with mainstream parties, they were willing to take a chance with Welfare. Some shared Erbakan's religiosity. Others were simply looking for a way to rebel—peacefully, as is the Turkish way—against stifling Kemalist orthodoxy.

Erbakan campaigned far more effectively than his secular rivals, who arrived at rallies in helicopters as if descending from Olympus, deigning to allow their supporters to see and hear them for a few minutes and then rising again into the clouds. For Erbakan a city rally was a half-day event involving visits to nearby villages, tea with respected elders, a speech laced with intoxicating promises of the "just order" to come and then a couple of hours of baby-kissing and earnest hearing of private grievances. Erbakan was the only candidate who gave the impression of caring for ordinary Turks. More important, he was the only one who stood for an idea. In that sense he was a refreshing reaction to the end of ideology in Turkey, to a system in which politicians no longer believed much of anything and competed simply for personal power. Unfortunately, his idea, depending on the day, sounded unrealistic, silly or downright terrifying.

"We will create an Islamic currency," Erbakan promised in one fiery speech a few weeks before the election. In another he went further, pledging "an Islamic United Nations, an Islamic NATO and an Islamic version of the European Union." In a third he vowed to launch a jihad to recapture Jerusalem, rescue Turkey from "the unbelievers of Europe" and finally seize the reins of world power now held by "imperialism and Zionism, as well as Israel and a handful of champagne-drinking collaborators in the conglomerates that feed it." Rapturous crowds cheered wildly.

The 1995 election turned out to be the closest in Turkish history, with less than two percentage points separating the top three parties, but that was not the big story. To the astonishment of almost everyone, Welfare finished first, taking slightly more than 21 percent of the vote. It owed its victory to a split between the country's two ethically bankrupt center-right leaders, former prime ministers Tansu Çiller and Mesut Yılmaz, whose parties took 20 percent each. Secular Turks were in shock. "This was the worst-case scenario," one newspaper columnist told me despondently after the results were announced.

Military commanders and other pillars of the Kemalist elite looked frantically for a way to keep Erbakan from the prime minister's job. They managed to push Çiller and Yılmaz into a coalition, but from their first day in power the titular partners fought like scorpions, and their government soon collapsed. Erbakan was back at center stage.

Although Welfare had finished first in the election, its 21 percent entitled it to less than a third of the seats in Parliament. To win the job of prime minister, Erbakan needed an ally. No secular leader wanted to join him, but he guessed there was one he could persuade: the utterly amoral Tansu Çiller. On the surface it seemed an odd if not impossible marriage. Çiller had run the most militantly anti-Islamist campaign of any candidate, warning that a Welfare government would "bury Turkey in darkness." She had even publicly revived an old charge that Erbakan was financing his movement by heroin smuggling. But under the circumstances, these two cynics needed each other. Erbakan was prepared to make any deal that would bring him to power; Çiller needed protection from a wave of corruption charges. Bring me your votes in Parliament, he told her, and we'll form a coalition that will make those nasty charges go away.

Çiller jumped at the offer, and the malodorous deal was struck. On a June afternoon six months after his victory at the polls, a beaming Erbakan emerged from President Süleyman Demirel's official residence in Ankara. "I have very good news for you," he told waiting reporters. "A new government has been formed."

All eyes were now on Erbakan. If he could reassure Turks of his commitment to the nation's hallowed secular principles, he might strengthen civilian authority, diminish the army's influence in politics and prove that politicians of all stripes could compete under the broad Kemalist umbrella. Even if in his heart he believed Turkey needed to change course to embrace the "just order" of which he so often spoke, he had to realize that his first step must be to win his people's trust. Nearly 80 percent of Turkish voters had cast their ballots for secular parties, and many feared and detested him. Now he had a chance to show that he embodied not religious fanaticism but simple Anatolian conservatism. By doing so he would be carrying out a mission of profound importance to Islam, Turkey and the cause of democracy.

The first sign that Erbakan would fail in this mission came the very day that President Demirel accepted his new government. Instead of reassuring the nation, Erbakan began dispensing utopian wisdom. He had not simply formed a government, he told reporters outside Demirel's residence, but reinvented Turkey.

"The other parties are finished," he declared. "In the first place, they have no identity, no character. They only want to imitate the West. That is a sickness. Their second mistake is their strongly capitalistic economic program, which helps a very small elite and leaves the rest of our people in misery. And their third mistake is that they are against religion. These parties have been hostile to religion for fifty years. They act as if there is no such thing as religion."

Turkey was now in a state of almost unbearable suspense. The entire nation was waiting for a signal that would show which way their new leader wanted to take the country. They did not have to wait long. Only a few weeks after taking office, Erbakan announced that he was departing on a foreign trip that would include a stop in Iran, then ruled by oppressive and fanatically anti-Western mullahs. When he got there, they welcomed him like a long-lost brother.

Upon returning home, Erbakan declared that his trip to Iran was only the beginning of a campaign for worldwide Muslim solidarity, which, he vowed, would return Turkey to the position of Islamic leadership that it had held during the centuries when Istanbul was the seat of the Muslim caliphate. Evidently he had convinced himself that he was free to pull Turkey away from its Western mooring. That was a wild miscalculation.

"A party that won only twenty-one percent of the vote has no right to change Turkish foreign policy," Mesut Yılmaz, leader of the center-right Motherland Party, protested. "There is no consensus in Turkey for such a change." Instead of heeding this and other similar warnings, Erbakan pressed on.

Soon after returning from Tehran he set off to embrace the Libyan tyrant Muammar el-Qaddafi, but he found Qaddafi in a foul mood. Far from showing gratitude to Erbakan for facing the wrath of Western powers by making this pilgrimage to his pariah state, the mercurial Bedouin used the visit as an opportunity to vent his hatred of every principle for which Turkey had come to stand. He received Erbakan and his party in a tent on the outskirts of Tripoli, and the moment they were seated he launched into a bitter tirade. "Turkey's foreign policy is wrong from A to Z," he shouted at the beginning of his harangue. "Turkey, a country under American control, has opened up its soil to American bases. As if that was not enough, it has concluded an accord with Israel, the enemy of Islam, and entered into military cooperation with it." He heaped scorn on Turkey for coming "under occupation" by Western powers, denounced its membership in NATO and issued a heretical call for cutting the country apart to give Kurds their own state. "Turkey has lost its will. Turkey's future lies not in NATO, U.S. bases and repressing the Kurds, but in its nobility and its past. Kurdistan should be established. I am talking about the Kurdish nation. This nation should have its place under the Middle Eastern sun."

The monologue was shocking enough, but Erbakan's response, or lack of it, infuriated even many of his friends. Rather than protest, he stared quietly upward as he listened, a beatific smile on his face. It was as if he loved the sound of words he wished to speak himself but dared not.

Turks, who have traditionally looked down on Arabs as ignorant and uncivilized, were enraged. Mass-circulation newspapers carried banner headlines like CATASTROPHE IN LIBYA, NIGHT OF SHAME and QADDAFI'S RAVINGS. A report in the secularist paper *Sabah* began, "A barefoot Bedouin stood in front of Erbakan and the Turkish delegation last night and hurled insults at Turkey." Even the Islamic-oriented *Zaman* was scandalized, with its correspondent writing: "Qaddafi's bitter words had the effect of a machine gun being fired at Erbakan. It was as if an atom bomb had fallen on the tent." One of Erbakan's own cabinet ministers described Qaddafi's words as "lunatic nonsense."

Erbakan gave not the slightest indication that he disapproved of anything his host had said. Floating blissfully above the drumbeat of criticism, he embarked on a series of domestic projects that seemed calculated to drive Kemalists crazy. First he proposed that female civil servants be allowed to wear head scarves, raising the specter of judges and city hall clerks dressed in clothing that Atatürk had banned decades earlier. Then he began making speeches encouraging young people to attend religious academies instead of public schools and urging that graduates of such academies be made eligible for placement in the officer corps. He started appearing in public surrounded by uniformed bodyguards from his Welfare Party, seeming to trust them more than the government's official security agents. Almost every day, he removed some Kemalist or other from a post in the bureaucracy and appointed a Welfare follower to fill the vacancy. On one religious holiday he received leaders of Islamic sects, several of them dressed in traditional robes, at his official residence. And in his most powerfully symbolic assault on Kemalism, he announced that he would build a grand new mosque overlooking Istiklal, the bustling pedestrian boulevard that runs through the center of Istanbul, and another in Çankaya, the neighborhood in Ankara that is dominated by the president's official residence. He could not have been more offensive had he proposed building one next to Atatürk's mausoleum.

Islamist mayors in cities and towns throughout Turkey were encouraged by the eagerness with which Erbakan was thumbing his nose at long-established conventions of Turkish life, and many launched their own local campaigns. One closed cinemas on the grounds that they were places where unholy ideas were propagated. Another banned the selling of turkeys, saying they were being eaten at dinners whose purpose was to celebrate Christian holidays. A third shut down a lingerie market because he found its display offensive. Several began to fill their administrations with men who had been cashiered from the army for fundamentalist leanings. Others terrorized merchants into shutting their doors at prayer time and ordered restaurants to close every day during Ramadan.

Soon after Erbakan took office I applied for an interview with him. My application and those of other Western journalists were politely ignored, leading us to conclude that Turkey's leader had no interest in meeting with representatives of Christian imperialism. Increasingly frustrated as months passed, I began telephoning people close to Erbakan to ask for their help. Finally I found one who said he could arrange a meeting. Then, one day in December, I received an extraordinary message. Erbakan would deign to see me, but only if I came on Christmas Day.

This was a deliberate insult and a reflection of Erbakan's own intolerance, but although I found it tasteless, I accepted. At the appointed hour I arrived at the ugly cement building that serves as the prime minister's residence in Ankara. Inside the door I literally bumped into Erbakan as he emerged from a small elevator. We bent down to remove our shoes together.

Erbakan was a white-haired, grandfatherly figure, surprisingly elegant in appearance. He moved delicately, gestured calmly and spoke softly. For most of our two hours together, he smiled indulgently as he drifted from cliché to cliché, not showing much in the way of analytical power or concentrated intelligence. His discourse was an odd combination of conservative Islam and leftist anti-imperialism. All he wanted, he seemed to be insisting, was to change the world.

"At the end of World War II, the Western powers and Russia met at Yalta and set rules for the coming era," he told me as he sipped from a small coffee cup. "But the West and Russia can't make the rules by themselves anymore. They have to sit down with the developing countries to establish a new order. The world needs a second Yalta conference. The first Yalta did its job, but its time is now past. Now the world must again be reshaped."

I didn't need to ask which country would lead this great realignment. "Turkey is at the center of the world," Erbakan told me. "Turkey is going to take the first step toward ending this double standard and injustice in the world."

Erbakan's dream of worldwide Muslim solidarity was wildly unrealistic. He was pursuing a phantom in a way that seemed calculated to outrage the Kemalist establishment. He even felt free to disparage Europe and its ideals, thereby challenging Atatürk's most basic precept. "Turkey has been a European country for centuries, and it is a European country today," Erbakan told me that evening. "Five hundred years ago our territory stretched to the outskirts of Vienna, and Constantinople was the largest city in Europe. Today part of our territory is geographically in

Europe. But, unfortunately, for a long time European policy toward Turkey has been very wrong. Turkey has been in NATO for more than forty years, but the West is constantly pushing us away. They treat us unjustly, and then they blame us."

Erbakan's profoundly subversive message was clear: Europe doesn't want us, so we have to look elsewhere for friends and allies. But on other issues Erbakan embraced the nationalist consensus, showing himself to be no true radical. He fiercely defended the army's conduct of the campaign against Kurdish guerrillas in eastern provinces, echoing the army's view that it was "not a war but a fight against terrorism." When I asked how he would deal with human-rights abuses, he shook his head sadly. "There is no particular human-rights problem in Turkey," he said with an indulgent smile, as if correcting a student who had come up with a wrong answer. "Western countries shouldn't talk to us about human rights. It's like an old record. When Western diplomats or cabinet members come to visit us, they take out this old record and play it. It has no meaning."

This interview showed me what already seemed clear from Erbakan's actions and public statements: that he was not only nutty but nutty in a highly provocative way. Where he might have dissented from established dogma and embraced the cause of democracy, he did not do so, choosing instead to fall back on the pat answers he had mouthed for years as a pillar of the establishment. None of this mattered to the Anatolian masses and urban poor, who viewed him as a holy warrior and didn't care about his position on issues that were merely political. But in facing the great challenge of modern Turkey, that of balancing Kemalism with the clamor for more democracy, he chose a course that managed to alienate both sides. To Kemalists he was a treasonous fundamentalist, to democrats a dreary apostle of the old order. I stepped out into the Christmas darkness convinced that he was too poor a political juggler to remain in power for long.

A few weeks later one of Erbakan's acolytes, who was the mayor of Sincan, a gritty town near Ankara, called an evening rally to celebrate "Jerusalem Day," a holiday that Iran's Ayatollah Khomeini had proclaimed in Iran during the 1980s. Several hundred people jammed a local theater to watch a skit depicting Islam's victory in the forthcoming jihad. They cheered wildly when the guest of honor, Mohammed Reza Bagheri, the Iranian ambassador in Ankara, arrived at the door. "Down with Israel!" they shouted. "Down with Arafat!"

Ambassador Bagheri sent the crowd into ecstasy with a fiery speech demanding that Turkey submit to *sharia*, the law of the Koran. "On behalf of Muslims all over the world, I say that we can wait no longer!" he cried, shouting to be heard above the delirious cheers. "Do not be afraid to call yourselves fundamentalists! Fundamentalists are those who follow the words and actions of the Prophet. God has promised them the final victory!"

For Turkish generals, this was the last straw. A couple of days later they ordered a phalanx of tanks to roll through Sincan's streets, and although they claimed afterward that the tanks had simply "taken a wrong turn," their message was clear. The mayor went into hiding but was soon found, arrested, charged with violating laws that forbade attacks on the secular state, tried and imprisoned. Ambassador Bagheri was sent packing.

The next weekend, feminist groups led a mass protest on the streets of Ankara. Thousands of women turned out to protest Erbakan's rule and proclaim their refusal to accept the social position he and his followers envisioned for them. As I circulated through the crowd, I found many women in a state of near-panic. Erbakan's proposal to encourage the wearing of head scarves, they said, was not a step toward free choice but the beginning of a pressure campaign that would ultimately force all women to cover themselves. I saw an older woman draped in a Turkish flag to which she had pinned a portrait of Atatürk, and asked her why she had joined the march. "I don't want to live under a black sheet," she replied. "We are the real Muslims, not those who want to turn back the clock."

With the atmosphere now so highly charged, every aspect of daily life became politicized. Newspapers and television news programs were filled with reports about the intensifying political conflict. Culture became a major battleground. When the Ankara Symphony Orchestra announced plans to play Beethoven's Ninth Symphony at a large meeting hall, the city's Islamist mayor ordered work on a nearby construction project intensified as a way of creating obstructions for those heretics who would presume to listen to such an expression of European decadence. Sensing a challenge, enormous crowds turned out, some picking their way through piles of torn-up asphalt. Inside the stadium they shouted insults at Erbakan's culture minister, who had made a series of speeches proclaiming the superiority of Muslim culture over that of the West. They cheered wildly at the sight of President Demirel, who as prime minister had opened scores of religious schools but, like the rest of the Kemalist elite, had changed with the wind and begun denouncing the spread of Islamic militance. Visibly moved by the response, Demirel leaned into a microphone and shouted, "This magnificent picture is the picture of contemporary Turkey!" The crowd responded by chanting, "Turkey is secular and will remain so!"

A dangerous chasm had opened within Turkish society. In tea houses and *meyhane* people spoke of little else. Although Erbakan was neither violent nor a religious fanatic, his effort to exploit religious feeling for political ends seemed highly dangerous. Sentiment had clearly swung against him, but what could be done? The answer was lamentably obvious. The army had to step in, and step in it did.

This time the generals did not launch an old-fashioned coup, which, they realized, was no longer possible in a country that belonged to NATO and claimed to live within the rules of democracy. Besides, they had no desire to run the country themselves. Their goal was to depose Erbakan and return power to traditional politicians who respected the rules of Kemalism.

The generals, through their National Security Council, had already officially directed Erbakan to change course, but he had ignored them. So in the spring of 1997 they began issuing "memoranda" listing his sins. Then they invited various groups—judges, civil servants, journalists and others—to "briefings" in Ankara at which they issued vivid warnings about the peril at hand. They never openly demanded Erbakan's resignation, but their pressure soon became irresistible. He surrendered after exactly twelve months in office, victim of Turkey's first post-modern coup.

This coup would have been unthinkable in any true democracy. Most Turks, however, breathed a palpable sigh of relief. The generals had acted on behalf of the Turkish nation, crushing a force that most people had come to fear but none could stop. Once again they had proven their indispensability. Erbakan's year in power had been a disaster. For a man who had spent so long in Turkish politics, he showed astonishing naïveté in believing that he would be allowed to pull Turkey away from the West. More important, he squandered a great opportunity to show a skeptical nation and its ruling elite that devoutly Muslim politicians could accept the ideals of republican Turkey. In fact, he did the opposite, fixing in the public mind the image of his movement as a threat to dearly held principles.

Being pushed from power was only the beginning of Erbakan's punishment. Later his Welfare Party was outlawed (making it the twenty-first party since the 1980 coup to be dissolved by judicial order) and he himself was banned from politics. Then, in an act of unseemly vengeance, a prosecutor dredged up a speech he had made long before becoming prime minister and persuaded a judge that it was subversive. Erbakan was sentenced to one year in prison, although a subsequent amnesty allowed him to avoid actually serving time.

As if toppling an elected prime minister were not enough, the National Security Council embarked on a sweeping campaign to cleanse Turkey of other forces it considered part of the "reactionary sector." It decreed the closing of more than two thousand private associations that it said were promoting dangerous principles, along with nineteen newspapers, twenty television stations, fifty-one radio stations, one hundred ten magazines, eight hundred schools, and twelve hundred student hostels. Then it went even further, naming one hundred private companies it considered subversive. Nearly all were based in the Anatolian heartland and run by observant Muslims whose only evident offense had been to contribute a portion of their profits to Islamic charities. One of these companies happened to be Ülker, the country's largest manufacturer of candy and biscuits—and, perhaps coincidentally, Tayyip Erdoğan's onetime employer. All were forbidden to bid for government contracts or receive any form of government support. The generals even tried to pressure Turkish Airlines into ending its practice of giving Ülker chocolate bars and cupcakes to its passengers.

Despite being officially branded as "reactionary," Ülker and the other ninety-nine blacklisted companies continued functioning as before by one ruse or another, as did most of the institutions that the National Security Council had ordered shut. Everyone associated with them, however, realized that the army had branded them enemies of the state. That made them more eager than ever to support a transition to democracy in which elected civilians, not generals, would decide who threatened the state and who did not.

Lashing out against supposedly Islamist associations and companies did not sate the generals and their allies. Working through prosecutors like the redoubtable Vural Savaş, who vowed to seek bans on parties he didn't like even if they won 99 percent of the vote, they began systematically targeting Erbakan's followers, most of whom had stuck together after Welfare was banned and formed a new Islamic-oriented party called Virtue. The first to be indicted was Şükrü Karatepe, mayor of Kayseri, a city of six hundred thousand in central Anatolia where dozens of pious Muslims had seized the chance Turgut Özal gave them and built companies that turned a sleepy backwater into a booming economic powerhouse. Karatepe was a moderate in the party and one of the few whose wife did not wear a head scarf, but after he allegedly complained that he was tired of attending ceremonies in honor of Atatürk—a remark he denied making—he was convicted of spreading subversion and sent to jail for five months. Then prosecutors moved on, indicting one supposedly subversive politician after another. Their biggest trophy was Mayor Tayyip Erdoğan of Istanbul.

It may have been reasonable for the authorities to presume that everyone in Erbakan's party shared all his views and also his confrontational style, but it was not true. Many younger figures in his movement recognized his mistakes even as he was making them. Abdullah Gül, one of his advisers, had privately urged him not to make his disastrous trip to Libya. Mayor Erdoğan, especially after the four months of private reflection he had the chance to enjoy in prison, became disenchanted with his anti-democratic and anti-Western rhetoric. Together these dissidents hatched a plan. At the next Virtue convention, they would depose Erbakan as party leader, replace him and his friends with a slate of younger, more pragmatic leaders who reflected the vigor of Anatolia's new counter-elite and transform the party into one that demanded democracy as well as respect for religious belief.

Their rebellion failed, but in the end their failure led to a success beyond what any of them could have dreamed. Unable to depose Virtue's traditionally Islamist leaders, they quit the party and formed their own, the AKP. As they were building it, a once promising political warhorse, Bülent Ecevit, cobbled together a weak coalition and became prime minister. Ecevit was an elderly, militant old-style secularist and utterly out of touch with Turkey's dynamic new society. In 2001 his bumbling set off a banking crisis that led to economic panic and devastated countless families. That intensified the conviction of many frustrated secularists that traditional political parties offered them no hope. As the 2002 election approached, some of them decided, often with great reluctance, to take the radical step of voting for Erdoğan and his new AKP.

Indoctrinated for generations with the principle that religious belief and religious believers are enemies of freedom, Turks slowly began concluding that the opposite might be true. Erdoğan's rhetoric so completely fused democracy with his mild brand of Islamism that it became difficult to say where one ended and the other began. There was never any doubt that he would attract votes from the Anatolian heartland, but what made the 2002 election campaign unique was the radical shift in perception that it set off in the minds of many worldly, secular Turks in Istanbul and other big cities.

This new AKP is led by people we were brought up to detest, these confused voters told themselves. Can it be that they actually support our democratic aspirations? Maybe the real obstacle to democracy in Turkey is not Islam but the encrusted authoritarian ideology that sees democracy and civil society as enemies. So maybe it's time to take the leap, to vote with our hopes rather than remain trapped in our fears.

Millions did that. This extraordinary coalition—pious Muslims from the provinces and irreligious sophisticates from big cities—swept Erdoğan to power. By doing so, they set off Turkey's second revolution.

Erdoğan took the oath of office as prime minister on March 14, 2003. In a series of speeches over the following months, he surprised many Turks—disappointing some but thrilling many others—by making clear that his chief priority would be not easing anti-religious rules but something quite different: leading Turkey toward membership in the European Union.

Erdoğan barnstormed across Turkey promoting his reformist agenda, and in his speeches he emerged as a refreshingly enlightened personality. He insisted that it was time for secularism to be "crowned with democracy," and that Turkey must evolve "parallel to the world's realities."

"My political views have always been in a state of constant evolution," he asserted in one speech.

Many of those who remained dubious about Erdoğan and his movement were reactionary defenders of the old order who cynically sought to foment unwarranted fears in the hope of reaping political gain. Other skeptics, however, harbored honest and deeply held concerns about where he was leading Turkey. They felt social pressure from the increasing number of women who wore head scarves, and they read with horror about newly popular resorts that catered to the pious by refusing to serve alcohol and dividing their beaches into male-only and female-only sections. Some feared that the new regime was embarked on a quiet but resolute campaign to Islamicize Turkish society.

The head scarf is tolerated in the Turkish heartland because it is part of the traditional female costume and does not necessarily symbolize religious orthodoxy. In the 1990s a new generation of young women, assertive and liberated but still religiously conservative, began pursuing opportunities that had never been available to their mothers and grandmothers but that, thanks to Kemalism, were available to them. They enrolled by the thousands at universities across the country, eagerly grasping the chance for education offered to them by the Turkish state. At the same time they insisted on wearing their scarves. Certainly some of them were being manipulated, consciously or otherwise, by fundamentalists looking for ways to upset the established order. But public universities are supported by taxpayers, and the young women who enrolled believed they had a right to attend regardless of how they dressed. They were wrong.

Istanbul University was built on the grounds of what was once the Ottoman defense ministry but is today a bastion of Kemalism. One day I met two aspiring doctors at the McDonald's across the street. Both had been expelled from medical school for refusing to remove their head scarves.

"Hello, I'm Stephen," I said as I greeted them, extending my hand. They only smiled and nodded in reply. These women considered even shaking a man's hand sinful. I hated that, but still I found myself sympathizing with them.

One of the two, Tülay Erdoğan (no relation to the prime minister), was twenty-three years old and had dreamed since childhood of becoming a doctor. But a few days earlier she had arrived to take an examination and was told that she could enter the room only if she removed her scarf. Suddenly she and several hundred of her classmates found themselves unexpectedly challenged. Nearly all of them refused to remove their scarves, choosing to quit school rather than uncover themselves.

"We love God, we read our Koran, we believe in our religion and we want to apply this religion in our lives," Ms. Erdoğan told me over a burger and fries. "What has happened in the last few weeks makes me very angry. I am protesting as much as possible because I really want to become a doctor. It's bad to become a fanatic, but they are pushing us toward fanaticism."

This young woman impressed me as highly intelligent and, although perhaps not exactly what Atatürk had in mind, a product of the Kemalist revolution. The triumph of Turkish secularism had made it possible for her to aspire to a career beyond the wildest dreams of girls in Saudi Arabia or Kuwait or Afghanistan. I admired her courage and would have liked to bid her goodbye in the traditional Turkish manner, with a kiss on each cheek, but under the circumstances that was of course impossible.

The arrival of the head scarf in such a citadel of secularism as Istanbul University was a challenge that Atatürk probably had not considered. Perhaps it would have outraged him. I prefer to believe, however, that the idea of women clamoring to become doctors would have seemed to him like a fulfillment of his dream. Turkish secularism no doubt requires that doctors in public hospitals be forbidden to wear head scarves, and along with them judges, lawyers, civil servants, diplomats and flight attendants on the national airline. But why college students?

"The head scarf is a symbol that represents an ideology," one member of Istanbul University's governing board, an economist named Toker

Dereli, told me when I posed this question to him. "Many people who like to see scarves would also like to see a regime like the one in Iran. That suggests a totalitarian approach."

Dereli seemed uncomfortable when I asked him if the university had been pressured to take this stand. "If the military has certain targets, unlike civilian sectors they follow to the end until the targets are reached," he told me. "I personally find it odd for someone to be banned from classes because of what she wears on her head. But you have to have been raised in Turkey in the 1930s and 1940s, when we were torn by so many ideological battles, to understand the fear we have of being pulled back to absolutism and religious rule."

The conflict over head scarves, along with the state's relentless campaign to harass, prosecute and jail Islamic-oriented politicians, produced a remarkable transformation in the minds of Islamist politicians. Under Erbakan's leadership they had shared the elite's suspicion of democracy, voting, for example, to strip several outspoken Kurdish deputies of their immunity so they could be expelled from Parliament and jailed in 1994. By the end of the century, however, as prosecutors began sending Islamist leaders to jail for saying forbidden things, they began to break away from this consensus, adopting the rhetoric of human rights and demanding the repeal of laws that limit freedom of expression. This presented the odd spectacle of a party campaigning for greater democracy while fending off charges from its enemies that it harbored a secret plan to impose fundamentalist rule and destroy democracy.

One of Turkey's leading journalists, Fehmi Koru, told me that when his wife studied at MIT, she had been allowed to wear her head scarf and even to take examinations at special times when regularly scheduled ones came on Islamic holy days, but that in Turkey she was denied teaching positions because of her scarf. The wife of Abdullah Gül, the most sophisticated of the young Virtue leaders, had a similar experience: in 1998, after her children had grown, she passed a university entrance examination but was not allowed to matriculate because she wears a head scarf.

I took a liking to Gül, and one day when a provincial prosecutor opened another case against an Islamist politician judged to have said something subversive, I called him for a comment. He said something very bland, and I pressed him. He replied: "Please don't ask me to say any more. If I say what I think, they'll open a case against *me*."

Kemalists may have thought they won a victory by striking such fear into the hearts of observant Muslims, but in the end it was no victory at all. They would have opposed fundamentalism far more effectively by reaching an accommodation with the Islamic political movement, a historic compromise under which believers would be allowed to practice, study and debate their religion freely in exchange for their explicit acceptance of secular rule. Instead they waged war against it. Frozen into immobility, unable to accept the evolution of their society and long accustomed to seeing enemies under every leaf, guardians of the old order relentlessly pressured even the most benign Islamist politicians. By doing so they blocked their country's progress toward democracy, alienated the conservative masses and ultimately became models of the very intolerance they claimed to detest.

The AKP's election victory in 2002 gave it the right to carry out social experiments. Some of these experiments, like loosening the restriction on wearing head scarves, unsettled many Turks who did not want to see their country slip back toward religious rule, yet their resistance has reinforced Turkey's stability rather than threatening it. The fact that a goodly number of strong and outspoken Turks remain suspicious of Erdoğan places a valuable check on his government and helps guarantee that it will not push religious aspects of its agenda too hard. When they protest his more extreme proposals, he pulls back. He and his comrades are pragmatists above all.

It is important to remember that the AKP is not a conventional party built around a clear ideology but a coalition of factions. Its supporters run the gamut from fundamentalists who would welcome the introduction of *sharia* law to secular democrats who feel little connection to Islam. Such a party requires a strong leader who not only strikes a balance among the factions but imposes his will once he decides. In Erdoğan, the former tough kid from Kasimpaşa's mean streets, it has one.

As Erdoğan was finishing his second year in power, I visited him at his office in Ankara. He was then fifty years old, tall and fair-skinned with a light brown mustache. What struck me most during our conversation was his burning sense of his own authority. He seemed to see himself, not his party or his government, as the force driving Turkey. When we talked about what had happened in the Anatolian city of Bingol after a recent earthquake, for example, he told me, "I built a new town for four thousand people who lost their homes," and "I built new schools right away, much better than the old ones." This was not a self-effacing man or one unsure of his mission.

Most of our conversation was about the reform packages Erdoğan was pushing through Parliament and the prospect of Turkey joining the European Union. I saved my most important question for last. How, I asked, did he respond to fears that he was not a reformer but rather a fundamentalist in disguise? As I spoke, I could see his jaw stiffen.

"This is the unfortunate mentality of marginal groups in Turkey," he told me sternly. "I was mayor of Istanbul for four and a half years, and if I had a hidden agenda, it would have been clear there. What I have done and am doing is clear to anyone. No one has a right to doubt what I think or believe. I laugh at those so-called fears. I'm proud of my achievements. This country is at a great moment in history, and I'm determined to seize it."

The movement Erdoğan leads is not, then, a simple uprising of religious believers against Turkey's secular elite. It is also the product of the rebellion of democracy against authoritarianism and of the periphery against the center. The combination of these rebellions has reshaped Turkey, as well as the very idea of what a party rooted in Islam can be and do.

On one of my first visits to a nargile salon, where Turks gather to smoke water pipes, I met a seventy-one-year-old pensioner named Ismet Ertep. He and the men who gather every afternoon at this salon beside the Bosphorus, along with the few women who join them, are heirs to a centuries-old tradition. Their worlds revolve around the soft sound of bubbling water, the sensation of drawing filtered tobacco smoke through long curled tubes and the love of contemplation and understated camaraderie.

"Smoking a nargile is nothing like smoking a cigarette," my new friend told me when I asked him to explain the attraction of this vice. "Cigarettes are for nervous people, competitive people, people on the run. When you smoke a nargile you have time to think. It teaches you patience and tolerance, and gives you an appreciation of good company. Nargile smokers have a much more balanced approach to life than cigarette smokers."

My travels in Turkey confirm these observations. Every time I arrive in a new town, I seek out the nargile salon. It is the ideal place, even better than the barbershop, to discover what is happening and what local people are thinking. The pace in these salons is slow, and time is plentiful. Usually there is not much noise. Conversation is only occasional, al-

ways soft and punctuated by long pauses. The sound of dominoes being played or backgammon tokens being moved is often all that competes with the pipes' gurgling. Some patrons work absently on crossword puzzles and others seem lost in reverie. No alcohol is served, only tea and sometimes coffee. Open windows keep the air fresh.

After a while, I realized that I enjoy nargile salons not just because they are good places to take the local pulse but because the sensation of smoking a water pipe is so seductive and satisfying. It starts when the elaborate hookah is placed before you, its bowl cleaned with a soft cloth and then filled with damp tobacco. Some patrons choose strong Turkish tobacco grown on plantations near the Syrian border, but I prefer aromatic apple or cherry blends imported from Egypt and Bahrain. After an attendant fills your pipe with the weed of your choice, he comes by carrying a copper tray piled with burning coals. He picks up a couple of them with a pair of metal pincers and sets them atop the tobacco plug. With a few puffs, you are under way.

It takes at least half an hour to smoke a pipeful of fruit tobacco, even longer for the more potent stuff. The smoke is noticeably cooler than cigarette smoke, and lightly intoxicating. Before long the water begins to turn brown; smokers say it is filtering out many of the harmful substances they would normally be inhaling.

Perhaps no habit is associated more closely with Turks than smoking tobacco. Herman Melville reported walking along Istanbul streets lined with cafés where "Turks sit smoking like conjurers." By the nineteenth century, when he visited, nargiles had become important status symbols. Offering one to a guest was a sign of trust, and withholding it could be taken as a serious insult. In 1841 a diplomatic crisis broke out with France when the French ambassador demanded a formal apology for not having been offered a chance to smoke with the sultan during a visit to the royal palace.

Today smoking is not only acceptable but almost mandatory in Turkey, especially for men. "A 'manly man' is one who is brave, loud, virile, does not hesitate to fight for what he believes in, does not show his emotions or cry, and knows no fear," the social historian Arın Bayraktaroğlu wrote in a treatise on the Turkish psyche. "He usually has a mustache, and drinks and smokes a lot."

Nargiles were first used in India, but they were primitive ones made from coconut shells. From India the custom spread to Iran and then to Turkey, where it flowered. A separate guild of craftsmen was established to make each of the nargile's pieces. The mouthpiece is traditionally made of amber, the tube of fine leather dyed in different colors, and the sphere that holds the water of glass, crystal or silver, sometimes decorated with floral motifs or other designs. In olden days the water itself used to be scented with perfume or herbs, but that custom has faded.

Turks took to smoking nargiles almost immediately after the first tobacco leaves arrived from America in 1601. Smoking quickly became a craze. People indulged at home, at work and in cafés. "Puffing in each other's faces, they made the streets and markets stink," wrote the contemporary historian Ibrahim Pecevi.

The authorities were not pleased by this development. At nargile cafés, then as now, people do not just smoke. They talk. In a society where the sultan's political power was supposed to be absolute and submission to it unquestioning, the specter of leisurely social gatherings where the topics of the day would inevitably be discussed and debated was unsettling. Ottoman rulers did not like being unsettled, and in 1633 Sultan Murad IV issued a decree that banned smoking on pain of death. An underground immediately took shape. Those afraid of being traced by smoke resorted to inhaling the aroma of chopped leaves. After fourteen years the ban was finally lifted. Tobacco soon became one of the empire's main exports, and Pecevi concluded that it had joined coffee, wine and opium as one of the four "cushions on the sofa of pleasure."

No one believes the nargile will ever regain its supremacy in the tobacco world. Indeed, logic suggests that the nargile salon should be a dying tradition in Turkey. The atmosphere inside is distinctly Oriental, the pace leisurely to the point of torpor. With Turks now turning ever more decisively toward Europe and modernity, they might be expected to shun such places. But although the number of salons is slowly declining, the tradition will not die. Every year brings a new crop of pensioners who have the time and often the desire to spend hours in quiet reflection. On some evenings I even see college students and other young people sitting and puffing. They embrace an experience that is at once solitary and convivial, that evokes nostalgia but also inculcates the values of peace, dialogue and tolerance that today's Turks must absorb if their nation is to fulfill its destiny.

In days gone by, some smokers used to fill their nargiles with illicit drugs. Some still do. I know a small hotel in Istanbul where there is a secret back room that the owner opens for friends and special customers. There they don rich Ottoman costumes, sit on embroidered velvet cushions and smoke a blend of fruit tobacco and hashish. The pleasure of such an interlude approaches that enjoyed by the sultans, who smoked a special mixture of opium, incense and crushed pearls.

"The important thing is not what you put in the pipe but who's with you when you're smoking," a sailor I met in one salon told me. "It's a complete experience. In a café like this one you find the good people, the old people, the interesting people. As long as there's a need for company and friendship, as long as people want to stop and think, there will be nargile cafés."

• FOUR •

GHOSTS

☪

The shore of majestic Lake Van, eight hundred miles east of Istanbul and even farther away culturally and psychologically, is a fine place to sit and reflect on the vicissitudes of history. This is Turkey's largest lake, covering a larger area than Luxembourg or Rhode Island. Around it lies magnificent scenery, with rugged peaks sloping down to wide, fragrant meadows that blaze with wildflowers during spring and summer. Crumbling ruins of ancient castles and fortresses give the region an exotic, almost spiritual aura. The lake itself is disturbingly beautiful, a great sea set incongruously amid a vast expanse of mountains and rocky prairie. Close by are Turkey's borders with Iran, Iraq and Armenia.

Cave paintings, inscriptions carved in rock and countless ancient artifacts testify to this region's rich history. Over the millennia dozens of peoples, some of them now lost to human memory, have lived in or passed through the region. In 840 B.C. the town of Van, which sits on the eastern shore of the lake, became the capital of the kingdom of Urartu, a confederation formed to resist rampaging Assyrians. It remained so for more than two hundred years, until it was overrun by the Medes, said to be ancestors of today's Kurds. Later it was an Armenian capital under the governance of the Medes, but today it is almost entirely Kurdish. Among the most popular spots is an island just off the lakeshore that is dominated by the stately ruin of an ancient church. On warm days, families row to the island in small boats and enjoy picnics in its shady groves.

During my first visit to Van, I bought a copy of the only guidebook available in local shops. It says the island church was "built during the reign of King Gagik, under Byzantine sovereignty, between the years of 915 and 921 by architect Manuel, who was a monk." There are descriptions of the intricate friezes that decorate the interior, but that is all. Readers seek in vain for explanations of who King Gagik was and what became of his people. This is no accident, because Gagik was Armenian, and by the time his church was built Van had been Armenian for centuries. It remained so until 1915, the year of apocalypse for Armenians in eastern Turkey. But the words "Armenia" and "Armenian" do not appear in the guidebook I bought. A historical atlas produced by one of Turkey's principal newspapers also makes no reference to the fact that Armenians were once the majority there. History is not always a pleasant subject for Turks. They revel in the glories of their past, as well they should, but choose to ignore what seems dark and dangerous. Their celebration of history is selective. Often they shy away from it rather than confronting its painful lessons.

In the spring of 1915, Armenians in this region made common cause with their Orthodox cousins in Russia, who hoped to seize eastern Anatolia and turn it into a Russian-Armenian province. The Ottoman authorities, understandably alarmed, ordered the deportation of populations "suspected of being guilty of treason or espionage." Soon bands of Ottoman soldiers and Kurdish tribesmen were storming through Armenian towns, forcing their citizens to flee the land of their forefathers and killing hundreds of thousands of them in an orgy of ethnic violence. In one of many eyewitness testimonies, an American diplomat posted in Van reported that these bands were "sweeping the countryside, massacring men, women and children and burning their homes. Babies were shot in their mothers' arms, small children were horribly mutilated, women were stripped and beaten."

Officially sanctioned textbooks in Turkey barely allude to this tragedy, so Turks who learned their history in school may be forgiven for not comprehending its scope. At the small museum in Van, which is de-

us everything. My grandfather said soldiers gave him a coin for every head of an Armenian that he brought to the command post. He told me there were bodies along the roadside everywhere you went. Kurds were promised that if they could get rid of the Armenians, they could have this land for themselves. In the end it didn't work out that way, but at that time our grandfathers were happy to help with the killing. Don't ever believe that this never happened, or that it was just a minor thing, or that both sides suffered equally. It did happen. Turks and Kurds did it, and Armenians were the victims. Many of them. Many, many, many."

The mood had turned somber, and although the sun had not yet sunk into the lake, I felt a chill. The other guests at my table nodded in agreement as the engineer spoke. "My family has a farm out in the hills east of here," another man said. "One day a couple of years ago my father was out plowing and he turned up some bones. We called the police, and the next day a truck full of soldiers came out to see what we'd found. They started digging, and they came up with five or six skeletons. Some of the skulls were crushed. One had a bullet hole in it. There were Armenian crosses and emblems in the hole. They loaded the bones and everything else into their truck and drove it away. We never heard anything more about it. You can be sure that if those had been bodies of Muslims, the newspapers would have been full of stories about new proof that Armenians had massacred Turks. The bones would be in a glass case at the museum. But what we found didn't fit the Turkish version of history, so it had to be ignored. It's very important for us to ignore things like this. There's a lot we have to pretend didn't happen."

In the 1970s and 1980s, terrorists calling themselves Commandos of the Armenian Genocide set out to murder Turkish diplomats in the United States and Europe and bomb targets like the Turkish Airlines counter at Orly Airport in Paris. The killing of diplomats in particular—thirty-four of them, a huge number in such a small, close-knit foreign service—embittered and outraged many Turks. Even now, decades later, the foreign ministry, which might otherwise be supporting overtures toward Armenia, remains deeply scarred by the trauma. Its anger is understandable, as is its frustration over the efforts of some Armenians, mostly in the diaspora, to take the events of 1915 out of their historical context and portray them as no more than unprovoked genocide.

But Turkey has not set out to refute one set of historical arguments with another. It simply refuses to confront this tragic episode.

Despite what both Turks and Armenians say, much of what happened in 1915 is still unclear. Fair-minded historians might be able to answer many of the remaining questions, but the Turkish authorities, apparently fearing what could emerge from such research, have done all they can to discourage it, including limiting access to Ottoman archives. This is frustrating not for the parties themselves—they are already convinced of their respective versions of the truth—but for the rest of the world.

Armenians have built a Genocide Museum in their nation's capital, Yerevan, and all state visitors are expected to visit it just as they must lay a wreath at Atatürk's mausoleum when they come to Turkey. In one glass case at the museum is a copy of a 1915 telegram in which Ottoman leaders ordered their commanders in eastern provinces to kill as many Armenians as possible and expel the rest. Turks claim that this document is a forgery and that no such telegram ever existed. An even better-known debate is over a quotation from Hitler, who is said to have assured his confederates that they could get away with genocide against Jews by asking, "Who today remembers the extermination of the Armenians?" Armenian historians say they have contemporaneous notes to prove Hitler uttered those words, but Turks say this is yet another clumsy fabrication. It should be relatively easy for historians to determine the authenticity of a key order issued by a national government or a remark made by a major historical figure, but emotion and the demands of national chauvinism on both sides overwhelm such pursuits, which, although they may seem merely scholarly, are in fact pregnant with meaning for the future as well as the past.

As Turkey matures, its leaders, and hence its people, will have to face their history more honestly. In the case of the Armenian massacres, they would certainly be right to assert that whatever happened in 1915 was not their doing but that of distant ancestors, since the Ottoman regime then in power has long since passed into history. But to be sincere, such an assertion would have to be accompanied by a recognition of the boundless pain that these events inflicted on the Armenian soul and a pledge to encourage fair-minded historical research. If Armenians can persuade Turks that they mean no ill to the Turkish Republic, Turks should be able to break away from their years of denial and look more dispassionately at their past.

Other nations, including some in Turkey's neighborhood, have already begun to do that. Soon after Bulgaria elected Philip Dimitrov as its first post-Communist prime minister, for example, he came to Turkey and displayed a remarkable willingness to confront unpleasant aspects of his country's history. During the Communist era, thousands of Bulgarian Muslims had been brutalized, robbed of their property and forced to flee to Turkey. When Dimitrov convened a press conference in Istanbul, the first question came from one of these refugees, who had become a reporter for a nationalist newspaper. The question was more of a tirade, not unlike those that Turkish diplomats sometimes hear from Armenians. Dimitrov's answer was startling.

"You are right," he said. "I apologize in the name of Bulgaria. This was not our fault, but the fault of the Communists. And I add that any of our citizens who wish to come back may do so and will receive all possible help from the state." With those few words, Dimitrov set Bulgaria and Turkey on a path toward friendship.

It would be naïve to suggest that a similar statement from a Turkish leader would pacify rabid Turkey-haters abroad. The reason Turkey must face its history, though, is not to satisfy outsiders but to become a complete nation, to emerge from its insecurity and accept what is bad as well as what is good in its history. More and more Turks realize this. As their country completes its march toward democracy, they are becoming steadily more interested in learning hidden truths about their past.

Facing the facts of what happened in 1915 will not be enough to quench their thirst. As it becomes possible for Turks to research and discuss and debate the 1915 killings without restriction, it must also become possible to turn over many other rocks, pull back many carpets and look into many dark corners. This process is never easy. Many Europeans are just beginning to face the truth of their parents' and grandparents' collaboration with Nazi occupiers. Others barely acknowledge the brutality with which their forefathers oppressed people in overseas colonies. Even in the United States, efforts to come to grips with the monumental crimes of slavery and the extermination of native peoples are far from complete. But countries, like individuals, cannot become whole until they confront the truth of who they are and what they have been.

No country has been brave enough to look at its own history without illusion. Many, however, have sought to purge themselves of at least some of their historical sin. The example of Argentina may be typical. Once an eminently civilized nation, it fell into barbarism under the rule of fanatic military officers during the 1970s. Argentines shamefully averted their eyes as military squads abducted thousands of law-abiding citizens and tortured them to death on military bases. But after the dictatorship was toppled, elected leaders appointed Argentina's most renowned novelist to head a commission of inquiry. Its report left many questions unanswered, and the government went so far as to give blanket pardons to both generals and torturers. Yet the report documented much about the machinery of military repression, and made it possible for Argentina to begin reclaiming its moral position in the world. Turkey must do the same if it hopes to grow into true maturity.

Confronting the truth of 1915 might actually be an easy way to begin this process, because the massacres of that year were directed and tolerated by a regime that was overthrown by modern Turkey's greatest hero. Since Atatürk himself condemned the Ottomans so harshly, it should not be impossible for his successors to condemn them for their crimes against Armenians. It will be much harder for them to face up to more recent history.

When the Turkish army staged its 1980 coup, many citizens breathed an enormous sigh of relief. Most realized that their country had been sliding toward chaos. Leftist groups, some of them frighteningly radical, were gaining strength, and rightists banded together to stop them, usually by the simple expedient of murder. People cowered fearfully in their homes as terrorists and counter-terrorists roamed the streets. Not a day passed without bombings and killings. But immediately after the government was overthrown and military officers began to rule by fiat, the violence ended. Once again the army had saved Turkey from itself.

It is still unclear how Turkey descended into such violent upheaval during the late 1970s. There is much debate over who supported the militant left and who encouraged and armed the rightist gangs that reacted so violently to the left's rising power. Even more painful are questions raised by the wave of arrests and torture after the coup. Thousands of Turks were taken into custody, stripped of their rights and held in appalling conditions for months or years. Many were never told what crimes they were supposed to have committed, much less given a chance to defend themselves. Today it is quite normal to find a journalist, politician, artist, businessman or university professor who turns out to have been one of the victims.

Several of my Turkish friends suffered this abuse. One of them is Orhan Taylan, a gifted painter who during the 1970s joined a leftist group opposed to military intervention in politics. After his arrest he was taken to a police station in Ankara for twelve days of beatings and torture by electric shock, then transferred to the nearby Mamak Military Prison, where a squad of soldiers welcomed him with a thirty-six-hour beating. Over the months that followed he and other prisoners were beaten regularly, deprived of sleep and forced to spend hours in a freezing courtyard while wearing only prison-issue trousers. Orhan believes this regimen was designed not to kill the prisoners, although two of his cell mates did die, but to ruin their health so they would not live long after being released. He spent more than three years in military custody, and when he was released he was so emaciated that friends did not recognize him, so broken that he could not speak at his trial. Ten years later he and the other members of his Turkish Peace Committee were acquitted of all charges.

In 1999 a provincial prosecutor announced that he was investigating the general who led the 1980 coup, Kenan Evren, with the intention of indicting him for subverting the constitution. A few days later the prosecutor mysteriously announced his retirement. Soon afterward the justice ministry not only quashed the investigation of Evren but threatened to indict the prosecutor himself for abusing his office.

Turkey's refusal to confront events surrounding the 1980 coup cannot continue forever. Criminal investigations may not be the best way to determine what actually happened during that period, but some way must be found. Turks need to know how their country fell into near-anarchy during the late 1970s and who ordered the imprisonment and abuse of Orhan Taylan and so many other citizens after the coup. They need answers not so they can seek revenge but so they can learn lessons to help them build a stable and peaceful future.

Turks must one day try to answer other, equally urgent questions. Most obvious are those surrounding the violent antagonism between partisans of Turkish and Kurdish nationalism. The war between these partisans was the dominant fact of Turkish life during the 1980s and 1990s, but it still cannot be freely discussed. In few countries has it been so difficult for so long to speak frankly about such an overwhelming issue. Kurds pass down stories of their sufferings from one generation to the next, but even the most sophisticated Turks know almost nothing about them.

"I was absolutely amazed when I started my research," the political scientist Kemal Kırışcı told me after he finished coauthoring a highly perceptive study of the Kurds. "When I began, I thought Kurdish violence had come more or less out of nowhere. That's what most Turks believe. But as I got deeper into my work, I realized that for the whole period from the founding of the Republic up to World War II there were Kurdish rebellions, one after another. I had to ask myself: How come I never knew any of this? Why wasn't it taught to us in school? Why are people in Turkey denied access to our history?"

War between Kurdish insurgents and the Turkish army raged for almost fifteen years, but journalists were forbidden to cover it and few outsiders know much about how it was fought. Certainly both sides committed gross crimes. Establishing the truth about these crimes is vital simply because such a seminal event in any nation's history cannot remain unexamined.

There have been many skirmishes in the Turkish government's campaign to deny or cover up what happened in the Kurdish war, but I have a favorite. One of my Turkish friends, a journalist named Nadire Mater, spent two years tracking down army veterans who had fought in frontline units. She gave each one she found the rare chance to tell his story. It was the first time that Mehmet, as the Turkish recruit is affectionately known, had ever been given such a voice. Nadire took pains not to insert herself into her work; she only turned on her tape recorder and sat back to listen. The stories she gathered were like those told by Americans who fought in Vietnam, Russians who returned from Afghanistan or, for that matter, soldiers who lived through any counter-insurgency campaign. Like most soldiers, they came to fear death, but they also mistrusted their officers, sometimes sympathized with their enemies and rejected the simplistic platitudes that sent them off to war in the first place.

Nadire published her interviews in a volume called *Mehmet's Book*. In many countries it would have been received as an authentic cry of pain from boys sent out as cannon fodder in a war they did not understand. In Turkey, however, its publication was considered a subversive act. Although it contained not a word of commentary, only the verbatim testimony of young men who had served their country in uniform, it was too much for the army to bear. Prosecutors could not find the veterans themselves—Nadire had promised them anonymity in exchange for their candor—so they vented their outrage on her. Her book was banned, and she was indicted for slandering the army, a crime punishable by up to twelve years' imprisonment. Only after more than a year of legal maneuvering, with the political climate easing as the war wound down, was she finally acquitted.

It had been hard for Nadire to find ex-soldiers who had fought Kurdish rebels and to persuade them to speak. Like many unhappy veterans, they had melted back into civilian life, closely guarding their memories and emotions. But finding civilian victims of the war is no trouble at all. The towns of southeastern Turkey are overflowing with them. To hear a heartrending tale of forced exile, torture or some other form of brutality, one need only stop a pedestrian or walk into a living room there. Each of these stories represents both a personal tragedy and a piece of modern Turkish history.

Because Turks were denied the right to read or write about this war as it was being fought, most perceive it today as a jumble of violence and terror. Those who lived through it, however, remember each day, each bullet, each torture session. Their dead brethren cry out from the tomb, not necessarily for revenge but for recognition. Who killed them? Who gave the killers their orders? Why, and by what authority? No war is as cruel as a civil war, and even atrocities must be seen in their proper context. Yet questions like these cannot go unanswered forever.

Some of the challenges that history poses to Turkey seep slowly into the public consciousness. Others shock the nation by bursting suddenly onto the front pages. That was what happened one rainy night in the autumn of 1996, when a Mercedes speeding through the western town of Susurluk crashed into a truck that was slowly pulling out of a filling station. The effect of that crash is still reverberating through Turkish society. The very name of Susurluk became a symbol of the obscure and chilling web of conspiracies that weave together the interests of gangsters, politicians and commanders of Turkey's most important military and security agencies.

Three men were riding in the Mercedes that night. One was a top-ranking police commander named Hüseyin Kocadağ, who had once run counter-guerrilla operations against Kurdish rebels and later became a director of Turkey's main police academy. The second was Sedat Bucak, hereditary chief of a feudal Kurdish clan who had gotten himself elected to Parliament and raked in millions of dollars by renting his private army to the Turkish authorities for use in their war against Kurdish nationalists. In the backseat, accompanied by his mistress, a glossy-lipped former beauty queen, was none other than Abdullah Çatlı, one of the country's most famous gangsters, a convicted heroin smuggler who had escaped from a prison in Switzerland and was being sought by Interpol. Çatlı was revered by ultra-rightists who credited him with murdering many "enemies of the state."

What was this odd trio doing together? That question was and is the heart of the Susurluk scandal. No one inside the car could answer it. Çatlı and his mistress were killed instantly. So was the police commander, Kocadağ. The only survivor, Bucak, did not shed any light on the affair because, he claimed, the impact gave him a severe and evidently incurable case of amnesia.

Traffic police who arrived at the scene of the crash found a small arsenal of pistols and silencers in the trunk, together with a diplomatic passport made out in Çatlı's name. Soon it was discovered that Çatlı had held not one but half a dozen diplomatic passports, each with a different name; several identity cards, each also with a different name; and a folder full of gun permits signed by top interior ministry officials. Evidence leaked from police files suggested that he had masterminded crimes ranging from the 1978 massacre of seven leftist students in

Ankara to the jailbreak a year later that freed Mehmet Ali Ağca, the contract gunman who went on to shoot Pope John Paul II in Rome.

Çatlı, it turned out, had been far from a freelance killer. Together with an unknown number of other thugs, he had been recruited by government security agents as an assassin. As payment for his services they allowed him to run his lucrative heroin-smuggling operation, launder his money through crooked casinos and kill his rivals whenever he chose, all without interference. To their credit, Turkish newspapers reported these facts as quickly as their reporters could confirm them. Soon every Turk understood why police commanders had protected Çatlı rather than arresting him and turning him over to Interpol.

A thorough investigation of the Susurluk scandal would stain the reputations of many important politicians and military commanders. Some Turks clamor for it, hoping that it would not only reveal ugly truths but also set Turkey on a new path toward political morality. Others fear the political devastation that would certainly follow. Bad as it may be to ignore and thus effectively pardon such crimes, they reason, it would be even worse to bring them to light. One newspaper columnist wrote:

> It is now obvious that the state has from time to time engaged in secret operations to commit illegal acts. Undemocratic-minded people, concocting their own brand of "patriotism," decided to use gunmen to eliminate people they saw as a threat. Most of the public believes that the truth about these gangs will never be fully exposed. Is it really an insoluble problem? No. But unraveling the tangle would upset so many powerful individuals and organizations that one tends to think maybe it is better kept as it is.

Susurluk was a key turning point in Turkey's modern history. For generations Turks had clung to a childlike belief that however confusing things seemed, the state probably knew best. Susurluk, meaning not only the facts of the scandal but also the state's refusal to allow it to be fully investigated, shook and began to destroy that faith. It stripped away the myth that security agencies exist to enforce law and that a clear line separates police from criminals. In the process it sobered many Turks and forced them to accept new truths about the society in which they live.

Although this episode set off great public outrage and the word *Susurluk* became an instantly understood code word for the dark matrix that binds political assassins to elements in the security forces, little seemed to change in the heart of "deep state." That became clear when, shortly after noon on November 9, 2005, nine years after the Susurluk crash, life in the hardscrabble Kurdish town of Şemdinli was shattered by a bomb thrown into the local bookstore. Because bookstores are by nature places where ideas are debated, those in southeastern Turkey have often been targets of thugs who wish to suppress free speech. This time, however, something extraordinary followed the bombing. The bookstore owner survived, and along with a crowd of outraged neighbors he managed to chase the three attackers to their car and capture them.

What they discovered confirmed their suspicions about who was behind anti-Kurdish terror attacks that had plagued their region for more than a decade. Two of the three bombers were government intelligence agents, and the third was a former Kurdish militant who had become a police informer. In their car, which belonged to the army, were grenades, automatic rifles, armored vests, maps of the surrounding area and lists of local citizens who sympathized with Kurdish causes.

This news outraged many Turks. Prime Minister Erdoğan professed to be one of them. He traveled to Şemdinli and vowed in a public speech to punish everyone involved in the bombing. *Nereye kadar giderse gidilecek*, he promised—"Wherever it takes us, we will go." This was a daring pledge. Most doubted he would be able to keep it. They were right.

The Turkish chief of staff, General Yaşar Büyükanit, not only refused to condemn the bombing but said he was personally acquainted with one of the bombers and knew him as "a good boy." Then, after a prosecutor secured long prison terms for the "good boy" and his two comrades, General Büyükanit called the verdicts a "murder of law" and arranged for the prosecutor to be fired. The case died there, without the investigation Erdoğan had been so bold as to promise.

Episodes like the Susurluk crash and the Şemdinli bombing have reshaped Turkey's national conscience, for they revealed the moral corruption that had infected the state, and many Turks came to suspect that truths the government had drilled into them for years might actually be lies. That allowed them to open their minds to alternative views of the 1915 tragedy. In the first years of the new century more than a dozen books touching on this subject were published in Turkey, bearing titles like *Armenians in Our Neighborhood* and *The Armenian Taboo*.

In 2005, eager to take advantage of this changing climate, a group of Turkish scholars and opinion makers announced plans to hold an academic conference in Istanbul at which, for the first time in modern Turkish history, all points of view about the Armenian massacre would be respectfully heard. Their central goal was to move this debate from the province of emotion into the realm of fact-based history. As the date of their conference approached, however, nationalists realized what they were doing and raised a great commotion. Using the power that the old elite still holds over Turkey's higher education system, they forced Bosphorus University to cancel plans to host the conference.

"We must put an end to this cycle of treason and insult, of spreading propaganda against the nation by people who belong to it," Minister of Justice Cemil Çiçek snarled, reflecting the reactionary strain that infected even the supposedly democratic new regime. Istanbul's governor warned that he would not be able to guarantee security for the conference. A prosecutor demanded that he be allowed to review all papers before they were publicly presented.

In a past era that would have been enough to scuttle the conference. Several private universities had opened in Istanbul, however, and one of them agreed to host the event. There was nothing the old guard could do other than to dispatch a few dozen protesters to shout insults and throw eggs at people as they arrived. Every session was packed. People listened raptly to speakers who read papers with titles like "What the World Knows but Turkey Does Not" and "The Roots of a Taboo: The Historical-Psychological Suffocation of Turkish Public Opinion on the Armenian Problem." For weeks afterward the press was full of reaction and analysis, much of it deeply soul-searching. Some commentators objected to parts of what was said at the conference, but nearly all welcomed the breakthrough to open debate on this painful topic.

"I felt that we were making history, that something incredible had suddenly happened," my friend Yavuz Baydar, a columnist for the mass-circulation daily *Sabah*, marveled afterward. "Everyone was conscious of it. This is not a taboo anymore."

Why did it take Turks so long to begin acknowledging that the pitiless slaughter of Armenians in 1915 was the result of a calculated plan devised by the dying Ottoman regime? There are four reasons.

The first is obvious. It is the same reason people in other countries rarely admit that their ancestors murdered and oppressed innocents. Few nations have the courage to face devastating truths of their own history. Turks are just as comfortable in their cocoon of denial as are the descendants of killers in other countries.

The second reason many Turks have mischaracterized or minimized the events of 1915 is simple ignorance. In public schools this subject is taught from the official point of view, so the Turks' outrage at hearing their ancestors accused of great crimes may stem not only from chauvinism or malice but also from the distorted history that has been drilled into them by schoolteachers, university professors, journalists, writers, military commanders and political leaders.

A third reason for refusing to accept the idea that their forebears were *génocidaires* is the Turks' fear of what would follow such an admission. Some Armenian-Americans insist that once Turkey makes an official acknowledgment or is officially condemned under international law, it must be forced to pay compensation to the victims' descendants. Others go further, suggesting that Turkey turn over swaths of land in eastern Anatolia to Armenian families, Armenian organizations or the Republic of Armenia. No resolution to the debate is possible so long as these threats hang over it.

The fourth and most underappreciated factor in this difficult conflict lies in the Turks' own history since 1915. Official propaganda has long sought to persuade citizens of the Turkish Republic that they are all Turks, but the truth is quite different. Many Turkish citizens have little or no Turkic blood. Ask one about his or her family background, and you may well hear a story about grandparents or great-grandparents who were forced to flee from ancestral homes in Crimea, the Balkans, Central Asia, Aegean islands, the Caucasus or another region overrun by anti-Muslim forces as the Ottoman Empire collapsed. Millions of these refugees—among them ancestors of Tayyip Erdoğan, who came from Georgia—flooded into Anatolia, forced to leave behind everything their families had spent centuries accumulating. Their experience of being driven from their native lands is seared into their memories. The outside world, however, is largely unaware of their histories of displacement and exile. It is ignorant of their suffering, just as many Turks are ignorant of how Armenians suffered. Instead of recognizing that many of today's Turks are descended from victims of ethnic cleansing, much of the world sees them as descendants of cleansers. To most Turks that seems outrageously unjust. It leads them to reject the pretensions of their accusers.

The question of what name to give the killings of 1915—slaughter, massacre or genocide—might properly be the province of philologists and international lawyers. That is not, however, how many in the Armenian diaspora see it. In the two countries where they are most numerous and politically powerful, France and the United States, they have waged a relentless political campaign to have their suffering officially labeled as genocide.

Years of campaigning by French citizens of Armenian descent—there are about half a million of them—led in 2006 to an astonishing victory. The French National Assembly officially declared that Ottoman Turks committed genocide in 1915, and voted to make it a crime for anyone to assert otherwise. This triumph in France inspired some of the four hundred thousand Americans of Armenian descent, working through their superbly effective lobby in Washington, to intensify pressure on the U.S. Congress. In pressing for a resolution defining the 1915 killings as genocide, which they have done yearly since the late 1980s, they presented Congress with two questions.

The first was whether the events of 1915 constituted genocide. Turks like to point out that while Armenians in eastern Anatolia were suffering in 1915 as part of the Ottoman campaign to crush an ethnic rebellion there, those in Istanbul and other western cities were allowed to live freely. But the United Nations, in a treaty adopted in 1948 and ratified by more than 120 countries, accepts a sweeping definition in which the murder of as few as two people, or even causing "mental harm" to two people, can constitute genocide if it is part of a campaign intended to destroy, even "in part," any national, ethnic, racial or religious group. That is a far cry from the definition in my *American Heritage* dictionary, which calls genocide "the systematic and planned extermination of an entire national, racial, political or ethnic group." By that definition, which corresponds to what most lay people believe, the slaughter of 1915 was probably not genocide. By the definition in the UN treaty, the standard of international law, it probably was.

The second fundamental question Congress must address is whether condemning evil-doers from past centuries should be part of its job. In 2006, as the Armenian-American lobbying campaign in Washington was reaching a peak of success, the Pulitzer Prize for nonfiction was awarded to a devastating book entitled *Imperial Reckoning* that makes the case that Britain committed genocide in Kenya during the 1950s. That Congress did not consider condemning the British for what the author of *Imperial Reckoning* called a "campaign of terror, dehumanizing torture and genocide" was in part because Kenyans do not have a powerful Washington lobby, and in part because doing so would place a moral obligation on Congress to decide whether France, Belgium, Germany, Holland, Russia, Serbia, Spain, Portugal, Cambodia, China or other countries are equally guilty—not to mention the United States itself, which was built on piles of Native American and African bones.

Few members of Congress reflect on such abstract concepts as moral obligation. Still, the resolution branding Turks as guilty of genocide almost passed the House of Representatives in 2007, thanks to the influence of Speaker Nancy Pelosi, in whose home state of California many prosperous Armenian-Americans live. Only the prospect that its passage might lead Turkey to reduce its cooperation with the American war effort in Iraq—70 percent of the cargo shipped to U.S. soldiers in Iraq was passing through a base in southern Turkey—allowed cooler heads to prevail.

The catastrophe of 1915—Atatürk called it a "shameful act"—is a central fact of modern Armenian history. Victims and their descendants have a right to make demands of modern Turkey. They deserve truth. They deserve an apology. Most of all, they deserve advocates who will promote the reconciliation that is their best hope for the future.

Lobbyists in the Armenian diaspora seem puzzlingly uninterested in advocating democracy in their ancestral homeland. Modern Armenia is a wretchedly poor, self-isolated backwater whose army crushes dissent and whose national life is shrouded in dank pessimism. Its population is steadily sinking and its level of development, measured by any political, social or economic standard, is far behind Turkey's. If its sons and daughters abroad had devoted to the cause of Armenian democracy even a fraction of the resources they have used to lobby Congress to pass a genocide resolution, Armenia might he a much happier place today.

Perhaps the most curious aspect of the campaign to brand Turks as guilty of genocide in 1915 is that it has never excited much interest in Armenia. That is partly because many Armenian citizens, unlike their cousins in France and the United States, are not descended from survivors of the 1915 massacre. But the more important reason is that they have immediate needs. Most live poor, heartbreakingly unfulfilled lives. They are far more interested in improving their future than in probing their past. According to a public opinion survey taken in 2007, only 3 percent of Armenians believe that forcing Turkey to admit genocide should be their government's top priority. Only 4 percent even placed it on their list of priorities.

Tens of thousands of ethnic Armenians still live in Turkey, and in Istanbul there are Armenian churches, an Armenian patriarch, an Armenian school, an Armenian hospital and an Armenian newspaper, *Agos*. The editor of *Agos*, Hrant Dink, was a wonderful exemplar of the Turkish-Armenian tradition. Turkish nationalists hated him because he was proud of his heritage and identity, and like too many of his colleagues, he had been forced to defend himself in court against the charge of "insulting Turkishness." Some Armenians in France and the United States scorned him because he campaigned relentlessly for reconciliation. In his editorials about the massacres of 1915 he urged them not to demand *ikrar*, or confession, from Turkey, but rather *idrak*, which means "perception" or "understanding."

"Turkey's democratization is much more important than its recognition of the genocide," Dink wrote in one newspaper column. "Only a country that is democratic can dare to deal with its history, discuss its problems, and feel empathy."

One night in 2006 I happily accepted an invitation from friends to enjoy one of Turkey's great delights, dinner aboard a yacht cruising the Bosphorus. Among the other guests was Hrant Dink, whose life had become less than delightful. He was being fiercely denounced in the ultranationalist press and received a steady stream of death threats. With an election campaign approaching, politicians were trawling for votes with chauvinistic anti-Armenian and anti-Kurdish rhetoric. I was not surprised that Dink seemed subdued and preoccupied. Feeling a sudden need to do more than just exchange pleasantries, I pulled him aside and told him how important his work was, how much support he had in Turkey and beyond, and what a journalistic hero he had become.

"I understand," he replied simply. "I do not stop."

On the afternoon of January 19, 2007, as Dink was returning to the *Agos* office on a busy Istanbul street, a gunman stepped out of the passing crowd and shot him dead. It was a stunning crime, the like of which had not been seen in Turkey for decades. Footage from a surveillance camera was broadcast on television. Soon afterward a man from the Black Sea town of Trabzon called police to report that he recognized the killer as his seventeen-year-old son, Ogün Samast. The young man was quickly arrested and confessed his crime. He said he had fired the fatal shots because Dink "insulted Turkish blood."

My first reaction was to blame "deep state." Even if the young killer had acted alone, he had certainly been encouraged by the hateful rhetoric of violent nationalists. He must also have been aware that police and army officers had for years tolerated and even organized murders of people they considered subversive. "Deep state has become a tradition," Prime Minister Erdoğan lamented. "We can describe it as gangs inside a state organization. This kind of structure does exist. Our state and our nation have paid a high price because we have not been able to crack down on these networks."

Outrage engulfed much of Turkey in the hours after Dink was shot. Newspapers carried banner headlines like THEY KILLED OUR

BROTHER and IT WAS TURKEY THAT WAS SHOT DEAD. More than one hundred thousand people turned out for a protest march through the streets of Istanbul, carrying posters with the victim's portrait and the words WE ARE ALL HRANT DINK—WE ARE ALL ARMENIANS.

For a very short time it seemed possible to believe that a perverted youth from the provinces, his mind twisted by criminally irresponsible politicians and others, had taken it upon himself to commit this horrific crime. But evidence quickly emerged suggesting that others were involved. A prosecutor indicted eighteen people, and the justice minister declared that Dink had been killed by "an organization." Former president Kenan Evren said he doubted the murder was "the act of a child or his friends." Erdoğan fired Trabzon's governor and police chief, and then suspended the chief of police intelligence in Istanbul, who had reportedly failed to act after being informed of a plot against Dink.

"The dark hand that killed him will be found and punished," Erdoğan vowed.

That promise sounded thrilling, but Erdoğan had made a similar one after the Şemdinli bombing and little had come of it. Soon it became clear that the same would happen in this case. Police files mysteriously disappeared. A prominent nationalist politician called the march by Dink's admirers "a freak show." Then an Istanbul television station broadcast a shocking video showing Ogün Samast, the confessed killer, with his jailers, who cheered and embraced him as they would a hero. In the background hung a Turkish flag and a banner bearing sentences of Atatürk's: "The nation's land is sacred. It cannot be left to fate." The police responded to this video not by punishing the prison guards but by launching an investigation into who had leaked it. Then the offending station's right to cover government events was canceled. "The murderer and his associates were not alone," the newspaper editor Ismet Berkan sadly concluded, but had "penetrated all segments of the state."

Violent nationalists who believe that journalists should be killed if they write forbidden words were not the only Turks who shared responsibility for Dink's murder. So did government officials who never found it necessary to condemn rhetoric that incited people to violence, never spoke out to defend the right of free speech and never demanded serious investigations of the car crash at Susurluk or the Şemdinli bombing.

By their silence they had emboldened radicals and encouraged them to believe that the state tacitly supported them. This set the stage for Dink's murder.

The virulence of these ultra-nationalists burst into public view at a provincial stadium a few days after the murder. A large crowd had assembled for a soccer match. Much of Turkey was still in shock, and during a break in the action, people began a chant in memory of the victim. "We are all Hrant Dink!" they shouted repeatedly.

Before anyone had time to absorb the full meaning of this welcome message of solidarity and defiance, it was drowned out by another cry, louder and more passionate: "We are all Ogün Samast!" thousands screamed. "We are all Ogün Samast!" This praise of the murderer was a chilling reminder that ultra-nationalism still moves too many Turkish souls. The fact that political leaders did not immediately castigate those who took up the repugnant cry allowed them to believe they had tacit support in high places.

One reason ultra-nationalists howled ever more loudly during the first years of the new century was that they sensed the tide of Turkish history turning against them. Their ability to enforce limits on public debate was fading. Nowhere was that clearer than in the growing willingness of Turks to look more honestly at their history, especially the history of Ottoman Armenians.

The intellectuals who organized that 2005 conference where questions of genocide were debated publicly for the first time were prominent among the Turks promoting this new openness. More intriguing was the mood among people in eastern Anatolia itself. Many of them grew up hearing chilling stories about the massacres of 1915 and therefore knew that the official history was untrue. But they also discovered a good reason to wish for renewed friendship between Turks and Armenians. If the land border between Turkey and Armenia were reopened—Turkey closed it to protest Armenia's seizure of the Nagorno-Karabakh enclave from Azerbaijan in the early 1990s—life in eastern Anatolia, the poorest part of Turkey, would certainly improve. Not only would trade boom, but Armenian tourists would stream in to visit sites that mark the zenith of their ancient civilization. Such tourists have, in recent years, arrived by roundabout routes, but if they could once again make the simple border crossing near the Turkish town of Kars, their number would undoubtedly skyrocket.

A couple of months after the 2005 genocide conference in Istanbul, I returned to Lake Van, one of my favorite spots in Turkey. From the shore I could see the island dominated by the ruins of the tenth-century Akhtamar Church, for nearly a millennium a seat of great religious and political power.

On my previous visits, the collapsed walls of this church had struck me as a vivid symbol of what had happened to the intimate ties that for centuries bound the Ottoman Empire's Turkish and Armenian communities together. This time, though, I saw something that would have been unthinkable only a few years earlier. Restoration workers, paid by the Turkish government, were repairing the church. Thrilled by the sight, I hired a boat to take me out to the island, where I watched craftsmen replacing the collapsed roof and cleaning the magnificent exterior relief carvings that Armenian artisans created ten centuries ago. I stared up at them in awe. Some depict biblical scenes, like Samson smiting a Philistine with the jawbone of an ass and David preparing to fling a stone at Goliath. Others portray contemporary life, like one that shows a man struggling with a bear beneath bunches of heavy-hanging grapes. I stared the longest at one that shows a figure labeled "Saint Gregory, Illuminator of the Armenians," holding a book stamped with a cross as John the Baptist blesses him. According to tradition, Armenia was the first nation to accept Christianity.

Few are the Armenians who would not wish to return and pray at this uniquely meaningful spot. That is not yet possible, since Akhtamar, now fully restored, has become a museum rather than a church. I nonetheless took its painstaking reconstruction as a sign of hope, a hint that the century of pain that has divided two peoples who lived and thrived together for so long might one day be wiped away.

Thetis, the sea nymph who was Achilles' mother, stared up at me one hot day as I walked near the banks of the Euphrates River in southern Turkey. Her face was at the center of an exquisite Roman mosaic that archaeologists had just uncovered, surrounded by a host of dolphins, crabs and other sea creatures. Around me the archaeologists were still digging in the sandy earth. They had found ancient columns, remains of walls and artifacts ranging from pottery shards to a magnificent bronze statue of Mars.

This had once been Zeugma, a city of seventy thousand people at the eastern edge of the Roman Empire. It sat astride some of the world's most important trading routes, and its merchants became very rich. They spent much of their money paying the most accomplished artists of the age to create elaborate mosaics on the floors of their villas, competing with one another to see who could commission the most elaborate and original ones.

In the third century Zeugma fell to invaders from the east and then was struck by an earthquake. Its people drifted away and nature slowly reclaimed and buried the city. Archaeologists pinpointed its location in the mid-1970s and began sporadic excavations, but it was not until a dam was built across the Euphrates half a mile away that anyone felt the need to begin intensive digging there. Zeugma, or at least what were its lower-lying neighborhoods, was about to be flooded by the waters of an artificial lake. The archaeologists wanted to save whatever they could, and soon after they began their work they realized they had stumbled onto one of the most important collections of Roman mosaics ever discovered. They hauled a dozen of them to the nearest museum, but an unknown number were lost to the advancing water without ever being seen.

Publicity about the find at Zeugma led an American foundation to launch a multimillion-dollar project there. Its directors believe that most of the ancient city lies beneath nearby hills that are above the new water level. They hope to spend several years excavating the site, and if their hunch is correct they want to turn it into an open-air museum.

The discovery of these mosaics reflected an aspect of Turkey that foreigners do not always understand. This country's land has been populated since the beginning of human history by an amazing number of civilizations—pagan, Christian and Islamic, coming from Greece, Rome, Egypt, Arabia, Persia and places even farther away. King Midas and King Croesus, Saint Paul and Saint Nicholas, Homer and Herodotus—all came from the land that is now Turkey. This is where Aristotle taught philosophy, where Diogenes searched for an honest man and where Florence Nightingale treated the sick and wounded. Many of history's greatest conquerors have won or lost wars here, among them Alexander, Darius, Tamerlane, Hannibal and Saladin. No other piece of geography on earth has been home to so many different peoples over so many centuries.

Before I began traveling in Turkey, I thought ancient Greece was in Greece as we know it today. Much of it was, of course, including Athens, Sparta and the city-states of the Peloponnese. But many of its greatest, richest and most imposing cities arose in what is now Turkey. Pergamon, whose astonishing temple to Zeus was excavated and carried intact to Berlin in the nineteenth century, is in Turkey. So are Ephesus, which housed one of the greatest libraries of antiquity, and Halicarnassus, once a crossroads of the world known for its towering lighthouse. Traveling along Turkey's Aegean and Mediterranean coasts, one is overwhelmed by the density of Hellenic ruins there.

My favorite of these ruins is Phaselis, once a thriving capital and now a quiet, stately and abandoned monument facing an implausibly gorgeous Mediterranean cove not far from Antalya, the region's main city. It is well enough preserved to convey a vivid sense of what it must have been like to live in antiquity. Founded by colonists from Rhodes in the seventh century B.C., *it quickly became a trading center rich enough to have its own mint, which not surprisingly produced coins depicting nautical scenes. Alexander spent several months there, choosing it over other towns in the region partly because he was deeply moved at the sight of its most impressive artifact, a broken spear supposedly used by Achilles. "The extraordinarily beautiful town had three harbors, straight avenues, a theater and plazas," he wrote. "Although it was winter, roses were in bloom everywhere."*

Phaselis's broad main street, paved with cut stones, is lined with the ruins of many Roman structures, including a gymnasium that opens onto a public bath, a long aqueduct, a gate dedicated to Hadrian and a classically proportioned theater with twenty rows of stone seats. When I was there a large tortoise was all that moved on what had been the stage, but when I closed my eyes I thought I heard a toga-clad poet chanting tales of seafaring heroes. Cleopatra is said to have visited Phaselis, and it takes only a bit of imagination to picture her in one of the seats.

What is most remarkable about Phaselis is that for all its splendor, it is little known and rarely visited. If it were the only ancient site in Turkey it would be jammed with tourists every day, but it is one of thousands. Turkey has so many places like this that it cannot even catalog them, much less excavate and protect them. It is hard to turn a shovel without discovering something ancient. Even in Istanbul, the long-planned subway system cannot be extended to serve some of the most densely populated neighborhoods because any tunnel there would have to be drilled through priceless ruins.

One summer I spent a week sailing around the peninsula west of Phaselis. Two thousand years ago this was the heart of an ancient confederation called the Lycian League, which at various times was under the control of Greeks, Romans, Persians, Egyptians and even bands of pirates. Near one seaside village I explored a necropolis where the Lycians buried their dead in above-ground tombs, some of them freestand-

ing and others carved into the sides of cliffs. Atop a nearby hill was a well-preserved Byzantine fortress built on the ruins of one from Lycian times. On my way down I stopped to admire the smallest ancient amphitheater I have ever seen, carved from rock in a neat semicircle and only large enough to hold about two hundred fifty people.

On that trip I spent one day inland. After driving about thirty-five miles in a rented car, I parked at the foot of a deep canyon in the Taurus range, which runs along much of Turkey's Mediterranean coast. Guided by a friend who had been there before, I walked for an hour along a Roman road and then across a farmer's yard where goats were grazing. Suddenly, emerging from a poplar grove, I found myself facing the ruined towers and walls of an ornate Byzantine church with two octagonal chambers in opposite corners. This church is not mentioned in any guidebook, and probably very few outsiders have laid eyes on it in recent centuries. How many undiscovered places like this there are across Turkey's vast territory!

Even the discovered sites are so remote and widely scattered that many are rarely visited. In Turkey I have followed routes taken by Julius Caesar and Saint Peter, walked among weird monoliths carved by Hittite sculptors three thousand years ago, crawled into caves used as churches by early Christians and climbed rocky hills up to crusaders' castles. Once I took a drive through eastern Turkey that in the space of just four days took me to unforgettable ruins from half a dozen great cultures.

My first stop was the huge fifteenth-century Ottoman cemetery at Ahlat, on the shore of Lake Van. It is filled with tall headstones carved with intricate Arabic inscriptions, mute messengers from times now only barely remembered, and at the same time objects of powerful beauty. From Ahlat I drove north along the Iranian border to the spectacular Ishak Pasha castle, built atop a mountain crag in the eighteenth century by a clan called the Çıldıroğlu, who, depending on which expert one believes, were either Georgians, Turks, Armenians or Kurds. I continued past snowcapped Mount Ararat to Kars, formerly a Russian garrison town, and then to the abandoned Armenian capital of Ani, which around the year 1000 was the seat of kings, bishops and one hundred thousand prosperous citizens; today it is surreal and abandoned, the shells of its great churches and palaces conveying a deep sense of the impermanence of grandeur. My last stops were in the verdant hills around Artvin, near the border with Georgia, which are dotted with awe-inspiring Georgian churches more than a thousand years old.

Nowhere else in the world can one possibly have a tour like this. Turks are rightly proud of what their land has to offer, but in one sense not proud enough. Their culture ministry is pitifully poor, barely able to pay its employees and maintain the country's most famous monuments, much less preserve the lesser-known ones or begin new excavations. The sheer number of ancient sites in their country has jaded them. Even some people at the highest ranks of the government don't seem to understand what lies on and beneath Turkish soil. All too many of their treasures are slowly disintegrating.

Some Turks are less than comfortable with their land's pre-Islamic history. They worry that if they celebrate their Arabian, Kurdish, Greek, Armenian and Georgian pasts, Turkey will seem less theirs. Taught from childhood that they are descended from Turkic tribes that followed the legendary gray wolf out of Central Asia in the tenth century, many of them have an insular Turkocentric view of the world, reinforced by the government's having changed hundreds of place-names to make them sound more Turkish. The mayor of Ankara (formerly Angora) has gone so far as to launch a campaign to change the city's symbol from one based on a Hittite design to one including a mosque; he says the Hittites were "not Turkish."

In fact, Turks are heir to every culture that ever existed in Anatolia. Their heritage is vigorous, cosmopolitan, diverse and unimaginably rich. They should embrace it wholeheartedly and become caretakers of all the glittering riches of Anatolian history.

• FIVE •

THE KURDISH PUZZLE

☪

An old man who is among the most respected denizens of the twisting Diyarbakır bazaar sat on a tattered sofa one afternoon and spun out his memories of Kurdish struggle. Speaking with a precision and energy that belied his years, he began his tale in the 1930s. There were patterns over the decades: rebellions crushed, villages burned, relatives arrested, friends lost to unknown assassins.

"Even though it's dangerous for me to say this, I have been greatly oppressed in my lifetime," he told me as he leaned his chin on his wooden cane. "I have been tortured many times. One of my sons died after forty days of torture by the police. All of this has happened to me and to so many of us because we claim our rights. Kurds don't even have minority rights in a region where we are the majority. But we have to keep demanding them. We can't stop. This war is our third since the great uprising in 1938. All have been fought for the same reason. Each generation produces a leader who fights for our rights."

Sitting silently nearby, taking it all in, were a handful of earnest-looking teenagers. They are the new generation of Kurds, eagerly absorbing stories that fire their political commitment. Watching this scene, I had the sense of a torch being passed. As long as Kurdish consciousness is nourished this way, no amount of military or political pressure applied by the Turkish authorities will be able to pacify these people.

Despite its poverty and the sense of intimidation that hangs in its air, Diyarbakır, with its winding streets, hidden courtyards and ancient city wall, became one of my favorite cities in Turkey. What truly enthralled me about the Kurdish region, though, was not its cities but the grandeur of its countryside. Much of western Turkey is either coastal lowland or rolling hills covered by farms and orchards. Central provinces are rugged and barren. The Black Sea region is cool, verdant and alpine. But no part of this country is as overwhelming as the east. Jagged peaks and precipices soar above gorges and lakes. In the warm months, dazzling colors and sweet fragrances assault the senses. When the snow falls it falls without pity, blanketing huge areas in deep drifts, cutting some villages off from the outside world and all but burying others. The landscape here is oversize, like the passions of the tribesmen who have lived amid it for millennia. It is not a geography that encourages moderation. Not coincidentally, it is also ideal guerrilla territory.

The Kurdish conflict is Turkey's festering wound, and to travel to Diyarbakır and from there through eastern provinces where Kurds constitute the large majority is to see the country's ugliest face. Convinced that they are fighting to defend their nation's very existence and desperately resisting the worldwide trend toward regionalism and local self-rule, successive Turkish leaders have willingly done whatever was necessary to crush Kurdish nationalism. Despite or perhaps because of this refusal to compromise, Kurdish consciousness is stronger today than it has ever been.

For thousands of years Kurds have lived in what used to be called Mesopotamia and what some now call Kurdistan, a name the Turkish government rejects because of its supposed political taint. Today they are estimated to number about thirty million, with half in Turkey, another quarter in Iraq, about 15 percent in Iran, 5 percent in Syria and the rest scattered in the region and beyond. Until recently most thought of themselves not as Kurds but as members of one clan or another. Only during the last decades of the twentieth century did they come to consider themselves part of a single nation or people. Governments of all countries in which they live view them with suspicion.

In the fourth century B.C. the Greek commander Xenophon came across tribesmen who may have been ancestors of today's Kurds, and later wrote: "They lived among the mountains, were very warlike and did not obey the king." That is the best one-sentence description of Kurds ever written, as true today as it was then. Although they have never had a country of their own, Kurds have no tradition of submitting to anyone.

In modern Turkey no one is discriminated against for being Kurdish. Many Kurds have reached the pinnacle of success in business, entertainment and even politics. Others could share this success by acknowledging that first and foremost they are Turks, but millions refuse to do so, and largely as a result of their stubbornness they are among Turkey's poorest citizens. Some live in muddy ghettos on the edges of prosperous, lovely towns like Safranbolu, far from their ancestral homeland. Most remain in the east, unemployed and unhappy.

"The Government has long denied the Kurdish population, located largely in the southeast, basic political, cultural and linguistic rights," the U.S. State Department asserted in one human-rights report. "As part of its fight against the PKK, the Government forcibly displaced noncombatants, failed to resolve extra-judicial killings, tortured civilians and abridged freedom of expression."

The revolutionary PKK, or Kurdistan Workers Party, was born not in the hardscrabble villages of Turkey's southeast but in Ankara. It was there that a Marxist firebrand named Abdullah Öcalan and a handful of his comrades met during the mid-1970s to begin building what would become the most effective rebel force ever to take up arms against the Turkish state. Kurds are poor, share a collective memory of rebellion and have used guns to solve their problems for as long as there have been guns. This, Öcalan concluded, made them the ideal base for a revolutionary movement in Turkey. He and his brothers in arms were infected by the same curses that have driven politics in this part of the world for too long: ethnic chauvinism, dictatorial arrogance and the impulse to mindless violence.

In 1978 this core of radicals, together with a handful of non-Marxist Kurds, formally established the PKK. After the 1980 military coup they moved their headquarters to Syria, where President Hafez al-Assad quickly recognized them as a useful tool in his country's long-running feud with Turkey. Encouraged by his patrons in Moscow, who were also looking for ways to undermine Turkish power, Assad gave the PKK training bases, weapons and generous financial support. Soon the guerrillas were ready to fight. On August 15, 1984, they launched their war with rocket and machine-gun attacks on Turkish government outposts in two eastern villages.

Within a few years the guerrilla force had attracted thousands of militants, and war had spread across eastern Turkey. The government responded by placing the region under "emergency rule," a form of martial law that permits censorship, detention without trial and the use of summary tribunals to try suspected subversives. But these efforts proved inadequate, and within a few years PKK units were moving freely through Turkey's eastern provinces, even naming their own mayors, judges and tax collectors. Energized by their success, Öcalan's men began assassinating Turkish schoolteachers who by the luck of a draw had been assigned to the southeast, newspaper vendors who dared to distribute Turkish newspapers and villagers they considered too friendly to the army.

In the early 1990s the government realized that what it officially described as a band of cutthroat terrorists was actually a disciplined military force that had won at least nighttime control of huge swaths of territory, enjoyed growing popular support in the combat zone and counted on backing not just from Syria but also from powerful groups in Russia, Iraq, Armenia and Greece. Its treasury was swollen by profits from heroin smuggling and by contributions, voluntary and otherwise, from Kurdish exiles in Europe. The PKK had come to embody the most terrifying Kemalist nightmare: a conspiracy of foreign powers and renegade locals aimed at dismembering the Turkish motherland. Military commanders told Prime Minister Tansu Çiller they could crush this threat only if they were allowed to wage war without quarter. Lacking the imagination to come up with an alternative, she eagerly agreed. Soon hundreds of thousands of Turkish soldiers were flooding eastward to launch one of the century's great counter-insurgency campaigns.

The army began by identifying hundreds of villages and hamlets suspected of being pro-PKK. Squads marched systematically from one to the next, calling residents together and announcing that the village was to be burned in an hour. Distraught villagers would try to gather what they could of their possessions while soldiers machine-gunned their cattle and set their fields and crop stores ablaze.

At the same time, security agencies enlisted gangs of nationalist gunmen and sent them off to assassinate civilians suspected of sympathizing with Kurdish nationalism. Police "special teams" and rural gendarmes were encouraged to use whatever techniques of torture they considered necessary, either to extract information or simply to intimidate perceived enemies into silence. The Kurdish political party was banned and its representatives in Parliament dragged from their offices, summarily convicted of treason and sentenced to draconian prison terms.

The brutality of these tactics is indisputable, as is the brutality of the PKK's rebellion. Yet the eagerness with which some foreign governments have condemned Turkey, justified as condemnation may be, is more than a little disingenuous. Turkey was facing a threat to its very existence as a unified state, and it responded the way other countries in the post-war world have responded when peoples under their sovereignty rose in rebellion. The Turkish campaign against the PKK was comparable in various ways to those waged by the Dutch in Indonesia, the British in Malaya, the French in Algeria, the Serbs in Bosnia and the Russians in Chechnya. Turks understandably react unpleasantly when those former imperial powers condemn them for using tactics they themselves perfected not so long ago.

Most Turks, eager to believe the best about their army and knowing only what the pro-government press told them about the war, perceived it as a heroic struggle against terrorism. Young soldiers by the hundreds were coming home in flag-draped coffins, and Turks began to view the PKK as a font of unspeakable evil. But in the southeast everything looked different. There people used the word "martyr" to describe not soldiers ceremoniously buried with military honors but guerrillas dumped into unmarked graves. During my trips through the vast war zone, which covered an area the size of New England, I never found a Kurd who did not consider the security forces guilty of repression, torture and murder. Everyone there either has suffered at the hands of men in uniform or knows someone who has.

This campaign naturally led many Kurds to hate the Turkish army and the state it represents. It also led many to view Abdullah Öcalan and his PKK as beacons of hope. By banning almost every kind of Kurdish organization, the government made it impossible for moderate Kurdish leaders to emerge. This policy allowed Öcalan, a figure of marginal intelligence and great political immaturity, to became the sole embodiment of Kurdishness. Even today he could easily be elected mayor of any town or city in southeastern Turkey.

Journalists must apply for permission to travel in the war zone, and most of the time I worked in Turkey, my applications were ignored. Once in the spring of 1998, for reasons I never understood, one was approved, and immediately I flew to Diyarbakır and set off by car toward the mountains. At the first military checkpoint outside town I was invited to sit at a picnic table while my credentials were checked. I found three officers there sipping tea. They were curious about my impressions, but rather than sharing them, I began asking questions. If the guerrillas had no support, I wondered, how had they survived and waged war for so long? Might there not be some ordinary Kurds who support them?

The officers looked incredulous. Obviously they found the very idea absurd. "There is no political or social basis to this conflict," said a major who told me he was serving his third tour of duty in the southeast. "It is all fomented by foreign countries. You say it is a war, but I have to correct you. This is not a war. It's a peace operation. We're defending the country from terrorism, just as armies do all over the world. The only difference here is that it's taking a little longer."

I spent half an hour chatting with these officers. They seemed genuinely convinced that the PKK was implacably evil, that it had not a shred of popular support and that the only option for the Turkish state was to fight on until it had wiped away every vestige of Kurdish nationalism. Amazingly, they believed this could actually be accomplished.

Word finally came that I should be allowed to pass. Perhaps I would be allowed to reach my destination, Lice, a remote town in the heart of the war zone, after all. This was a thrilling prospect, because Lice (pronounced LEE-jeh) had been closed to outsiders for years. Even members of Parliament had been refused permission to visit. Lice is not just a hotbed of Kurdish nationalism but a legend, a rumor, a place few have ever visited but many believe they know.

For years the area around Lice was controlled by the PKK, and when the army began its scorched-earth campaign in the early 1990s, the town was among the first targets. Soldiers first razed the outlying villages, then set fire to nearby forests in which guerrillas had found refuge and finally, one day in 1993, burned down the town itself. Ninety percent of its ten thousand suddenly homeless residents fled to Istanbul or other cities, carrying identity cards that listed Lice as their birthplace and thus marked them instantly as suspicious or worse. They have been replaced by refugees from destroyed villages who were herded into town and allowed to build new homes on the rubble.

The checkpoint at the edge of Lice was manned by plainclothes officers from "special teams," men whose job it was either to ferret out terrorists or to repress and torture Kurds, depending on one's perspective. They were tough-looking guys, beefy and with no necks. Unlike their counterparts in Diyarbakır, they made no effort to cover the pistols on their hips. After a few minutes, several of them climbed into an unmarked car and told me to follow them. As I drove into Lice I turned to my Kurdish translator, who had doubted we would ever be allowed in. He was smiling nervously and shaking his head in disbelief.

We were led to the local police station, and as I crossed the threshold I felt an involuntary shudder. Who knew how many unfortunates, guilty or otherwise, had been brought through this door for rough, perhaps very rough, interrogation sessions? Inside, a thickset fellow named Hasrettin Bayraktar introduced himself as the chief of security in Lice. He seemed friendly enough as he asked me what I wanted to do, who I wanted to see, what I knew about Lice and what I hoped to learn.

I told him I had no agenda and simply wanted to look around and chat with townspeople. He assured me I was free to do so, and told me Lice was all but pacified. "Things are much better than when I got here three years ago. We lost a lot of people to migration, but not many are leaving now. We have a factory here. People are free to farm their land. When people don't work they get bad ideas in their heads, but now that there are more jobs, fewer people think like that."

Most people in Lice know better than to talk to strangers, but I was able to discover a few of the town's secrets. A strict eight o'clock curfew had been in force for years. Food distribution was controlled by the police, who feared that if free sale were allowed, people would buy extra and smuggle it to the guerrillas. A female suicide bomber had killed herself and wounded a few soldiers at a grocery store a couple of months before.

In one overgrown lot I picked up a piece of glass that had melted into a strange shape during the great fire that destroyed the town. I asked a man passing nearby who had set that fire. He shrugged and said he didn't know. When I asked if the fire might have been sparked by a bolt of lightning, a mischievous smile crept over his face. "Lightning," he mused, turning the idea over in his head. "That must have been it. Lightning."

I was torn between my curiosity and my desire not to cause trouble for the people I spoke to in Lice. Most would say only a sentence or two, always choosing their words carefully, and then hurry off. When I asked one man if the police considered everyone in Lice either a terrorist or a potential terrorist, he kept on walking as he nodded and answered, "That's the way it is." I found a refugee from a burned village and asked who burned it. He stared at me for a moment and then asked in reply, "Who burned *your* village?"

Lice has only one main street, dotted by cafés where unemployed men spend much of the day drinking tea and smoking. Across from an enormous statue of Atatürk, standing on a base that bears the admonition THE NATION IS ONE AND CANNOT BE DIVIDED, I found several men sitting on a sidewalk smoking nargiles. One of them looked to be well into his seventies but told me he was just fifty. Like most people in town, he had no work. Unlike most of them, he spoke freely.

"First the villages were torched, then it was our turn," he began. "They saw this place as some kind of temple, and they wanted to destroy it. It was a way of showing that they have the power to do whatever they want to us and we can't do anything back. Now the town is like an open prison. We can't talk and we can't move without being watched.

"But we still feel free," he went on. "Real freedom comes from inside you. I can still think what I want. I know I was born a Kurd and I'll die a Kurd. They can't take that away from me. So in spite of everything I'm a happy man. I'm winning my own personal war, because they haven't been able to crush my mind." He puffed his bubbling pipe and seemed absolutely tranquil.

I was deeply moved by his strength of character, but also worried. Wouldn't police agents come to bother him the moment I was gone?

"They will," he replied simply. "I'm ready for that too."

At that moment a new customer arrived and sat down. It was immediately clear that everyone knew him as a police informer, and with a quick hand gesture my friend signaled that our interview was over. I smoked for another couple of minutes, finished my tea and took my leave.

The Turkish army's vast numerical superiority in both men and weapons made its victory over the PKK only a matter of time. By the end of the century the military tide had turned, with soldiers painstakingly winning control of one mountain after another. It was a costly victory, not just in blood and treasure but also because it deeply alienated the people of southeastern Turkey and blackened the country's image abroad. The generals probably realized that this would be the price of victory, but they saw no other option. In the early years of the conflict, the PKK had declared its intention of turning southeastern Turkey into an independent Marxist state. Later Öcalan claimed several times that he was ready to negotiate a cease-fire and accept political compromises, but by then it was too late. The army had taken too many casualties and was determined to destroy his rebel force regardless of political cost.

As the war wound down, the PKK could claim a curious legacy of abject failure mixed with astonishing triumph. Its fighting force had been reduced to ragged bands cowering in foreign hideouts and unable to launch anything more than hit-and-run attacks inside Turkey. Its popular support network had been broken by the government's savagely effective military campaign. Perhaps most important, it had utterly failed to evolve into a democratic movement embodying the aspirations of a long-suffering people. Instead, thanks to Öcalan's megalomania, it was a rigid Leninist force that not only used terror against its enemies but punished its own dissenting members with torture and summary execution.

Despite these failures, however, the PKK could claim what were from its perspective two great victories. First and most transcendently,

Kurds emerged from the war with a greater sense of their own identity than ever before in their history. An entire generation of Kurds has grown up knowing that Kurds have been at war with Turks. Even those who did not support the rebellion have come to believe that there is such a thing as a Kurdish nation and that they belong to it. Whatever may be said about Öcalan's ruthlessness and corruption, he must be recognized, for better or worse, as the figure who lit the fire of Kurdish consciousness in countless souls.

Öcalan's second triumph was his success in luring the Turkish army into the brutality of counter-insurgency warfare. Armies fighting to defeat guerrilla uprisings use a classic set of tactics: they burn villages, shoot cattle, destroy food depots, displace populations and torture and execute suspected collaborators. Turkish security forces did all this and more. They won their war but, in doing so, earned worldwide opprobrium and polarized their own people. Öcalan wanted to inflict a deep wound on Turkey, and he succeeded.

For most of the war years Öcalan lived in Syria, supposedly a guest of the dictator Assad but in effect his prisoner. Like every other leader in the region, Assad had no use for Kurds and did not hesitate to repress his own Kurdish population whenever necessary. His support for Öcalan had nothing to do with the Kurdish cause and everything to do with his fear of Turkey's rising power. He knew that by encouraging Öcalan's rebellion he could tie down huge numbers of Turkish troops and bleed the Turkish economy.

Since the early 1980s Turkey had been diverting water from the Euphrates for large-scale irrigation and hydroelectric projects, ignoring Assad's bitter complaints that the diversions were turning the adjacent region of Syria into a desert. Assad calculated that if PKK guerrillas fought well, he might be able to force Turkish leaders to accept a deal in which he would end his support for their rebellion if Turkey would adopt a more generous water policy. In his dreams he may even have imagined that a PKK victory might help Syria regain Hatay, an ethnically Arab province of southern Turkey that sticks down like a thumb into Syria. Hatay was considered part of Syria from the Roman era until the early twentieth century. In 1939, however, departing French colonial rulers held a referendum asking local people whether they wanted to be left under Syrian or Turkish sovereignty. Most chose Turkey, and as a result France bequeathed Hatay to the Turks. To this day many Syrians believe Turkey stole it by rigging the referendum, and their official maps still show it as a Syrian province. Assad decided that sponsoring Öcalan was a fine way to punish Turks for their perfidy and perhaps extract valuable concessions from their government.

By the late 1990s the military balance between Turkey and Syria had shifted decisively. The Turkish army had bought hundreds of tanks and jet fighters, complemented by a host of high-tech weapons systems, and could claim to be the only modern fighting force in the Middle East other than Israel's. Syria was weak by comparison, friendless since the collapse of the Soviet Union and as backward militarily as it was politically. Turkish generals decided it was time to decapitate the PKK by demanding that Syria surrender Öcalan.

This campaign began the way all such campaigns begin in Turkey, with a speech by a general. In this case the messenger was General Atilla Ateş, chief of staff of the Turkish army. His threat, delivered in the autumn of 1998, was simple: Syria must expel Öcalan or risk war with Turkey. To underline his seriousness he sent ten thousand soldiers to mass along the Syrian border. Assad buckled almost immediately, and suddenly Öcalan was gone from Damascus. For a few days no one knew where he was, but intelligence agencies soon tracked him to a dacha outside Moscow. President Boris Yeltsin wanted him out of Russia, and a group of Italian leftists with connections to the Italian government, then led by ex-Communists, came to Öcalan's aid. They brought him to Rome, and a couple of days after his arrival Prime Minister Massimo D'Alema said that extradition was out of the question since Italy's constitution forbids extraditing anyone who could face the death penalty in his home country. Turks were outraged, and their anger intensified as prominent Europeans began to suggest that since terrorists were turning to peacemakers in other places, maybe Öcalan could do the same.

"He calls himself a guerrilla, but what could he do when his people were being systematically killed?" asked Danielle Mitterrand, widow of the French president and a longtime supporter of the Kurdish cause. She suggested that if Öcalan was to be put on trial, Turkish generals should be in the dock with him.

Within hours of Öcalan's arrival in Rome, throngs of Kurds living in exile there converged in front of the hospital to which he had been admitted for a checkup, waving Kurdish flags and chanting pledges of eternal love for their leader. Soon they were joined by thousands of their compatriots who arrived in buses, trains and auto caravans from other parts of Europe. So passionate was their emotion that they even set upon and beat Turkish journalists who had come to cover the story.

"If so many Kurds are coming to support him, then it cannot simply be a terrorist issue," reasoned Cardinal Achille Silvestrini of Rome. "It is a European issue."

What had at first looked like a triumph for Turkey became, almost overnight, a public relations disaster. Öcalan took up residence at a seaside villa and started receiving visitors as if he were a head of state. European politicians focused on the Kurdish problem in ways they never had while Öcalan was living in remote obscurity in Damascus. Some suggested that instead of being tried he should be invited to an international forum where he could present his case to world opinion. Prime Minister D'Alema urged Turkey to "find a solution to this long and bloody conflict by following the examples of Northern Ireland and the Basque country." Hans-Ulrich Klose, chairman of the foreign affairs committee in Germany's parliament, called Öcalan's capture "a good opportunity for solving the country's problems with the PKK and making the necessary reforms in Turkey." The European Parliament called for an international conference on the Kurdish issue.

Turks furiously rejected these ideas as intolerable infringements on their sovereignty. Whipped into a nationalist frenzy by politicians and the press, they turned their anger from Öcalan to Italy. Wild-eyed demonstrators burned Italian flags and Versace neckties in street-corner bonfires. Some of them, carrying placards that showed Prime Minister D'Alema with long fangs as he consumed Turkish children, or maps of Italy drenched in blood, tried to storm Italian diplomatic missions. Others jammed rallies where they joined in impassioned chants of "Damn Italy! Damn Italy!" Fruit dealers offered customers the chance to stomp on imported Italian lemons. Leaflets signed "Turkish Youth" urged patriots to stop eating pizza and spaghetti. Television transmitted pictures of these excesses across Europe, where they naturally appalled everyone who watched. Turkey's case against Öcalan was forgotten, replaced in the popular mind by images of Turks as mindless fanatics bereft of the manners expected of those who would sit at the European table.

But Turkey's leaders had learned from their successful intimidation of Syria that flexing their considerable muscle could bring results. They turned up their pressure on Italy, not just on the streets but in the boardrooms. Turkish companies began to cancel contracts with their Italian partners, and the army announced it would no longer accept Italian bids on lucrative procurement contracts. Leading Italian politicians became uncomfortable with the position in which their country suddenly found itself, and Prime Minister D'Alema soon came to share their misgivings. One day, eight weeks after Öcalan had arrived in Rome, he was suddenly gone. A few days later a private plane on which he was a passenger appeared in the air above Rotterdam, but air-traffic controllers there denied him permission to land. So did their counterparts in several other European cities. Frustrated in another attempt to find a home, the fugitive vanished again.

Exactly twelve days after that bizarre flying circus, on the morning of February 16, 1999, my telephone rang and a friend in Ankara told me excitedly that Öcalan had fallen into Turkish hands. At first I had trouble believing it. Quickly, like almost everyone else in Turkey, I switched on my television. A few minutes later Prime Minister Bülent Ecevit, who had taken office just a month before, appeared on the screen. He seemed to be struggling to contain his emotions as he read from a paper he held in his hands.

"Ladies and gentlemen, I have an announcement," he began. "The terrorist has been in Turkey since three o'clock this morning."

For a short while I was so confused and amazed that I could not focus on the details. When they emerged they made a wild story of betrayal and derring-do. It turned out that after his failed attempt to find a European government that would grant him asylum, Öcalan had secretly been taken under the protection of Greece. His plane refueled at a Greek airport, remained there for a few hours while senior officials made a series of frantic telephone calls, and then took off for, of all places, Kenya. Öcalan entered Nairobi with a false Cypriot passport and was whisked to the Greek embassy compound.

By offering one of their diplomatic missions as a clandestine shelter for a fugitive wanted not only in his homeland but also by Interpol, Greek officials broke both international law and the most elementary rules of diplomacy. They did not act out of any deep conviction that Öcalan was a wronged innocent, or even out of serious sympathy for the Kurdish cause. They simply believed in the age-old axiom that holds that the enemy of one's enemy is one's friend. Öcalan had greatly weakened Turkey, and, by their Machiavellian calculation, this made him a uniquely valuable asset.

Greek intelligence officers, however, made a terrible mistake in choosing to hide their man in Nairobi. The American embassy there had been bombed with horrific loss of life only a couple of months before, and more than one hundred agents from the CIA and other secret services were in town for the investigation. Öcalan himself was no cleverer. Once inside the Greek compound, he insisted on strolling around the grounds rather than remaining out of sight. He refused suggestions that he move out of Nairobi to a remote spot in the countryside. Most incredibly of all, he began using his cell phone to call people he thought might help him find a permanent base somewhere. He could hardly have made his presence more obvious if he had sent change-of-address cards to foreign embassies.

When Kenyan officials learned that Öcalan was illegally on their territory, they immediately demanded that the Greek ambassador remove him. No one other than a handful of intelligence agents is sure what happened next. According to the most widely disseminated version, Öcalan was hustled into a car one night and told that he was headed for the Nairobi airport. Probably he believed he was going back to Greece, or if not there then to some new sanctuary arranged by his Greek patrons. But before his car had driven far it was intercepted by a team of commandos. They pulled him out, threw him into their jeep, raced to the airport and hustled him onto a waiting Turkish plane.

How could this have happened? Greek diplomats angrily denied that they had given up hope of protecting Öcalan and knowingly led him into a trap. Kenyans denied that they had known about the operation in advance. Israel denied rumors that the Mossad had designed it. The United States denied that its agents had provided any "direct assistance." In the end, the truth or falsity of those denials was unimportant. What mattered was that "Operation Safari," as the Turks code-named it, had succeeded. After more than a decade as Turkey's most wanted fugitive, Öcalan came home a prisoner.

No Turkish film ever packed the emotional power of the three-minute video that showed commandos leading the blindfolded revolutionary onto a private plane at the Nairobi airport, handcuffing him to his seat and then unmasking him to show his sweat-drenched face. For two days and nights television stations broadcast it almost continuously, as if viewers needed to see it a dozen times in order to believe it, another dozen to unleash their jubilation and then a dozen more to focus their hatred.

Even more astonishing than the pictures was the soundtrack. This monumental figure, object of one of the world's last Stalinist personality cults, hero to thousands of Kurds and demon to millions of Turks, a man who could order executions between dinner courses without the slightest disturbance to his digestion, blubbered like a child.

"I really love Turkey and the Turkish people," he told his captors. "My mother was Turkish. Yes, if the truth needs to be told, I love Turkey and the Turkish nation and I want to serve it. If I have the chance, I would be pleased to serve. Let there be no torture or anything. I would be happy to serve."

Öcalan was groggy when he spoke, possibly under the influence of drugs. The video had obviously been heavily cut and edited. Nonetheless, there was no sign of the defiant revolutionary who had vowed for years to lead his people to liberation or death. It was a pitiful spectacle.

Much of the world was riveted by the Öcalan case, and the Turkish authorities might have won great good will had they bent over backward to observe every legal nicety. Instead they did the opposite. Prosecutors subjected the prisoner to ten days of intense interrogation without benefit of counsel, and then allowed two lawyers to see him for twenty minutes on condition that they discuss only his health. The next day one of the lawyers was arrested, ostensibly on an old charge of collaborating with the PKK, and the other quit for fear of his life.

Emotions were running very high in Turkey, as I was able to see in travels through the countryside during those weeks. One day I visited the conservative town of Kayseri and had lunch with a young engineer who lived there. As we sipped our lentil soup, I asked him if local people were debating a possible death penalty for Öcalan. Oh, yes, he replied, it was the hottest topic in town. So, did most favor an execution or not? My friend gazed at me, first blankly and then incredulously.

"Maybe I didn't understand your question," he said. "There isn't any debate about whether or not to hang him. The debate is over whether he should be hanged after a trial or right away, without a trial." As I was taking this in, he added offhandedly: "Personally, I favor hanging him without a trial. What has he done to earn a trial? What kind of trial did he give to all the people he killed?"

It was inevitable that the process of trying Öcalan, finding him guilty and sentencing him to hang would display all the peculiarities of the Turkish judicial system. The evidence against him was overwhelming, so perhaps it would have been best, as some dreamers suggested, for the government to have rid itself of the case altogether by sending it to an international tribunal. But Prime Minister Ecevit declared that Public Enemy Number One would be tried for treason by what he called "the completely independent Turkish judiciary, which no one can influence in the slightest."

Upon his arrival as a prisoner in Turkey, Öcalan was brought to an island called Imralı, a pleasant speck of earth in the Sea of Marmara, the small body of water south of the Bosphorus that separates Turkey's European and Asian provinces. Imralı had for years been used as a low-security prison where pickpockets and other minor criminals served their sentences while strolling about freely, taking the sea breeze and watching passing freighters. They became the first victims of Öcalan's new status, because they were immediately packed off to more conventional jails to make way for him. Öcalan became the sole inmate, moved to a different cell each night.

A handful of brave or foolish lawyers, a couple of them veteran supporters of the Kurdish cause and the rest young idealists imbued with the odd notion that every defendant is entitled to good counsel, signed up to defend the prisoner. From the beginning they faced extreme obstacles. Gangs of rowdies pelted them with rocks as they waited for ferries to take them to Imralı, and when they arrived they were allowed only brief interviews with their client, always monitored by hooded officers. Several quit in disgust, unwilling to play their role in this scripted drama.

Hundreds of journalists and others with varying credentials applied to cover the trial, and I found myself among the lucky ones given a courtroom seat on the first day, May 31, 1999. I awoke before dawn and drove to the port of Mudanya, where we had been told to assemble. Photographers and television crews had gathered in droves near the dock to film us boarding our ferry. Crowds of angry mothers shouted curses at us, as if our interest in covering the trial somehow made us complicit in their sons' deaths.

A new courtroom, modern and air-conditioned, had been built on Imralı especially for this trial. As is normal in Turkish security courts, the judges and prosecutors sat together on a raised dais; they are considered to represent both the state and the cause of justice. Below them sat defense lawyers and spectators. A booth made of bulletproof glass had been built for the defendant, like the one in which Adolf Eichmann had sat during his famous trial in Israel.

We spectators took our assigned seats and sat for a while, murmuring among ourselves. Then, without any warning or announcement, a side door opened and Öcalan shambled out, alone and seeming a bit disoriented. He looked around the room, opened the door to his booth and sat down inside. He wore a suit and blue shirt with no necktie. The paunch he had developed during his years as a pampered deity had disappeared. He looked thin, haggard and quite defeated.

I had expected the relatives of his victims, several dozen of whom had been invited to attend the trial, to explode in anger when they finally were able to see the man they blamed for their grief. They did not, obviously having been warned against it. But everyone in the hall was riveted by the sight of this near-mythical figure in mortal form.

Prosecutors began with a monotonous reading of their case, which comprised an abbreviated history of the PKK interspersed with accounts of various battles, ambushes and killings. After several hours of this, the presiding member of the five-judge panel called for a lunch break. We expected the afternoon session to be equally boring, but soon after it began Öcalan unexpectedly rose to his feet and began to speak. The judges did not interrupt his extraordinary monologue.

Speaking at first tentatively and then more quickly, as if he feared the judges might silence him at any moment, Öcalan admitted that his guerrillas had committed all the acts attributed to them by the prosecution, and added: "I could list many more that you haven't mentioned." But he said he now realized that he had led the Kurds down "a dead-end street."

"Now is the time to end this conflict, or it will get much worse," he said. "I want to dedicate my life to bringing Kurds and Turks together."

For several years before his capture Öcalan had been declaring temporary cease-fires and making various overtures to Ankara, so perhaps we should not have been so surprised when he depicted himself as a would-be peacemaker. Yet there was something quite astonishing about this towering figure of resistance, this fearsome warrior who for years had held a great army at bay, transforming himself into a meek supplicant rather than thundering defiance, defending his people as oppressed victims and warning that thousands were waiting to pick up the banner of Kurdish resistance. I thought of the Wizard of Oz, a pipsqueak who hid behind a curtain and pulled levers that made him appear to be a terrifying giant, all the while dreading the moment when someone would be bold enough to peek behind the curtain.

"We want to give up the armed struggle and have full democracy," Öcalan told the court. "I will work with the Republic of Turkey toward the goal of peace and brotherhood. In the past I was the one to blame, the one responsible. But that is not the case today. I call on both sides to stop the bloodshed of armed conflict. Call it a cease-fire or whatever you want. Turkey's future is at stake."

What should the Turkish state do to placate angry Kurds? Öcalan's demands were suddenly quite moderate: "Barriers against the Kurdish language and culture should be removed. Today the best policy would be to give the Kurds linguistic and cultural freedom. Kurds should not hesitate to use this democratic chance in the best way possible. I call upon the state not to block the way."

Öcalan used the word *devlet* in this last sentence, which meant that he had chosen to appeal to something bigger than the judicial system, bigger than the Turkish government, bigger than the people. He was offering to collaborate with that incorporeal but holy entity that is at the center of Turkey's consciousness. This was truly astonishing, almost incomprehensible.

"I will serve the state, because I now see this is necessary," Öcalan continued. "These are my most important words. My service is important if it extinguishes the fire." Later on he said he wanted "to work for brotherhood and the state" and declared that the PKK was ready to "give up its stance against the state."

Then came his offer. "If I am given the means," he declared, "I can bring the fighters down from the mountains in three months. But the state cannot do it. Let us join together to end this danger. The PKK should see that the only solution is living together in a single country, together and without weapons. I realize that I am saying this too late, but what can I do now? Maybe I can help. The best shelter for Kurds would be a democratic Republic."

Öcalan spoke for forty minutes, interrupted occasionally by mothers of war victims who, unable to restrain themselves, had burst into tearful tirades, shouting curses and waving photos of their dead sons. After he sat back down, the chief judge began to question him. His answers came in jumbles of sentence fragments and disconnected words, betraying not only a lack of poise and intellect but also the effects of so many years living as a demi-god, with no one contradicting him, scorning him, speaking sharply to him or demanding that he justify himself. The judge did all those things, and for Öcalan the situation was so unfamiliar that he could not respond coherently.

From that point the trial moved quickly toward its inevitable denouement. Prosecutors elaborated their charges, but since the defendant had already in effect pleaded guilty, there was little left for them to say. After five days the prosecution rested and the judges called a fifteen-day recess. When the court reconvened, defense lawyers protested the legitimacy of the proceedings but were overruled. Öcalan spoke once more, repeating somewhat more coherently the themes he had struck on the opening day. There was another recess of several weeks, and when the court reconvened it handed down the death sentence that had been a foregone conclusion from the day of his capture.

Just as there was never any doubt that Öcalan would be sentenced to die, there was never any real prospect that the sentence would be carried out. European leaders appealed for a stay of execution, and Prime Minister Ecevit calmed his people's emotions by assuring them that the state would find it "more useful" to keep the prisoner alive. The press was mobilized to reshape public opinion, and it managed to do so in a remarkably short time. Öcalan seemed likely to spend many years in his island cell.

With that decision, the matter was more or less laid to rest. Nearly all of the few thousand remaining PKK guerrillas heeded their leader's call to stop fighting. Most withdrew to Kurdish bases in northern Iraq, and the rest simply melted back into the Kurdish population within Turkey. After so much blood and suffering, the war was over.

The greater question of how to resolve the conflict between Turkish and Kurdish nationalism, however, remains unanswered. In the summer of 2005, when Prime Minister Erdoğan flew to Diyarbakır to deliver a speech about Kurdish issues, he was shocking in his candor about this intractable problem. He promised to "resolve every issue with more democracy," and he spoke words unlike those any Turkish leader had ever uttered.

"A great and powerful nation must have the confidence to face itself, recognize the mistakes and sins of the past, and march confidently into the future," he said. "The Kurdish issue does not belong to a part of our nation, but to us all. It is also my problem . . . We accept it as real and are ready to face it . . . We are ready to listen to anyone who has something to say, and ready to consult anyone who has a sense of justice . . . Turkey will not retreat from the point we have reached. We will not step back from our process of democratization."

Erdoğan's speech, especially his use of the word "sins" to describe aspects of the state's policy toward Kurds, provoked howls of protest from Turkish nationalists. But many Kurds were thrilled. Some began to sense that a new era might be dawning. Eager to see if it was, I set out on an extended tour of Turkey's southeastern provinces.

In the bad old days of the 1990s, I remembered, security at the Diyarbakır airport was so tight that arriving foreigners were routinely pulled aside, questioned about the purpose of their visit, and often, if their answers were not satisfying, ordered back onto the plane. When I arrived in late 2005, fighter jets were still parked on the military side of the airport, but we civilians were free to disembark without controls and to go our own ways.

The city also felt different. Gone were the knots of armed soldiers and plainclothes police officers who used to watch everything and everyone. Tanks no longer stood menacingly on downtown street corners. People did not seem exactly happy—that was not possible in a place where 60 percent of the population was unemployed and nearly every family had a relative in prison, recently released from prison or in the mountains with the PKK—but they were not utterly hopeless.

Under a great tent that had been erected in one of Diyarbakır's main plazas, a book fair was under way. I had never known of such an event being held in the Kurdish region and stepped eagerly inside. At the first stand I visited, wedged between Turkish translations of *War and Peace* and *For Whom the Bell Tolls*, I found a selection of books with titles like *History of Kurdistan* and *Turkey's Kurdish Problem*. No such books could possibly have been sold here during the 1990s, when the very word "Kurdistan" was taboo and the term "Kurdish problem" was taken to refer to an illegal form of separatism.

"Before, we were afraid to speak out," a Kurdish writer named Lutfi Baski told me at the fair. "The government was insisting that there were no Kurds, that there was no Kurdish language or culture. They arrested us and closed our organizations. Now, so much has changed, especially in the last few months. Our problems haven't been solved, not at all, but at least we can talk about them honestly. It's a huge difference."

Later that day I walked past City Hall and saw a large banner advertising a conference being held inside. Its subject was "The European Union Accession Process and the Kurdish Problem." When I walked inside, a local politician was delivering a passionate harangue.

"For many years the Turkish state called us criminals, saying it was not possible to have a dialogue with us and that we had to be crushed," he told the rapt crowd. "This is the repeated tragedy that caused the Kurdish problem. The only reason Kurds were forced to begin armed struggle was the way the Turkish state has treated Kurds at every stage in the history of this country!"

A police agent stood at the side of the hall videotaping the proceedings. That would once have been enough to intimidate bold speakers like the one I heard. Now, though, people acted as if he were not there. "They watch us just as they did before, but they can't do anything to us anymore," one man told me. "This is a democracy now. We're becoming European. The state can't touch us."

The next morning I visited the mayor of Diyarbakır, Osman Baydemir, a young politician who since his election in 2004 had become a leading spokesman for the rising generation of Turkish Kurds. "Revolutionary steps are now being taken within the framework of democracy," he told me. "But in a country where change comes slowly, we need an outside influence to push us along. The prospect of getting into the European Union gives us that external pressure. It's why more has changed for us in the last few years than in the entire period since the founding of the Turkish Republic. It's also our main hope for the future. This problem can only be solved peacefully, but who can make Turks and Kurds realize that? Only the EU."

Just a few months before, on October 3, 2005, leaders of the twenty-five European Union countries had agreed to begin formal membership negotiations with Turkey. All understood that the talks would last for years and that the final outcome was far from guaranteed. Yet in the Kurdish region, people were behaving as if they were already under Europe's protection.

The European Union, one of the most successful peacemaking institutions of the modern era, eased transitions from dictatorship to democracy in Spain, Portugal and Greece, and then it helped manage the peaceable breakup of the Soviet empire. Nowhere, though, did the prospect of EU membership have so sudden and profound an impact as it did among Turkey's Kurds. It raised hopes for an end to a festering conflict that had taken tens of thousands of lives, devastated a generation and blackened Turkey's name in the world.

While the Kurdish war raged, it was difficult to discover what Kurds in southeastern Turkey felt about the PKK. I was reluctant to ask them, since spies were everywhere and an unguarded comment could lead to arrest or worse. During my trip through Kurdish provinces in 2005, though, I found Kurds willing and even eager to express thoughts they had kept hidden for years.

I set out from Diyarbakır one bright morning, drove alongside the Tigris River and made my first stop in the town of Silvan. This had been an especially violent place, where shadowy ultra-right groups, working with government security agents, carried out some two hundred "mystery killings" during the 1980s and 1990s. Now it seemed as free from fear as the rest of the Kurdish region. I asked a man in a tea house which political group people in Silvan favored; and without hesitating he replied, "One hundred percent PKK."

Many Kurds I met told me they sympathized with the PKK. A surprising number said they had sons, brothers, or friends who had "gone to the mountain." Others told of being arrested or abused for sympathizing with the PKK. Perhaps the most important reason the PKK has attracted so much popular support, however, is that it is the only organization Turkish Kurds have. For years the Turkish state banned almost all Kurdish political, social and cultural groups. That left the field to the PKK.

Many Kurds I met professed to know little about the PKK's militant Marxist background, its years of separatist demands or its many acts of terror. They consider it a benign movement dedicated only to defending their communal identity. So the group with which the Turkish state categorically refuses to deal is precisely the one that many Kurds consider legitimate.

The poorest and most remote of Turkey's eighty-one provinces is Hakkari, which is nestled next to the Iraqi border more than a thousand miles from Istanbul. During the war years it was a battleground. I tried several times to visit but was always turned back at military checkpoints. On my 2005 trip I was stopped only once. A young soldier checked my passport and then sent me on my way with the words *Gule gule*—"Go with a smile."

Many of Hakkari's residents consider themselves Kurds first, then Turks. In this they differ from millions of their fellow Kurds who have moved westward and established themselves in Turkey's big cities, where many of them are by now well assimilated. In Hakkari, people cling to their Kurdish identity.

The bravest person I met in Hakkari was a young lawyer named Rojbin Tugan. She attended law school in Istanbul, won high grades and after graduating was hired by a prominent Istanbul firm. Less than a year later, anguished by reports of the violence that was spreading in the Kurdish region, she quit her job and returned home. By the time I visited her, she had for nearly a decade been one of the few human-rights lawyers in this part of Turkey, doggedly representing clients who claimed that soldiers or police had abused them. The relentless harassment she suffers, ranging from police officers opening her suitcases and waving her underwear in the air to streams of death threats against her and her relatives, would be enough to crush a weaker soul. Yet despite having little protection other than her own sense of moral duty, she has persevered. In Hakkari and much of southeastern Turkey, she is a heroine.

Rojbin Tugan invited me for dinner at the apartment she shared with her parents. For most of the evening we talked about the physical and spiritual devastation that overwhelmed the Kurdish region during the 1990s. She has dealt with many horrific cases and strongly identifies with the Kurdish cause. Her brother was serving a prison term after being convicted of membership in the PKK. Yet as I was leaving, she surprised me with a burst of optimism.

"I am very hopeful for Turkey's future," she said. "These last few years have been like paradise. I can travel on the roads and not have to worry about being back before dark. When the doorbell rings, we answer it without being afraid. When someone in my family goes out shopping and isn't home in an hour, I'm not terrified. We used to be without hope, but there have been so many changes."

Just a few weeks after our dinner, the bomb attack in Şemdinli, not far from Hakkari, shook Turks into realizing that "deep state" was still using terror in its rear-guard campaign to disrupt the process of reconciliation in the southeast. It set off violent protests in both Hakkari and Diyarbakır, with thousands of people shouting pro-PKK slogans. Their intensity showed that many Kurds were angry at what had happened to them, but also that they were free to express their anger.

I found more evidence of this phenomenon in the town of Sirnak, a provincial capital near the Syrian border. In a barbershop I heard graphic accounts of what people described as a four-day military sweep through the town that had begun on August 18, 1992, and ended with scores dead and much of the town burned. "Who are the real terrorists?" a barber indignantly asked me. "Our organization, or the security forces that burn and torture and kill? Why do Europe and the United States call our PKK fighters terrorists?"

"What do you call them?" I asked.

"Kurds," he replied simply.

The men in this barbershop were so outspoken that even my Kurdish traveling companion, who lives in Diyarbakır, was amazed. He told me that as recently as a year earlier, a conversation like this in a public place would have been unthinkable. I asked the barber what had changed, and he answered immediately. "We're becoming part of Europe," he said. "If we're European, we can say whatever we want."

Wherever I went in southeastern Turkey, I found encouraging signs of rebirth. Roads were being widened, and schools were being built. But the region needed psychological as well as physical reconstruction.

"We have an exercise at the women's center where I work," Nurcan Baysal, a social worker in Diyarbakır, told me at dinner one evening. "We put a group of women together and ask them to close their eyes for three minutes and think of things that have happened to them because they are women. By the end of three minutes, every woman is crying. Then come the stories: my village was burned, my husband was tortured, my son was killed. This war devastated our society. Even now, there is no work for people here. The girls become prostitutes. The boys are thieves. They're proud of it. They come to me and say, 'I'm happy because I was able to steal some money today and bring it to my family.' Our people are suffering. We have deep and painful wounds that will take a very long time to heal."

It is hard to imagine how these wounds can heal unless there is some form of amnesty for PKK fighters. Without it, thousands of young men and women can never come down from their mountain hideouts and return to civilian life. The idea that they might be allowed to do so without punishment, however, is abhorrent to many Turks. For any form of amnesty to work, these Turks would have to change their minds. The PKK would also have to change.

"It is objectively impossible to deny the power of the PKK in this region," one thoughtful Kurd, Dagistan Toprak, a businessman and former deputy mayor of Diyarbakır, told me at a café overlooking the majestic city wall. "If we're going to have real peace here, though, the PKK needs to adjust itself to the new world situation. The Turkish state is becoming more democratic. The PKK needs to do the same. It should give up the idea of armed struggle and open respectful dialogue with Kurds who think differently. It also needs to renovate its leadership. This organization was formed with a cold war mentality. It needs to evolve."

With this new climate in southeastern Turkey, some PKK leaders said they were eager to negotiate with the Turkish state. One senior PKK figure told an interviewer that the group had given up "extreme socialist ideas" and now sought only to assure that Kurds can live "in a democratic way." In view of other statements, and the sporadic attacks PKK fighters were still carrying out, that claim seemed dubious. In any case the army maintained a firm policy of rejecting all overtures from the PKK.

Many Kurds I met dreamed that one day PKK militants might return to their homes under protection of an amnesty. The PKK has never made clear whether it is ready to accept this prospect. Certainly the Turkish state is not; nor are most Turks. The European Union, having classified the PKK as a terrorist organization, can hardly pressure Turkey to negotiate with it. Still, I found Kurds buoyed by a boundless, almost childlike hope that the EU would lead them out of their conundrum. Even Selahattin Demirtaş, chairman of the Human Rights Association in Diyarbakır, whose office is decorated with portraits of assassinated comrades, told me that he fervently believed in the transforming power of the EU. "If our own government were the only hope for accomplishing all this, I don't think it would be possible," he told me. "But there is a powerful external dynamic in this process now, the European Union. That gives us great hope."

I returned to Istanbul filled with that hope. Prospects for a decisive change, even for a final end to this horrific social, political, cultural and military conflict, were more promising than ever. Before long, though, they began to unravel. Two years after my energizing tour of the Kurdish region in 2005, old feelings of depression and hopelessness were shrouding it once again. The pace of reform slowed. Mayors of several Kurdish towns were arrested on charges of supporting subversion. The leader of Turkey's most prominent nationalist party, Devlet Bahçeli, described pro-Kurdish members of Parliament (nearly two dozen had won election in 2007) as "supporters of terrorists." My friend Rojbin Tugan summed up the new climate in a deeply depressing newspaper column.

"We are breathing the air of hell," she wrote, tears seeming to drip from her pen along with ink. "Turkish racism is stronger than ever. Everything is tense. We feel defeated . . . Kurds are despised. It seems to have been forgotten that we too are citizens of this country. This intensifies the threats we face and fills me and many around me with deep doubts."

What happened? Why did the optimism that Kurds felt in 2005 become a fleeting burst of sunshine rather than a permanent change in climate? There are three answers.

One devastating blow came from Europe. While citizens of Turkey, especially Kurds, were rejoicing in the new level of freedom that was attributable in no small measure to their country's drive toward membership in the European Union, the EU was moving in the opposite direction. European politicians, especially in France, Germany and Austria, began saying that Turkey should never be admitted to their club. In referendums, French and Dutch voters turned down a proposed EU constitution, partly because of their unhappiness at the prospect of Turkey's membership. Then, at the end of 2006, the EU took the dramatic step of suspending talks on key aspects of Turkey's application.

Nowhere did Europe's reversal have a greater impact than in the Kurdish region. Police crackdowns resumed, and all who called for more Kurdish rights were once again branded as traitors. Diplomats in faraway Brussels, claiming perhaps sincerely to represent the democratically expressed wishes of their constituents, undermined the nascent democracy that had been settling over southeastern Turkey.

Another blow came from the Turkish state. Its capture of Abdullah Öcalan in 1999 had given it an ideal opportunity to begin forging a peaceful and democratic solution to the Kurdish conflict, reaching out in magnanimity to grant Kurds new social and cultural rights, perhaps even offering some form of amnesty to PKK fighters. Öcalan's statements at his trial suggested that he was ready to help this process. But the army at that time still exercised complete control over all policy related to Kurds. Military commanders never wavered from their fierce conviction that the Kurdish challenge could be met only with unrelenting force and that to suggest anything else was treasonous.

The bizarre effect of this attitude was to make the Turkish army the effective ally of the PKK. Both knew that war would increase their power and that a democratic solution brokered by civilians would weaken them. Caught in a paradigm of violence that had entrapped them for a generation, these supposed enemies combined to undermine the prospect for a peaceful settlement in the years after Öcalan's capture.

Perhaps the most decisive factor in the re-ignition of Turkish-Kurdish conflict was the American invasion of Iraq in 2003. The Turkish government understood perfectly well that this invasion would not only set Iraq afire but fragment power there, which would allow the PKK to establish protected bases in Iraqi regions bordering on Turkey. It warned the Bush administration that this planned action would open a deep breach between the United States and Turkey and set off a new, deeply destabilizing Middle East crisis. President Bush and his aides brushed these warnings aside with the same response they gave to other warnings they heard in 2003: We are determined to invade Iraq, we are powerful enough to resolve whatever problems might emerge afterward and anyone who believes otherwise is "defeatist."

This, then, was the sequence of events that crushed Kurdish hopes in the early years of the new century. The Turkish state, still dominated by the military, refused to seek a peaceful settlement to the conflict in the period after Öcalan's capture; the American invasion of Iraq placed northern Iraq under the rule of Kurds who gave the PKK a protected sanctuary from which its fighters launched attacks on Turkey; and the European Union removed the great incentive for democratization in the Kurdish region by freezing key accession talks and warning that it might never accept Turkey as a member.

The inevitable crisis to which these misbegotten policies gave birth erupted in late 2007. Guerrillas from the PKK began to slip down from their hideouts in northern Iraq and launch attacks inside Turkey, killing and capturing dozens of Turkish soldiers. Turkey exploded in anger. Citizens poured onto the streets demanding that Prime Minister Erdoğan answer decisively by attacking PKK sanctuaries in Iraqi Kurdistan. He added his voice to the clamor of outrage, but much to his credit he refused to order the massive attack that would have made him a national hero. He realized that such an attack would not succeed in wiping out the PKK threat and might well trap the Turkish army in a dangerous quagmire. It would give new power and authority to military commanders, thereby undermining his transcendent goal of solidifying civilian rule. It would also further weaken Turkey's already dimmed chances of entering the European Union. Erdoğan had not allowed the EU's insults to deter him from pursuing eventual Turkish membership.

Prime Minister Erdoğan had told Kurds that he was ready to consider a peaceful solution to their conflict with the Turkish state. Whether he was truly sincere remained a matter of much debate. His margin for decisive action narrowed, however, as PKK attacks enraged the Turkish people. Yet although many Kurds in the southeast still support the PKK, their support is weakening. Most wish to live in a peaceful, democratic Turkey. How to give them that right remains one of the nation's central conundrums. Turkey will not be truly free or stable until it is resolved.

I couldn't tell what time it was when three scary-looking cops appeared in front of the cell into which they had thrown me the night before. It must have been mid-morning. I had maintained a semblance of composure during an intense all-night interrogation and lain awake since, but at the sight of these men unlocking my cell door I unaccountably lost it.

"No!" I shouted, clutching my knees in my arms and bracing for a beating. "No! Don't! Don't do it!"

That was the worst moment of my worst day in Turkey. I had been arrested while engaged in the highly suspicious activity of driving aimlessly around the war zone. The army liked fighting its Kurdish campaign without anyone watching, so prying eyes were most unwelcome.

My adventure, like most adventures in what is never supposed to be called Kurdistan, began in Diyarbakır. I had arrived there by plane, checked in to a hotel that was built in the sixteenth century for Silk Road traders and telephoned trusty Hasan, a Kurdish college student who was bold or foolish or penniless enough to spend his spare time working as a translator for whatever outsiders turned up in town. We greeted each other warmly, and after a few glasses of rakı *decided to visit a local lawyer who tried to keep up with events in the surrounding countryside. He told us he knew little more than we did but could pass along a few rumors. On a scrap of paper he wrote the names of three villages where people were supposedly unhappy. Had these villages been forcibly evacuated? Had their men refused to help the army? Had atrocities been committed there? No one knew.*

The next morning Hasan and I began winding our way northwest from Diyarbakır. By asking villagers and farmers, we figured out more or less where we might find Gümüşsorgü, one of the hamlets our lawyer friend had mentioned. We were about to reach the top of the hill behind which it was hidden when we were stopped at an army roadblock. Obviously we were not going to be allowed to find out what sort of outrage, if any, had been perpetrated there. As we had done at several other roadblocks that day, we agreed to turn back. But this time the soldier in charge would not let us leave. Instead he brought us into his blockhouse and ordered us to sit.

We were held there for a couple of hours while radio calls were made, and finally were told that we would be escorted to the regional military headquarters. An armored personnel carrier drove along the dirt road ahead of us and a soldier rode in our backseat, his automatic rifle pointed at my back to discourage any thoughts of escape.

At the headquarters we were met by a very agitated lieutenant who was apparently the regional commander. For more than an hour he harangued us, jumping around the room and demanding to know why we had violated his security regulations. I showed my government-issued press card and told him he was making a mistake, but he would have none of it. Our transgression was too egregious for him to deal with, he said. We would be brought to the provincial capital, Batman, for interrogation.

"This is crazy," I told him, "but I'll tell you what. If the commander in Batman really wants to talk to us so badly, we'll show up there at nine o'clock tomorrow morning and answer his questions."

"Don't tell me what to do!" he shouted. "You're not getting away that easily. On your feet!"

Only then did it begin to dawn on me that this might develop into more than an inconvenience. Night was falling, and as Hasan and I stepped outside we saw not one but four armored personnel carriers waiting to escort us. Two rode ahead, the other two behind. Soldiers with machine guns at the ready scanned the roadside, perhaps waiting for my imagined confederates to spring an ambush and try to free me.

In about an hour we reached Batman, a miserable town fifty miles north of the Syrian border that, like many other towns in the region, was swollen with refugees. No one looked up as our caravan passed through the streets; evidently the sight of soldiers atop lumbering war machines was nothing new here. Finally we stopped at a gate and then passed under a large arch bearing the word JANDARMA.

Men in uniform are not widely loved in the Kurdish region, but local people perceive differences among them that are often lost on outsiders. Soldiers from the regular army often behave with a modicum of respect and act according to rules which may at times be harsh but are nonetheless predictable. The police, as in many parts of the world, are tougher. Worst of all is the gendarmerie, which is officially a military body but functions more as a rural police force. Ask a Kurd into whose hands he would least like to fall and the answer will probably be "Jandarma."

Despite my growing concern, I could not help smiling when I saw that two lines of soldiers, a total of twenty-four men, had been assembled to oversee my arrival. Never had any military body taken me so seriously.

Under the watchful eyes of these recruits, I was brought down a set of concrete steps to the subterranean jail. I knew that because I was a foreigner, nothing too serious would happen to me. Yet I could not help thinking of the many unfortunate Kurds, both guilty and innocent, who must have been dragged down this staircase on their way to brutal abuse.

I was led into a small room that quickly filled with unshaven interrogators. There were eight in all, and soon the cell was ripe with their sweat and mine. One sat behind a small desk and pecked continually at a typewriter that was placed next to my ear. The others shouted questions.

Who was I? Why had I been prowling the back roads here? Where was I going? Who had sent me? What was I hoping to find? Who was I planning to meet? What messages was I carrying? What was I delivering or picking up?

Now the ordeal was beginning in earnest. Over and over I explained that I was a journalist accredited by the Turkish government, but my hosts were not impressed. They took turns glowering at me and shaking their heads in disbelief. Finally one said, "We think you're a spy for the PKK."

To be suspected of collaborating with Kurdish rebels is about the worst thing that can happen to a Turkish citizen, and it isn't taken kindly among foreigners either. I knew that no one in the world had the slightest idea where I was, and I asked to use a telephone. "Too bad," one of my hosts replied dryly. "All our phones are out of order."

Hours passed, and my interrogators kept shouting. One or two would leave the room for a time and then return. At one point they took me out to be photographed and fingerprinted. For a time they videotaped me, warning that if I did not agree to speak before the camera they would hold me "for a long time—a very long time." Slowly I began to realize why police everywhere in the world use the tactic of long, intensive and repetitive interrogation: it works. I was isolated from the world and completely in the hands of the men facing me. My resistance was weakening, and I felt a strong urge to confess my crimes. All that stopped me was that I had none to confess.

At one point the men ordered me to empty my pockets. With intense interest they scrutinized every card and paper. Suddenly one of them cried out, "İşte!" *which means something like "Here it is!" The others quickly gathered around him and, one by one, nodded and smiled triumphantly. If I had been carrying a PKK membership card, I would know that it had been found. Since I was not, however, I wondered what could have provoked such a reaction.*

"If you aren't working for the PKK," the chief interrogator asked, waving a slip of paper at me, "then what's this?"

I looked at it and couldn't fathom their excitement. "It's nothing," I said. "It's a receipt from the Pera Palace bar in Istanbul. Look, right here at the top: 'Pera Palace.' "

"Sure, but what's this you have written on it?"

"It says 'Jean-Paul Marthoz.' That's the name of the guy I had a drink with. I have to write the name for my expense account."

"But keep reading. What does it say under the name?"

Jean-Paul Marthoz worked at the Brussels office of Human Rights

Watch and had been in Istanbul to attend a political trial. He had called and asked to meet me, and I had bought him a drink at the Pera Palace.

"It says 'Human Rights Watch,'" I said, still not comprehending.

"İşte! *PKK!"*

"No, not PKK. Human rights."

"That's what I said. Human rights. PKK."

I stopped to absorb this. The men facing me obviously considered the phrase "human rights" to be a synonym for terror. To them, meeting with someone from a group that used that phrase in its name was the same as meeting with a PKK agent.

The interrogators next told me they were going to search my car. They took me outside to watch while they probed the radiator, tested the tires, opened the first-aid kit and ripped out the seats. Suddenly there was another cry of "İşte!" *One of the searchers had found the scrap of paper on which my Diyarbakır friend had scrawled the names of three villages.*

"These are PKK villages," one of the interrogators shouted at me. "What were you going to do there? Who were you going to meet?"

This was another revelation. According to the official version there was no such thing as a "PKK village," nor could there be, since the PKK was devoted only to mindless terror and had no civilian base. I had learned something in a basement prison that I could not otherwise have learned: just as there are friendly villages in the southeast, there are also hostile ones where people sympathize with the enemy.

At four o'clock in the morning, after seven hours of harsh though not physical interrogation, I was led to a cell and locked in. I'm not having any fun, I told myself, but I'm definitely in better shape than the last guy who was brought here and the next guy who will be brought here.

A few hours later the cops showed up at my cell door. They smiled at my terrified reaction, opened the door and asked me to step out. I followed them back to the room where I had spent such an unpleasant night. The interrogation began again, but this time each question was asked only once, and in a civil tone. I was made to sign many papers, and after an hour was told that a decision had been made to release me. Outside I was reunited with Hasan, who told me that the cops had threatened to come for him some night and punish him for "working with foreign motherfuckers who want to destroy this country." We were led to our car, which had been partly reassembled, and I was given the key. I turned the ignition and drove very slowly toward the gate, still not sure I would be allowed to leave. But the gate opened and we drove to freedom.

We passed through the streets of Batman in silence, breathing deeply and looking anxiously behind us. At a small shop we stopped for fruit juice and cigarettes.

"That was awful," I told Hasan after we got back into the car. "That was terrible. I can't believe that happened."

Hasan shook his head in disbelief. Then he broke into a broad smile. "Believe me, that was nothing," he said. "It could have been much worse. Much, much worse."

• SIX •

FREEDOM RISING

When the film *Saving Private Ryan* opened in Istanbul, one of my Turkish friends called and suggested we go to see it. We arrived just before showtime, and the only seats available were in the front row. We sat in awe as larger-than-life images of soldiers hitting the Normandy beach swarmed above us in torrents of mayhem and blood. Afterward, over a dinner that lasted well into the night, we talked of World War II, then of war in general, then of the Kurdish war and finally, inevitably, about Turkey and its inability to give all its citizens the freedom that is their birthright.

My companion that night was the novelist and inveterate cinephile Orhan Pamuk. Most of our evenings together followed the same pattern: a movie and then hours of conversation that was as varied and deeply satisfying as the food we ate while talking. Literature was always my friend's favorite topic, but inescapably we always ended up talking about Turkey.

Politics has never been Pamuk's great interest. He fits into that glorious category of writers whose sole obsessions are reading and writing. Never did he set out to be a human-rights advocate or an exemplar of Turkey's long, anguished grappling with the principle of human rights. But the realities of Turkish life turned him, most unwillingly, into a political figure. He rose to prominence as Turkey was beginning its epic transition to full democracy. Like every thinking Turk, he was drawn into it.

In another time or place, Pamuk might have been happy to lock himself in his light-filled studio overlooking the Bosphorus, where books spill from shelves and are piled high on the floor. When not writing, he would look forward to nothing more than dipping into his favorite book, *Anna Karenina*, for the hundredth time. But he could not exist in another time or place. Although he deals with universal themes and speaks to readers around the world, he is very much a product of his environment. The tremors that have shaken Turkey during his lifetime—military coups, civil strife, tensions between secularism and religious belief, and above all the dizzying rush toward democracy—have profoundly shaped him and the way he views the world. He is a public man, and even a political figure, not out of choice but because the times forced that role upon him.

Turkey has always had a tortured relationship with its thinking citizens. Often it holds up their intellectual achievements as examples of how far the country has progressed toward modernity and how fully they measure up to those of the West. Inevitably, though, thinkers in Turkey find themselves confronting the state's failure to grasp the full meaning of democracy. They demand that it give every citizen the freedom to speak and act freely. That has turned many of them into dangerously threatening figures. Orhan Pamuk is prominent among them.

Like many countries, Turkey likes to honor its distinguished cultural figures with symbolic awards. In 1998 President Süleyman Demirel issued a list of eighty-five writers, painters, musicians and others judged worthy to hold the title of "state artist." Pamuk's name was on the list, and I called to congratulate him. Not so fast, he replied; he had decided to reject the honor.

"There is a moral issue here," he told me. "This state does not have clean hands."

Over the next few days, news of Pamuk's decision spread, and interviewers from newspapers and television stations pressed him to explain it. He answered frankly, accusing the state of repressing freethinkers and even naming several who were at that moment serving prison terms for having uttered forbidden opinions. It was one of the first times a figure of such stature had been so bold.

"For years I have been criticizing this society for its approach to the Kurdish problem, for its failure to move toward real democracy, for its violation of human rights and banning of books," he told me the next time we met. "Intellectuals, pro-Kurdish writers and even fundamentalists are in jail for writing books and articles. I thought this was a good time to separate myself from this happy public, which lacks a sense of self-criticism and immerses itself in crazy nationalism."

In the years that followed, and especially after Tayyip Erdoğan rose to power in 2002, human-rights conditions in Turkey improved dramatically. Most impressively, the incidence of jailhouse torture, which had for decades been accepted as almost normal, declined to almost nothing. But the issue Pamuk raised in the late 1990s was still unresolved a decade later. In an era when almost everything changed in Turkey, laws restricting free expression did not.

"I live in a country that values and honors its generals, police officers and statesmen," Pamuk complained, "but plagues its writers with prosecutions and jail sentences."

During the early decades of the Turkish Republic, restricting public discourse was probably necessary. Many citizens were shocked by Atatürk's radicalism, and some might have responded if they had been encouraged to rebel against his "sacrilegious" regime. That threat has now evaporated. Rather than lift restrictions on free speech, however, the state searches ceaselessly for new excuses to maintain them.

In the 1960s and 1970s the pretext for restricting free speech was the threat of Communism. Later it was the Kurdish war, and after the war wound down it was the supposed rise of Islamic fundamentalism. These arguments are strong. No state happily allows citizens to denounce the armed forces in times of national emergency, and none refuses to defend itself against those who detest its most cherished principles. The restrictions that Turkish leaders have imposed on public discourse, however, inhibit debate over vital issues the nation must confront if it is to keep pace with the rest of the world. As long as they are in force, democracy in Turkey will remain incomplete.

The irony is that today, public discourse in Turkey is astonishingly free. Politicians attack one another virulently, newspapers campaign loudly against abuses of power and late-night television programs feature intense debates over national issues. For all its failings, the Turkish press is the great platform for civil society, and there are some among Turkish journalists who would be heroes in any country. But all Turks who speak out in public understand the limits, explicit and implicit.

Laws that embody these prohibitions are vaguely worded and selectively enforced. A newspaper column judged inoffensive one year might lead to a jail sentence the next. Older and well-established commentators in mainstream papers are often allowed more leeway than brash newcomers working for smaller publications whose loyalty to the state is suspect. Yet everyone who writes, publishes, speaks in public or otherwise expresses opinions feels the chilling shadow of the law.

Turkey's constitution stipulates in its preamble: "No protection shall be given to thoughts or opinions that run counter to Turkish national interests, the fundamental principle of the existence and indivisibility of the Turkish state and territory, the historical and moral values of Turkishness, or the nationalism, principles, reforms and modernism of Atatürk." A handful of repressive laws have been written in the spirit of that preamble. They forbid the publication of "articles that threaten the internal or external security of the state"; "articles inciting people to break the law"; articles that "make people unwilling to serve in the military"; and articles or statements that "publicly insult or ridicule the moral personality of Turkishness, the Republic, the Parliament, the Government, ministers of state, the military or security forces or the judiciary." Also forbidden are radio or television broadcasts that undermine "the national and spiritual values of society"; political party platforms suggesting "that minorities exist in the Turkish Republic based on national, religious, confessional, racial or language differences"; and, of course, anything that "insults or curses the memory of Atatürk."

Three laws are used to prosecute most of the journalists, intellectuals and politicians whose imprisonment has been one of the most deplorable aspects of modern Turkish life. One, used frequently against those who propose new ways of dealing with Kurdish nationalism, is Article 8 of the 1991 Anti-Terror Law, which bans "written or oral propaganda, along with meetings, demonstrations and marches, that have the goal of destroying the indivisible unity of the state." The second, which was for years the main prosecutorial weapon against Islamic-oriented politicians, is Article 312 of the penal code, forbidding "incitement to hatred on grounds of race or religion." Broadest of all is Article 301. Under its provisions, jail terms of up to three years are prescribed for "public denigration of Turkishness" or "denigration of the government of the Republic of Turkey, its judiciary, or its military or security structures."

It was probably inevitable that Orhan Pamuk would find himself accused of violating one of these laws. It happened in 2005, after he told a reporter from a small Swiss newspaper that "thirty thousand Kurds and a million Armenians were killed in these lands." One morning a few months later he awoke to news that he had been indicted for making a statement that "explicitly insults" the Turkish state, a crime that carries a sentence of up to three years in prison. He did not take it lightly.

"It's a scandal, a shame," he told me. Laws like the one under which he was charged, he said, were "hidden hammers that prosecutors want to keep in their drawers so they can hit whenever they want."

When Pamuk's case finally came to trial, the small gang of ultranationalists who congregate outside courthouses to insult offenders was out once again. They surrounded him and shouted insults as he arrived. One woman smacked him on the head. Inside, the harried judge ruled that his case could proceed only with approval from the justice ministry.

"Traitor!" Pamuk's enemies shouted at him as he left the courthouse. "Turkey is ashamed of you!" As he sped away, his car was pelted with eggs.

This spectacle was lavishly covered in the world press, confirming everyone's worst stereotypes of Turkey. Leaders of the European Union were appalled and said so. A couple of months later the case was finally dropped. Another sixty Turks, however, remained under indictment for offenses similar to his. Among them were the author of a book suggesting that Atatürk had treated his wife unkindly; a Kurd who dared to say, "My heart bleeds for each soldier and guerrilla who gets killed" (he was charged with "making PKK propaganda"); and members of a punk rock band who produced a hit song criticizing Turkey's rigid system of college entrance exams and ending with the shouted words, "Let me tell you something / Screw your exam system!"

A year after Pamuk's case was dismissed, I checked court dockets for a single week and found three such cases scheduled for trial. One was against the author and publisher of a book called *The Language of Suffering*, which alleges that Turkish laws discriminate against women. The second was against a journalist who wrote a column asserting that "the state made a mistake" in its treatment of Kurds. Rounding out the week was a case against the author, editor and publisher of a collection of essays entitled *Treatment of Armenians in the Ottoman Empire*.

Around the same time those cases were scheduled, I myself, apparently for what I wrote in the first edition of this book, was implicated in the crimes of "insulting and ridiculing the state" and "insulting the memory of Atatürk." Those were the charges in a case brought against the heroic Istanbul publisher Ragip Zarakolu, who has been repeatedly prosecuted for the contents of the books he issues. The work for which he was being prosecuted this time was *The Truth Will Set Us Free: Armenians and Turks Reconciled*, by the British-Armenian author George Jerjian. In court Jerjian told the judge that it was foolish to prosecute the book's publisher instead of the author, and then said he had based his text on information reported by "eminent scholars and writers such as Dr. Vahakn Dadrian, Dr. Taner Akçam and Stephen Kinzer, a Turcophile American journalist." He called us "writers who want the truth to emerge for the benefit of society and their fellow citizens." His words might be interpreted as placing me in legal jeopardy, but I felt honored to be so named.

When cases like these were filed in the 1980s and 1990s, they were integral parts of a multi-faceted campaign by which "deep state" sought to keep Turks in a tight ideological straitjacket. In the first years of the new century—the dawning of what might be called the Erdoğan era—that campaign fell apart, and most egregious human-rights violations ceased. Prosecutions of people who spoke uncomfortable truths, or uncomfortable lies, never did. Prime Minister Erdoğan himself, despite all his proclamations about his determination to create a new Turkey, conspicuously failed to push for the repeal of laws restricting free speech. In fact, he fell into the habit of suing journalists he believed had slandered him. By one count, he won judgments totaling more than $200,000 in the two years after he filed his first suit in March 2005, against a cartoonist who depicted him as a cat tangled up in strands of wool. Nonetheless he congratulated Orhan Pamuk when, at the end of 2006, Pamuk became the first Turk to win a Nobel Prize. President Sezer, reflecting the old elite's disdain for freethinkers, did not see fit to do so.

Writers and other journalists were intensifying their campaign against restrictive laws, and daring to believe they would soon triumph, when the Turkish-Armenian journalist Hrant Dink was murdered in 2007. That crime, and the failure of national leaders to condemn it unequivocally, shocked them out of their optimism. "The death of my brave friend, who had a heart of gold, has made my life miserable," a disconsolate Orhan Pamuk told reporters who gathered outside Dink's office in the hours after his murder. "I am furious at everyone and everything, and I feel a shame that has no limit."

A few days later a prominent extremist who was summoned for questioning on charges that he helped arrange Dink's murder shouted to journalists as he left, "Orhan Pamuk had better be smarter!" Another militant posted a video on YouTube showing photos of Pamuk alongside images of Dink's body, with a Turkish flag in the background and the slogan "More Will Die." Soon afterward Pamuk accepted a teaching position in the United States.

In the weeks after Dink's murder, the government began providing bodyguards to more than a dozen writers who remained in Turkey. All were in danger for the same reason. They had challenged long-established ideas of what it means to be Turkish, ideas that some consider eternal and not subject to challenge. One was Atilla Yayla, a college professor who had been charged with "insulting the legacy of Atatürk" for asserting that Atatürk's one-party rule in the 1920s and 1930s was "a period of regression, not progress." Another was the writer Perihan Mağden, who had defended the right of military conscripts to claim conscientious objection as a ground for refusing to serve. A third was Ismet Berkan, a newspaper editor whose criticism of the government's effort to suppress debate on the Armenian question had brought him a stream of anonymous death threats. All hated the idea of relying on bodyguards, but several made strong public statements promising to press ahead just as before. Berkan vowed to redouble his campaign against "those who want to cut Turkey off from the rest of the world." The renowned political science professor Baskin Oran, who had been charged with threatening "fundamental elements of the Turkish Republic" after he suggested that people respect the country's ethnic diversity by replacing the word "Turks" with the phrase "citizens of Turkey," went so far as to ask his friends abroad not to judge his country too harshly. In the space of a few decades, he pointed out, Turkey was trying to make enormous political and cultural changes that Europe had taken centuries to make.

"Our country is becoming a better place with every passing day," Oran insisted, "even if our route to paradise passes through hell."

Cases against writers and other freethinkers are usually not prosecuted with Prime Minister Erdoğan's encouragement. In fact, many are part of a campaign to undermine him. Under Turkish law, any citizen may file a criminal complaint if he or she can find a prosecutor to accept it. Most of the charges against people who speak or write in ways that challenge old taboos are brought by a small cadre of ultranationalists who comb through the statements of Turks they dislike, find ones they consider treasonous and then "shop around" for a sympathetic prosecutor.

These prosecutions achieve two purposes at once. They intimidate freethinkers, and they also make Turkey seem less democratic to outsiders. This latter effect is vital, because it hinders Turkey's efforts to join the European Union and, in a broader sense, to show that it deserves full membership in the world's democratic community. For those who want to keep Turkey as it has always been, the outside world is a threat. Anything that keeps Turkey apart from it, and out of the European Union, serves their cause.

The old establishment is also determined to prevent Turkey's leaders from trying new approaches to the country's festering Armenian and Kurdish challenges. As long as Turkey refuses to admit that Ottoman leaders ordered the mass deportation of Armenian citizens in 1915, and as long as it insists on a military solution to the Kurdish problem, it will remain isolated and be unable to claim its place at the banquet of world democracy. The old elite has no appetite for that banquet. It has managed to limit debate on these issues so successfully that even today any Turk who dares to say, "We should admit that our great-grandfathers slaughtered Armenians," or "We should embrace our Kurdish citizens instead of sending our army to fight them," is liable to be prosecuted.

The bitter, atavistic and sometimes violent form of ultra-nationalism that is spreading in Turkey is fueled by a deep skepticism about the outside world, and by a conviction that outsiders are pursuing a secret, all-encompassing conspiracy against the Turkish nation. "The Turk has no friend other than the Turk," nationalists like to say. To those who reject their worldview they respond with another mantra: "Turkey is the country in the world that produces the greatest number of traitors." Everywhere they look, they see forces that threaten Turkey.

"If we take these types of nationalists seriously," the Turkish-Armenian columnist Etyen Mahçupyan wrote after Hrant Dink's murder, "then we can easily say that Turkey is gradually heading toward national insanity."

Turkey's ultra-nationalists count on support not only from intransigent prosecutors but also from two institutions that in other countries serve as guarantors of an open society: the education system and the press. Schools and universities demand strict adherence to dogma; a young friend of mine who wrote a paper urging that Kurds be granted more cultural and political rights was rewarded with quiet advice to leave school or face expulsion. Most newspapers and newspaper distribution companies are owned by conglomerates that depend on the state for contracts and subsidies, and therefore bow deeply before it. The minds of Turks will not be free until the control that "deep state" has traditionally exercised over these two institutions is broken.

Why do increasing numbers of Turks see so many threats to their country and insist on taking such extreme actions to resist them? Powerful forces in the world, they insist, are devoted to killing Turkey by cutting it apart. Wherever they look, they see evidence of this plot. In the 1990s, when environmental protests forced the cancellation of plans to build a nuclear power plant in a coastal region laced by earthquake faults, the director of the national energy commission said the protesters were "people who want to divide Turkey." Soon afterward, when Istanbul was eliminated as a contender for hosting the 2008 Olympics, the chairman of the Turkish Olympic Committee blamed "those who want to divide Turkey." This odd belief, the product of an insular and deeply self-defeating fantasy, has become a guiding principle for Turkish nationalists. Some go so far as to believe that democracy itself is an anti-Turkish plot, a clever trick that outsiders have devised to destroy the Turkish nation and people. According to this view, Kurds, Christians and others who are not ethnic Turks, along with those who defend their rights, constitute a fifth column dedicated to ripping Turkey apart. Outside of Latin America, there are few places in the world where conspiracy theories are as elaborate and as fervently embraced as they are in Turkey.

By ending the practice of abusing prisoners in police stations and detention centers, Prime Minister Erdoğan shook off a stigma that had hung over Turkey for generations. He would achieve something equally profound if he were to wipe away laws that restrict freedom of speech. After that must come an even more delicate task: exposing the bloody past, including the role of security forces in promoting anti-Kurdish terrorism. But to make Turkey a true paragon of human rights, the state must also confront the deep poverty that still imprisons many Turkish citizens. This is not simply, as some suggest, a challenge of development. To live free of misery is also a human right.

A gaping social and economic chasm divides Turkey's vibrant entrepreneurs and cosmopolitan urbanites from the millions of poor and isolated Turks in rural areas, especially in the mainly Kurdish southeast, where a huge underclass is still waiting for the benefits of national prosperity to trickle down. Turkey's race toward economic development has been astonishingly successful, but not all citizens have enjoyed its benefits.

Besides consolidating the right to free speech, granting cultural rights to Kurds and others who cling to their ethnic identity, breaking the hold of criminal gangs on parts of the state security apparatus and bringing a measure of economic justice to the impoverished southeast, Turkey faces one other great human-rights challenge: giving women the freedoms that men enjoy. Atatürk is justly celebrated for having outlawed polygamy, encouraged women to throw off their veils, abolished the Islamic court system under which women suffered systematic discrimination, given women the right to vote and taken other epochal steps to bring Turkish women into the modern age. Nonetheless Turkey remains a deeply patriarchal society.

Women's groups sprang up across Turkey in the 1990s, and when Tayyip Erdoğan's government announced plans to write a new penal code, they proposed sweeping changes to redress deep inequalities in the old one. The government proved remarkably open to their suggestions, and the new code, approved in 2004, was nothing less than revolutionary. All references to chastity, morality and decency in old laws were removed. Sexual harassment, rape within marriage and sexual assault by security officers became crimes for the first time. Legal discrimination against women who are unmarried or not virgins was banned. The practice of giving murderers reduced sentences if their crimes were "honor killings"—revenge on women or their lovers for violating traditional codes—was ended. Female sexuality was for the first time defined as a matter of individual right.

"These are the most radical changes in the legal status of Turkish women in eighty years," the nonprofit European Security Initiative concluded in 2007. "This was not just a revolution in the legal status of women. It was also a sign of profound changes in Turkish democracy. The entire process was conducted in a highly transparent fashion, with intense debate and inputs from across society."

The report added, however, that Turkey still "has a long road ahead of it in narrowing its gender gap." In 2006 a study by the World Economic Forum placed Turkey 105th among 115 countries in gender equality, measured by a host of criteria ranging from the percentage of women in the workforce to rates of female illiteracy. Scholars estimate that about one-third of Turkish women suffer from domestic violence. Yet that a governing party with roots in Islam has been so eager to reshape gender relations—and no "secular" party ever showed such eagerness—is another expression of its pioneering spirit.

Most Turks were rightly thrilled by these monumental advances in the cause of women's rights. A shadow hung over them, however. Profound as they were, they were not enough to ease the suspicion with which many secular women continued to view the Erdoğan government. The fact that the ruling party pledged its support to the cause of gender equality, and never proposed a female candidate for Parliament who covered her hair, was not enough to reassure them. They zealously defend their right to live as most Western women do. Some in the new regime scorn their zeal as excessive, but it serves as a valuable counterbalance to militantly religious factions within Erdoğan's party.

Every Turkish leader since the 1950s has promised to wipe away the stains that have led outsiders to brand their country a chronic abuser of human rights. Some did nothing to turn their words into reality. Others tried but failed because the army and the rest of the old elite blocked their efforts. Only after the civic uprising swept Tayyip Erdoğan to power did Turkey begin to lose its stigma. During Erdoğan's first years in power, its citizens became freer than they had ever been.

As true democracy took hold, though, some Turks began asking themselves a troubling question that one female architect posed to me over a lamb dinner one evening: "Democracy for what?" Democracy, she pointed out, is not an absolute good. She reminded me that Turks had watched neighboring Iraq be cast into bloody chaos by outsiders whose stated goal was to bring democracy. In Turkey, she told me, democracy was starting to seem like a way for the majority, long suppressed and isolated from power, to create a country where the secular and tolerant values she prized might slowly be abandoned. They could do this, she said, by simply arguing that the majority no longer supported those values—or never did.

A few days after our conversation, news came that the gifted Turkish pianist Fazil Say, whose triumphs in concert houses around the world have been held up as an example of how completely Turks have become part of world culture, no longer felt welcome in his homeland. "Our dream is dying a little in Turkey," Say told a German newspaper reporter. "Wives of our cabinet ministers wear head scarves. The Islamists have won. We're thirty percent, they're seventy percent. I'm thinking about where else I could live."

Say's interview set off a political firestorm. Prime Minister Erdoğan quickly rebuked him, saying that "an artist who is born here should stay here." But the deputy leader of Erdoğan's party, Dengir Mir Mehmet Firat, professed to be undisturbed by the prospect of Say's leaving Turkey. "I wouldn't cry if he did," Firat shrugged. Even some other cultural figures took issue with Say. As the controversy spread, the techno-Ottoman visionary Mercan Dede, who incorporates Sufi music and dance into his mesmerizing performances, said, "The AKP has given us the best government I've seen in this country in my lifetime. Turkey is becoming more democratic every day."

The future is dawning over Turkey. It holds exciting promise but also ominous threats. At every turn it is fighting battles against the past. Which side will win is still disturbingly uncertain.

Everyone in the seaside village of Adrasan knows Ali Taşgan, but not by his real name. Nearly half a century ago he exchanged it for a one-word moniker that he shares with ten thousand of his countrymen: Koreli. The restaurant he owns, which sits directly on the Mediterranean sand, is also called Koreli. So are dozens of other restaurants in Turkey, along with all manner of businesses, including a grocery in the Black Sea town of Rize, a tea house in the bustling southern city of Adana and a tire dealership at a busy intersection in Istanbul. At many Turkish ports there is at least one vessel, usually a skiff or small fishing boat, called Koreli. *I have seen the name painted on trucks, buses and automobiles, and also above doors in remote villages. Among Turks of a certain age it is a badge of honor and commands instant respect.*

Koreli *is the Turkish word for "Korean," but neither Ali Taşgan nor any of the other Turks who bear that name has a drop of Korean blood. They are veterans of the Korean War, the first and only foreign war in which soldiers of the Turkish Republic have fought. The bravery they exhibited on Korean battlefields earned Turkey a permanent place in the grateful memories of South Koreans. It also deeply impressed countless soldiers who were part of the Allied force fighting North Korea and China on that remote Asian peninsula. "Whenever you had a real tough or dangerous mission, you'd call in the Turks," an American veteran once told me. "Didn't matter how freezing it was or how many bullets were flying through the air. They'd go anywhere."*

Nearly eight hundred Turks were killed in combat during the Korean War and are buried in cold Korean soil. That is a sobering toll and, to those who appreciate the virtues of soldierly courage, proof that Turks still burn with the fire that once made them some of the world's most fearsome warriors. Time has shown, however, that the true legacy of the Korelis had nothing to do with their willingness to race across minefields or charge uphill toward machine-gun nests. They were the first large group of Turks since the founding of the Republic who left their country and saw the world beyond. With their return, Turkey changed forever.

Atatürk believed that the domestic challenges his new nation faced were so urgent and overwhelming that it could not afford to devote its energy to foreign affairs. The Ottomans had ruled a vast empire, but their limitless ambition, symbolized at the end by their mad alliance with Germany in World War I, was ultimately what destroyed them. Chastened by this history, Atatürk sought to avoid foreign entanglements at all costs. During his fifteen years as president he never set foot outside Turkey and never entertained a single one of the world's great statesmen. Pushing his people toward modernity was such a huge challenge, he realized, that it would be foolish for him to try to project power or influence abroad at the same time. He focused his attention on developing Turkey, and imposed rules that made foreign travel all but impossible for those few Turks who could afford it.

Atatürk's successors faithfully followed his isolationist precepts. Remembering their disastrous experience in World War I and afraid of making another such blunder, they kept their country out of World War II until it was nearly over. But after the war ended they realized that they could not look inward forever. They sent a delegation to the conference at which the United Nations was formed, and Turkey went on to become a founding member of the world body. A few years later, when the Security Council approved the "police action" in Korea and appealed to all nations to join the American-led fighting force there, the Turks decided to respond. Over the course of the war fifteen thousand young men, almost none of whom had ever heard of Korea, left Turkey to fight there.

"I had no idea where Korea was," Ali Taşgan told me as we sat under the stars at his restaurant, listening to waves gently lapping onto the beach a few feet from our table. "No one is happy to go to war, but we had the feeling that we were on the side of freedom."

Like the other Korelis, Ali reached Korea after a long and eventful trip by land and sea. Just past his eighteenth birthday, he saw things he had never imagined and met people whose lives were astonishingly unlike his. When he arrived at Pusan, part of a force sent to replace a three-hundred-man Turkish unit that had taken two hundred twenty-five casualties, his world continued to expand beyond anything he could have imagined. For nearly two years he lived among Koreans, Americans and other foreigners, at first dumbfounded and then fascinated by how different they were from everyone he had ever met. When the war ended, he and his Turkish comrades in arms returned home worldly and restless. They brought a beautiful virus to Turkey, and it has been spreading ever since.

Each of the Korelis was welcomed home by awed neighbors. Almost no Turk had ever known people who had traveled so far. To them, what these veterans had done in the combat zone was secondary; more important was the simple and astonishing fact that they had seen and learned so much. As soon as they returned they became local wise men. "The village elders, men I had been brought up to respect, were coming to me for advice," Ali Taşgan told me. "I was twenty years old, but somehow it seemed right. They had never been more than a day's mule ride from home. I had been to the other side of the planet. It made sense that they should listen to me. I wasn't just Ali anymore. I was Koreli."

As is often the case with subtle movements that build quietly in many places, the Korelis' return was not at first recognized as a profound social phenomenon. Soon, however, this breach in the dam of Turkish isolationism widened. Turkey's appearance on the world stage drew the attention of powerful foreign governments, especially that of the United States, and after 1952, when Turkey became a member of the NATO alliance, thousands of foreign soldiers and sailors passed through Turkish cities and towns. Turkish leaders began to accept the responsibilities of their nation's partnership with powerful allies.

Less than a decade later, Turkey was drawn further beyond its bor-

ders as the economies of northern Europe, especially that of West Germany, started to boom. Factories destroyed in the war were being rebuilt, new businesses were emerging and old entrepreneurial classes were reasserting themselves. These resurgent economies needed more labor than their own countries could supply, and for that the West Germans and their neighbors turned to southern Europe, mainly to Turkey. By the late 1960s hundreds of thousands of Turks, most of them from small towns and villages, were providing the muscle that powered the "miracle" of Western Europe's economic rebirth. When they went back home for their annual vacations and described their experiences to their neighbors, they became a force for change, as the Korelis had been, but far greater in number and influence. The infidel, they told their friends back home, had built a society as free as it was prosperous. Turkey's way of doing things was not the only way, perhaps not even the best way.

For a time the Turkish elite did not hear this message, much less understand its far-reaching implications. The dominant politicians in that period, most notably Süleyman Demirel and Bülent Ecevit, believed they could keep Turks as far from the international mainstream as they had been before World War II. As late as 1980 a Turk could obtain a passport only with difficulty and could not take more than one hundred dollars out of the country. Possession of foreign currency or foreign goods, even a pack of American cigarettes, was a crime. Turkish companies produced only for the domestic market; import and export were almost unknown. There was only one television station, owned and operated by the state.

Those conditions could not survive, and after the iconoclastic Turgut Özal came to power in 1983, he threw open doors and windows that had been tightly shut for decades. Suddenly Turks began to travel wherever they pleased, as both tourists and traders, and foreigners flooded into Turkish cities and onto Turkish beaches. In an amazingly short time Turkey became an important factor in regional affairs, first economically and then politically and militarily. But although Özal deserves credit for recognizing that his country needed to break out of its self-imposed solitude, he only delivered the final blow to the old system. The first blow, the first assault on the wall that had imprisoned Turks within their borders, must be credited to Ali Taşgan and the other returning Korelis.

Their stories led their friends and neighbors to wonder why Turkey was still insisting on keeping itself apart from the world. Korelis paved the way for the masses of "guest workers" who took jobs in Western Europe and who, although not always welcomed there with open arms, came home with new ideas about freedom, democracy, social justice and human rights.

Perhaps inevitably, new generations of Turks feel no special kinship with the Korelis, and certainly little gratitude toward them. To them the Korean War belongs to a forgotten era, its veterans more like relics than heroes. There are still plenty of cafés and restaurants where a Koreli can count on a free meal, a bottle of rakı *and a warm welcome, but they are places run by old people. Today, as the Korelis age, many feel forgotten by a state that sends them pensions worth no more than sixty dollars a month and by a nation that has no time to celebrate their sacrifices. Some have even been ridiculed, told they were crazy to have allowed faceless generals to ship them halfway around the world to fight in a war that meant nothing to them or their country.*

"Young people don't respect what we went through," a veteran named Selahattin Sanlı complained as he showed me the scars he still bears from his war wounds. He lives in lonely retirement in Ankara. "Many aren't even aware of it. Nowadays they don't even give up their seat on the bus when they see the veteran's badge on my jacket."

What Ali Taşgan, Selahattin Sanlı and their compatriots have done for Turkey! Nearly all were born into peasant families for whom travel and social mobility were unimaginable concepts. They saw more as teenagers than their parents and grandparents and great-grandparents saw in their entire lives. When they returned, they used their experiences to fire the curiosity of their people. Every modern Turk, everyone who revels in the opportunities Turkey now offers its citizens, is deeply in their debt.

• SEVEN •

GUARDIANS

☪

For some reason Turks shed their inhibitions when they board an intercity bus. As the Anatolian landscape rolls by hour after hour, they spill intimate secrets to total strangers who happen to be seated next to them. After a time I found this forced intimacy too taxing, so when I boarded a bus for the three-hour trip from Konya, home of the whirling dervishes, to Ankara one midsummer day, I chose to sit next to a young man in uniform. I thought a soldier would surely keep his own counsel, and this one did. He nodded to me as I sat down but spoke not a word.

Long-distance buses in Turkey are equipped with every convenience, including an attendant who brings passengers tea, cold drinks, and even lemon-scented cologne. Soon after our bus left Konya, however, it became clear that the air-conditioning was out of order. Everyone began to sweat, and much clothing was removed. But although the officer sitting next to me squirmed and wiped his brow like everyone else, he did not take off his beribboned jacket. After an hour, with evident uncertainty, he went so far as to loosen his tie just slightly. When we made a rest stop along the road, he pulled it tight again even though he was going no farther than the toilet.

This officer had been considerate enough not to bother me, but I found myself unable to return the favor. Why, I asked him when we were once again aboard, didn't he shuck the jacket, loosen the tie and relax along with everyone else? Why worry about appearances on a bus, or when walking a few steps to the bathroom and back?

"I'm an officer in the Turkish army," he told me quite seriously. "Other people can look sloppy, but not me. When I'm at the stadium and my team scores a goal, I can't jump up and scream like everyone else. I can't run after buses or elevators. I can't hang around in bars and make passes at women. That's the kind of thing civilians do. It's okay for them, but not for us. We're different. We're dignified. We have a mission. We discipline ourselves because we're responsible for the future of this country. Naturally we have higher standards." He stared out the window for a long time, then turned back and added, "Much higher."

One of the greatest achievements of the democratic ideal has been its success in subordinating military power to civilian control. Where democracy rules, army officers do not. They cannot even decide when, where or how to use their power in the field. Those decisions are left exclusively to the people, who through their elected civilian leaders hold a monopoly on political power. When a general in a democratic country speaks out on matters of public policy, he is reprimanded or fired and suffers the opprobrium of his people.

The process of asserting civilian control over armies has been under way for several centuries, and it has become normal for democrats around the world to view military involvement in politics as the antithesis of freedom. The long and horrific periods of military rule through which dozens of African, Asian and Latin American countries suffered during the second half of the twentieth century are taken as confirmation of this basic principle. Democracy is always assumed to suffer when military officers start trying to shape their country's destiny. Conversely, as generals become quieter and more submissive, nations become more democratic and their peoples happier and more free.

For most of its life, the Turkish Republic challenged this stereotype. Its founding revolution was led by army officers, and their breathtaking success in building a modern state on the ruins of the Ottoman Empire ranks among the twentieth century's greatest achievements. Turks realize that, and for generations felt deep gratitude and a genuine connection to their army.

By the twenty-first century, however, this bond was fraying. As Turks broke away from rigid Kemalist ideology, some began to lose their admiration for its most fervent defender, the army. That army, which had always guarded the achievements of Atatürk's revolution and tried to guide Turkey on a steady course toward social progress and the embrace of universal ideals, became a victim of its own success. As its political power became intrusive and suffocating, Turks began to reject it. They have learned the lessons of democracy and want to live by them.

This leap of consciousness confronts the Turkish army with its greatest challenge. A new political order now expresses the people's will for civilian democracy untainted by military power. Military commanders, schooled in the old days when generals were used to telling presidents and prime ministers what to do, are grappling with this new reality. Many are unhappy with it. Their ability to resist it, however, ebbs with each passing day.

Military conquest was the basis of Ottoman power. The greatest sultans were the greatest conquerors, and the empire's decline began with sultans who found military campaigns less appealing than the pleasures of hearth and harem. When the empire collapsed after World War I, the decadent ruling class virtually abandoned the idea of the Turkish nation and kept silent as foreign powers divided Anatolia among themselves. Thanks only to the valor of officers and the peasant soldiers they recruited, national honor was redeemed and the Turkish ideal salvaged.

Since then Turkish officers have defended their country against a host of foreign and domestic threats. Between 1960 and 1980 they toppled four governments, each time with considerable popular support. Although their record is not unblemished, it is one in which today's generals take justified pride. They see little reason to abandon ways that seem to them to have been remarkably successful.

For eighty years military commanders were the ultimate arbiters of life and politics in Turkey. Elected officials could act without their consent but not over their objections. They did not run the government and intruded only into areas of public policy that they considered vital to national security. But since they themselves defined "national security," in practice theirs was the decisive voice whenever they wanted it to be.

The army relaxed its hold on power during Turgut Özal's decade in power, but after his death in 1993 there suddenly proved to be no steady hand on the tiller of government. Irresponsible and corrupt party leaders spent their time bickering and amassing personal fortunes while the Kurdish rebellion reached a peak, the economy collapsed and inflation skyrocketed.

Prime Minister Tansu Çiller, a young American-educated economist in whom the army had at first placed limitless hope, turned out to be a scatterbrained rogue. After the 1995 election, when she made a cynical backroom deal with the Islamist leader Necmettin Erbakan, giving him the support he needed to become prime minister, and in exchange seeing corruption charges against her disappear, their new government veered dangerously away from principles shared by most Turks. Not just generals but many civilians concluded that a disciplining force needed to step in and set the country back on course. That force could only be the army. The generals responded with gusto, forcing Erbakan to resign and then setting about to limit politics so that such a figure would be prevented from ever again attaining power. The worst legacy of Erbakan's disastrous year in power was that it convinced the army that Turks were still not ready for democracy.

In the last years of the twentieth century, the Turkish army, acting always with the enthusiastic support of its friends in Parliament, the government bureaucracy and the judicial system, launched a new and vigorous offensive against what it considered dangerous trends in Turkish society. Acting in unison, this elite banned political parties, sent journalists and politicians—including Tayyip Erdoğan—to jail, harassed Kurdish activists and crushed efforts to repeal laws that limited personal freedom. Those steps were not new, and in fact had been depressing aspects of Turkish life for as long as Turkey had existed. What was new was the political climate. Most Turks had begun to chafe under the restrictive nature of their state. Many doubted that the threats facing their nation were really as dire as the military men made them out to be. As they came to understand what democracy is, they realized how far their country was from it. They believed they had reached the point at which they could be trusted to make their own decisions, even to make their own mistakes.

Army commanders, however, remained unconvinced. They considered themselves Atatürk's heirs and justified everything they did by claiming to be the only ones who truly understood what he wanted for the country. But were they upholding his vision or preventing its realization? Their narrow view of what constitutes national security and their terror of free inquiry and debate continues to stand in contradiction to Turkey's needs, now more than ever.

From the moment Turkish cadets enter military high school at the age of fourteen, they are inculcated with a sense of mission. Like the officer I met on the bus from Konya, they consider themselves purer than most civilians, less tainted by greed and dishonesty, more willing to make sacrifices for the good of the nation. They are a priesthood that lives and grows together, largely isolated from the rest of society. Most of the people they know are other cadets and officers. They live in their own neighborhoods and follow one another's careers intently. Many of the ambitious among them even choose their wives from military families.

Cadets are educated quite differently from other Turks. Like aspiring officers everywhere, they are taught the values of discipline, order and hard work. They also enjoy immeasurably better facilities than pupils in normal public schools. The buildings in which they study are modern and well maintained. Their computers are new, their science laboratories well equipped and their libraries full. Their teachers are wise and experienced, not like the ill-trained and poorly paid ones who must make the best of pitifully inadequate resources at many civilian schools. But the greatest difference lies in what they are taught. Cadets are told over and over that they are Atatürk's children, a selfless cadre set forth in a dissolute world. They learn the values of state and nation, not necessarily those of humanity and the individual. The most successful among them emerge with a deep sense of mission, an almost mystical conviction that Turkey's fate, not just militarily but also politically and spiritually, depends on their superior wisdom.

At the academy, cadets are taught strategic doctrine that presents a world fraught with danger. Threats are everywhere. Foreign powers plot endlessly to subvert, divide and weaken Turkey. Bad Turks, the enemies of Atatürk, lend themselves to these plots. To defend the nation in the face of such dire challenges, the army not only must have masses of tanks, helicopters and artillery but also must reconcile itself to the thankless task of regulating society, of suppressing dangerous ideas and individuals who seek to lead the nation astray. With this message drilled into them day after day and year after year, cadets naturally become officers who revere abstract ideals like "state" and "duty" more than humanistic values like individual rights and the supremacy of civilian power. They do not see the vibrant, self-confident and boldly ambitious Turkey that many civilians see. Rather they see a nation surrounded by enemies and populated by simpletons who are easily manipulated. The army and the army alone, they are taught, stands between this fragile nation and utter doom.

This outlandish perspective, like much of Kemalist doctrine, was once quite reasonable. In the 1920s and 1930s Turkey was indeed a fragile and besieged nation, and there was no social class or political force better than the army to defend it. The educated elite was small, and there was neither a middle class nor anything resembling civil society. All that has now changed. Turkey is bursting with energy and overflowing with people who can guide a nation at least as capably as military officers can. Army commanders do not seem to recognize that Turkey is racing past them and their stagnant worldview. Because their institution encourages the strictest orthodoxy and punishes creative thinking, it is drifting slowly away from its nation.

Each year about nine hundred Turkish cadets are commissioned as lieutenants. Only about thirty will ultimately become generals, or "pashas," as Turks still call them. Their progression through the ranks is determined partly by their command capacity and military expertise, but also according to their perceived fidelity to the rigid principles of Kemalism. An officer who prays, shuns alcohol or is married to a woman who wears a head scarf not only is an unlikely candidate for advancement but runs the risk of being cashiered. The same is true for any who question the accepted view of the army's role in Turkish society. As officers rise through the ranks and compete ever more intensely for the fewer and fewer available promotions, they naturally feel pressure to seem—and to be—more fiercely Kemalist than their rivals. The self-perpetuating elite this system has produced is highly resistant to change.

To portray Turkish generals as hopeless reactionaries, though, would be quite mistaken. The average general is better educated, more worldly and in some ways more liberal than the average politician. Hundreds of regional party bosses, mayors and members of Parliament are fanatic nationalists, ignorant demagogues or scheming crooks. Few generals fit into any of those categories. This truth is depressing because of what it says about the political class, but at the same time it is encouraging. It means that the military commanders of today and tomorrow know Turkey must change, even though they deeply fear that change. No one repeats more often than they do the old cliché about Turkey being a special case that cannot risk opening its society as completely as more comfortably located and traditionally democratic countries can. In their hearts, though, more than a few realize that the contradictions inherent in their self-image are sharper today than they have ever been.

Turkish officers command a huge force of more than half a million soldiers, bigger than any army in Europe and the second largest in NATO after that of the United States. Most are draftees, required by law to serve between one and two years in uniform. Over several generations the system of universal male conscription has effectively bound the citizenry to the army and led most Turks to view it as a part of their everyday lives. When they see a soldier they understand instinctively that he is Mehmet, the fellow from down the street or over in the next village.

Conscription was originally imposed not only to create a large army but also as a socialization tool. For generations it was invaluable in giving sons of peasants a glimpse of modernity, training in basic social skills and exposure to the ideals of patriotism and discipline. But today those functions are filled by education, travel and mass communication. Many Turkish youths have come to view their military service as a waste of time, almost a joke.

Partly in response to this mounting unhappiness, in 1999 the army instituted a system under which young men could buy their way out of military service for fifteen thousand German marks, the equivalent of about eight thousand dollars. Those who cannot afford such a sum naturally resent this system, but even many who take advantage of it slip into cynicism and frustration. After making their payment these men must spend twenty-eight days on a military base as a kind of token service. Many come home with stories that portray the army as an almost ridiculous institution.

"We never learned a thing about tactics or how to fight," a friend told me after returning from his twenty-eight days at Burdur, an army base near the Mediterranean coast. "In the morning we heard speeches about why Turks are the best soldiers in the world; it's because we are Turks. Then there were speeches about how joining the European Union is the strategic goal of Turkey. In the afternoon, four or five times a week, we had belly-dance and striptease shows. Everyone had to pay four million lira [then about seven dollars] for a ticket. At first some of the recruits from Anatolia didn't want to go because they didn't have enough money and didn't like the idea of seeing naked women. But anyone who didn't go had to march around the base in the hot sun all afternoon, so after the first few days everybody came. We had more than a thousand people in a huge hall. And during the shows, subofficers would go around selling Coke and ice cream. It was all a way to get money from us. After four weeks of this I came home. Do you think I came home respecting my military? Of course not. I came home thinking it's a stupid organization run by stupid people."

The Turkish army is able to get away with practices like this because it is not subject to outside control. Logic suggests that long ago officers should have begun to take advantage of this freedom not simply to extort money from recruits but to enrich themselves. Quite remarkably, however, they have not. Unlike many civilian politicians, the generals do not take bribes or extort money from contractors. When they retire they do not live in mansions, and their children do not attend expensive schools or drive flashy cars. Instead they set an example of probity and expect everyone in uniform to follow it.

Not all do, especially those whose service has taken them to traditionally lawless southeastern provinces. The war against Kurdish rebels led many people into crime, including some officers. When fighting was at its peak during the early 1990s, some used brutish tactics and collaborated with terror groups in ways that deeply alienated millions of Kurds. Others succumbed to temptation and made lucrative arrangements with the smugglers who for decades have been moving huge quantities of Iranian and Afghan heroin to Europe across well-worn paths in eastern Turkey. One captain who retired from the army and returned home to my neighborhood in Istanbul after serving for six years at posts near the Iranian border bought himself a twelve-villa vacation complex overlooking the Sea of Marmara, an unimaginable luxury for someone with no income other than a soldier's salary. Some of his old friends were so disgusted that they refused to speak to him again, but he didn't seem to mind.

Turks know these cases are exceptions and rightly consider their army to be fundamentally honest. Many also consider it decent and humane, although they have never heard the full story of how the Kurdish rebellion was suppressed. The Turkish army does not risk losing its prestige or its position in national life by being brutal, repressive and rapacious, like armies that became despised in countries from Indonesia to Chile to Zaire. But it is finding for the first time that a gap has developed between it and the Turkish people.

In one sense the Turkish army is beginning to resemble the elite Janissary corps that guarded Ottoman sultans and formed the backbone of military power during much of the imperial period. Originally Janissaries were servants of the state, but gradually they accumulated so much power that they became its masters. "The sultan trembles at a Janissary's frown," went an old Turkish proverb. Ultimately the Janissaries degenerated into brigandage and cruelty, and their corps was destroyed by Sultan Mahmut II in 1826—an episode known in Turkish history as the "auspicious event." Today's Turkish officers have never approached the lawlessness into which the Janissaries degenerated, but freethinking civilians tremble at a general's frown, and many Turks believe that the officers' withdrawal from politics would be an "auspicious event" every bit as crucial for republican Turkey as the first one was for the Ottomans.

Not long ago, nearly all Turks viewed their army as a valiant force of selfless patriots dedicated to defending the nation against its many enemies. Today growing numbers of young people view universal conscription as outmoded and harmful to the cause of national development, forcing them to waste time they might otherwise use studying or working. Among the citizenry at large, doubts run even deeper. More and more Turks are concluding that their army has failed to keep pace with their aspirations, that despite its stated commitment to Europe and European values it has become an obstacle, perhaps even the main obstacle, to modernization and democracy.

Some Turkish generals believe that foreign powers have never given up their secret desire to carve up Turkey for themselves, as they tried to do at Sèvres in 1920. They suspect that the European Union in particular uses human-rights issues and the status of Kurds as wedges in a campaign to destroy Turkey's unitary state and ultimately its nation. Closer to home, the generals see even more dire threats. In their view, Iran is directing a massive destabilization campaign designed to bring Turkey under the rule of reactionary mullahs; Syria plots to capture the ethnically Arab province of Hatay and adjacent regions rich with water and other resources; Iraq harbors Kurdish guerrillas waiting for the right time to launch a new offensive; Armenia directs a worldwide defamation campaign aimed at blackening Turkey's name and ultimately seizing its eastern provinces; even Greece cannot be trusted, its relatively recent desire for cooperation across the Aegean only a feint that may hide nefarious intentions. Worst of all are the threats from within Turkey itself. Bad children of the Turkish nation are cooperating with Turkey's foreign enemies, the generals believe, cynically disguising themselves as democrats, human-rights advocates, peaceful religious believers and defenders of cultural pluralism.

For a long time Turks were inclined to accept these views, mainly because they had great confidence in their military officers and assumed they must know best. That changed during the 1990s, as Turks began hearing younger and newer voices. They saw a world different from the one the generals saw, one where foreign powers did not necessarily wish Turkey ill. More important, they developed a self-confidence that encouraged them to believe they could govern themselves rather than having to live within limits the army set for them.

The rise of Tayyip Erdoğan and his AKP changed the political landscape in which the army was used to maneuvering. This new force, with its insistence on curbing military power, clearly had the support of masses of Turkish voters and could not easily be crushed. These voters saw through the army's attempt to portray the AKP as an insurgent clique of Muslim fundamentalists, and instead saw its rise for what it was: a democratic rebellion against suffocating dogma.

During his first years in power, Erdoğan brought his country economic stability and a broader, though still not a full, measure of democracy. Most thrillingly, through a series of maneuvers he emasculated the National Security Council, wiping away the institution through which the armed forces had dominated national life for so long. Generals naturally resented this reform. It intensified their conviction that their new prime minister was a subversive fundamentalist bent on bringing down the entire edifice of secular democracy.

Unable to intimidate Erdoğan as they had intimidated previous prime ministers, the generals used their faithful ally, President Ahmet Necdet Sezer, a former judge, to block him whenever possible. Turkey's president has limited but important powers. He (there has never been a female) names the military chief of staff, can veto laws passed by Parliament, appoints high-court judges and presides over periodic hearings at which the army purges officers who are considered too religious. He also rules on the appointment of university rectors (a power that was used with diabolical effectiveness during the 1980s and 1990s, when rectors became ideological enforcers, insisting that students and professors toe the official line rather than allowing them the terrifying right to free inquiry). "These powers in the hands of a politician from a party with an Islamist background would threaten the generals' hold on deep state," one newspaper columnist wrote.

Turkish presidents are elected by Parliament, and when President Sezer's term expired in 2007, Erdoğan made clear that he would use his parliamentary majority to install someone who supported his reform agenda. Then he announced his choice: Foreign Minister Abdullah Gül, his closest political comrade. Gül is a thoughtful, worldly figure, the son of a factory worker from the booming Anatolian city of Kayseri, but his nomination produced howls of protest for one reason: his wife wears a head scarf. The idea that a covered woman would defile the secular sanctuary of Çankaya, the presidential residence, was intolerable to the old elite. President Sezer went so far as to assert that the secular system was facing "its greatest threat since the founding of the Republic in 1923.

"Those who want to push Turkey back into a primitive order talk about democracy," he warned, perfectly epitomizing the old Kemalist mind-set. "A well-organized plot is being carried out with the aim of undermining the military."

In a series of public statements, Gül tried to calm these fears. "The president must be loyal to secular principles," he said at one press conference. "If elected I will act accordingly." When asked about the head scarf, he defended it as an expression of free will, calling women's decisions about whether to wear one "individual choices" that "everybody should respect." That made sense to most Turks but drove others to distraction. "The army will never let him become president," a Turkish friend assured me.

I wondered how, short of a coup d'état, the generals would be able to block Gül. Soon I had my answer. First the Constitutional Court, a pillar of the old establishment, issued a tortuous ruling that twisted long-established parliamentary rules in ways that made it impossible for the majority to elect its favored candidate. Then the military high command issued a statement that would be unthinkable in a truly democratic country. Turkey, the generals warned, was being threatened by "a reactionary mind-set whose sole aim is to erode the fundamentals of our state."

A few days later the chief of staff, General Yaşar Büyükanit, spoke even more directly. "Our nation has been watching the behavior of separatists who refuse to embrace Turkey's unitary nature, and centers of evil that systematically try to corrode the secular nature of the Turkish Republic," he ominously declared. "Nefarious plans to undermine Turkish secularism and democracy nature emerge in different forms every day . . . The Turkish armed forces remain as determined as ever to maintain a social, democratic and secular Turkey."

In the old days, such a statement from the high priests of Kemalism would have brought everyone to heel. Erdoğan was unimpressed, however. When asked his reaction, he said what most Turks felt: that the generals' intrusion into politics was "a bullet fired at democracy." The government spokesman, former justice minister Cemil Çiçek, called it "utterly wrong" and urged the generals to be "more sensitive and careful" in the future. Gül, as is his wont, was calmer. "No one finds these arguments convincing anymore," he told reporters with a dismissive smile.

The confrontation escalated when organizations representing the secular elite convened mass marches in several Turkish cities. A total of more than a million people paraded through the streets chanting, "Turkey is secular and will remain secular!" They seemed painfully out of touch with much of the nation, with their dogma of secularism above democracy as the nation's guiding principle. Yet the demonstrators, most of them women, could not fairly be dismissed as Kemalist reactionaries. Their fear that Turkish democracy might bring with it a new, oppressive form of public religiosity is as much a part of Turkish life as the rise of Erdoğan and his new regime. Because their protests came as a consequence of the confrontation between the armed forces and Turkey's elected leaders, however, the regime took them as a challenge.

Turkish politicians in the past had retreated whenever the military asserted its power, so many Turks expected Erdoğan to withdraw Gül's name and nominate someone else. Instead he did the opposite. Understanding that this was a key moment, he told the generals, in effect: You say my party has no mandate to choose a president. Fine, let's have another national election. It will show whether voters support me and my AKP or the discredited old parties that have been licking your polished boots for too long.

In the 2007 campaign, Erdoğan barnstormed the country and held mass rallies in fifty-five of Turkey's eighty-one provinces. His AKP organized a nationwide army of volunteers to knock on doors and spread their message—something traditional parties had never deigned to do. Voters rewarded him with a resounding mandate. It was an unprecedented rebuke to the generals and their Kemalist vanguard. A majority of Turks had finally rejected the state's age-old warning that religious politicians posed mortal threats to secularism.

Erdoğan's AKP won 47 percent of the vote, making it the first governing party in Turkish history to win more votes in its second campaign than in its first. It took 341 of the 550 parliamentary seats. This was an almost unimaginable act of defiance, and a deep humiliation for the armed forces. Turks said with their votes that they no longer cared what their "pashas" wanted and would decide for themselves what was best for their country. This gave most Turks a thrilling sense of liberation, but it terrified many others.

"The dominant feeling among secularists," the columnist Meral Tamer wrote in her post-election commentary, "is one of shock, impotence, fury and despair."

Part of the reason so many Turks voted to re-elect the AKP in 2007, and by extension to support the choice of Abdullah Gül as president, was that Gül was such a reassuring personality. I had had many conversations with him during his years as a member of Parliament, sometimes over dinner at Kıyı, a classic seafood restaurant that overlooks a lovely Bosphorus cove. Over *meze* and drinks—*rakı* for me, cola for him—I came to know him as a reflective and thoughtful conciliator, committed to democracy but also eager to avoid confrontation.

"Gül has limited charismatic attraction for ordinary Turkish voters, but he is softer, more polished and more willing to compromise than Erdoğan," the Turkish scholar Gül Berna Özcan observed. "He has the short and square body of a wrestler who could endure a slow fight and use tactical delays to gain position. Erdoğan, on the other hand, is tall and clever but also childishly impatient; like the former footballer he is, his political style is pushy and restless."

By campaigning so fiercely to block Gül's rise, trying to scare people into remaining faithful to old ways, the armed forces overplayed their hand. The old era was coming to an end. Erdoğan did not put it quite that way, but his terse victory statement made the point with words every Turk could interpret. "A structure doomed to uncertainty has been overcome," he said.

Newly strengthened, the AKP was easily able to place Gül in the presidency. Parliament elected him on August 28, 2007, and he took office without incident. In his inaugural address he said he considered secularism "a rule for social peace no less than it is an empowering model for different ways of life within democracy." Military commanders, still in shock, refused to attend the inaugural reception. They waited two weeks before congratulating him on his victory, and when they finally did, they also warned that the armed forces would remain the "absolute defender of secularism."

That statement, though, was worded in a way that suggested the commanders felt chastened by the rebuke Turks had given them at the polls. One phrase was especially intriguing. Instead of insisting that they would enforce their will regardless of what people wanted, the generals said only that they were determined to be "one of the sides in this debate." It was a welcome sign that they were adjusting to new realities instead of trying to dictate the limits of national debate.

Just as many Turks and their friends were thrilling to the idea that the old elite had finally agreed to loosen its hold on power, however, the past came snarling back. In 2008 the country's highest court announced that it would hear a complaint charging that the AKP had violated the constitution by seeking to impose an Islamic order. The complaint asked for a breathtakingly radical remedy: a ban on the AKP and an order forbidding dozens of its leaders, including President Gül and Prime Minister Erdoğan, to continue in politics. There may be no other country where a court would seriously consider banning a ruling party that commanded such broad support. Doing so would be a form of coup d'état clothed in the guise of judicial legitimacy.

The oddest aspect of this judicial campaign is that, as previous closings of political parties have shown, it would have little practical effect. Each time this has happened in the past, the party quickly regroups under a new name and returns to active politics, with its banned leaders still in charge from behind the scenes. Closings actually tend to increase parties' popularity, because they allow the victims to pose as objects of persecution at the hands of an oppressive elite. Religious-oriented parties and leaders have been especially skillful in manipulating this image.

Even if it is not true that the AKP harbors a secret agenda to turn Turkey into an Islamic republic, as some Turks believe, it is difficult to avoid the conclusion that many of its leaders have an incomplete understanding of democracy. They insist on democratic rights for their followers, but seem less eager to guarantee them to others. During their years in power, their enthusiasm for sweeping reform has measurably ebbed.

Part of this is the fault of the European Union. The EU accession process gave Turkey a theoretical and ideological framework for democratization. As long as this framework held, it provided a built-in guarantee that the AKP would embrace policies of transparency and civil rights for all, and crush radical elements in its ranks. This pulled Turkey steadily away from its old military-dominated political system and ever closer to democracy, just as it did in Spain, Portugal and Greece. When the EU turned away from the idea of Turkish accession, democratization quickly began to seem less urgent. So did suppressing fundamentalist factions within the AKP.

The AKP itself, though, shares the blame for Turkey's slow polarization. Its leaders are vulnerable to triumphalism, as they showed by insisting that one of their own, Abdullah Gül, be chosen as president rather than a figure who would have been acceptable to all Turks. They have contributed to tensions that threaten both their country's political progress and its economic stability.

The AKP rose to power because it addresses voters' real concerns. It dominates the political landscape and will, under one name or another, continue to do so for years to come. It is a social reality that cannot be made to disappear by judicial fiat. Court decisions and political bans cannot resolve the tensions that have begun to spread through Turkey, and may well exacerbate them. Both sides in this escalating conflict—the AKP and the old Kemalist ruling class—have shown a stubborn unwillingness to follow the path of dialogue and compromise. This places them at odds in a domestic conflict that, if it continues to escalate, could destabilize Turkey and place its grand achievements at risk. That would lead many Turks and their friends abroad to resurrect an old lament that many believed had become obsolete: "Turkey is the country that never fails to disappoint." Making sure it remains obsolete—making sure that, this time, Turkey builds on its success instead of committing political hara-kiri just as it reaches a pinnacle of success—is the central challenge facing the country's political class today.

I knew Hamza Akmeşe was a real man when I noticed that he doesn't care how much camel saliva drips onto his shoulders. He loves his beast and would probably take it to bed with him if he could. A little spit, even a lot of spit, doesn't bother him.

The day I met Hamza he was furtively surveying the competition before a big camel-fighting match in Selçuk, a town near the Aegean coast that is known to foreigners only because it is on the road to the ancient ruins of Ephesus. He quickly realized he had nothing to worry about. "My camel is strong," he told me. "He has a good body, good technique, and he knows how to use his front legs for tripping."

Turks are becoming steadily more European and that is good, because it means they are embracing ideas and perspectives that will make their lives richer and more fulfilling. But they will never be completely European, and that is also good. They have a different heritage, a different psychology. Like many Europeans they love soccer, but they also have more exotic sporting tastes, and camel fighting is one of them. Hamza Akmeşe, who has been in the game for forty years, compares its hold on Turks to the hold bullfighting has on Spaniards. "It's our tradition," he told me as he led his hulking creature toward the ring, bells on its humps, a mirrored blanket covering its back and colorful pom-poms woven into its tail. "It's very big, very important."

Turks migrated from the steppes of Central Asia a thousand years ago, but something of their past remains within them. It must be a kind of collective imagination; it cannot be a personal gene, since most people in Turkey today have no Central Asian ancestry at all. As they hurtle toward modernity, they are also looking back. The prospect of becoming European thrills them, as well it should, but they also find it vaguely disturbing. They do not want to lose what makes them different and special, which is why so many thousands of them turn out every Sunday during the three-month winter season to watch camels fight.

The owner of a fighting camel is invariably a celebrity in his village. Children admire him, men defer to him, women compete for his attention. He may shine shoes, sell vegetables or work in an office, but when he is with his camel he is an incarnation of Turkishness. Fighting camels have names that express valor and fearlessness, like Thunderbolt, Falcon, Destiny, Black Ali and Jackal. They are not to be trifled with, and neither are their owners.

Fans of camel fighting can discourse endlessly about the sport's finer points. They compare bloodlines, assess technique and trade rumors about young camels that seem to be developing into future champions. To the untrained eye, however, the game's subtleties are not immediately visible.

A match resembles an outsize version of sumo wrestling. It begins with two camels, the largest of which can weigh well over a ton, being led toward each other. Sometimes one bolts and runs away, thereby forfeiting the match. More often, they crash into each other and begin shoulder-to-shoulder pushing. For a minute or more, there is little movement as the contestants strain against each other. Their owners urge them on, spectators cheer and an announcer breathlessly calls the play-by-play. Finally one of the animals collapses onto the ground. The winner's owner is awarded a carpet.

"I have piles of them at home," one successful owner told me the day I was in Selçuk. "They're all machine-made and not so good. I give them away. But this isn't about money or carpets. It's about keeping something alive that was given to us by our grandfathers and great-grandfathers."

Yet camels are not and never were the animals most central to the

Turkish identity. As long as there have been Turks they have been known for their horsemanship, and watching men on horseback is still one of the Turk's great pleasures. There are of course country clubs where the privileged practice the stylized delicacy of dressage and the tightly controlled ritual of show jumping. But in the Turkish heartland, especially on the plains of wild provinces like Erzincan and Bayburt, once home to ancient cultures and still places where tradition is strong, it is the wild sport of cirit *that captivates and thrills.*

Cirit *matches are lightning-fast, played by riders who gallop toward each other in clouds of dust, hurling wooden javelins. They win points by striking an opponent or forcing his horse to veer off course. Like the owners of fighting camels, they are heroic figures, at least in their own minds. Many seem as if they might be more at home in untamed, horse-crazy places like Afghanistan or Kyrgyzstan than in Turkey. The growing popularity of their sport, which is now played even in Ankara and Istanbul, reflects the resolve of Turks not to lose their old identity as they embrace a new one.*

People are thought to have begun riding horses more than four thousand years ago in Central Asia, and the first to do so were probably ancestors of today's Turks. So were the first mounted archers, who began roaming the rugged highlands north of the Caspian and Black seas in the eighth century B.C. *Turkic tribesmen spent much of their lives on horseback. Children were put on sheeps' backs before they could walk so that they would become accustomed to the feel of riding. Adults ate, drank, conducted business, held meetings and even slept on horseback. The ancient Chinese knew them as "horse barbarians."*

Mounted cavalrymen called sipahi *were the backbone of the Ottoman army that spent centuries winning victory after victory. They were considered almost helpless when on foot but invincible when mounted. To gallop at full speed, turn backward and shoot a deadly arrow at a distant foe was only their most famous skill.*

The sipahi *rode off to war almost every spring, and their commanders devised* cirit *as a form of off-season training and exercise. In those days competitors had to hurl spears through rings while galloping and shoot arrows at suspended brass spheres. Their sport declined in the early twentieth century as new forms of warfare replaced mounted cav-*

alry and machines weakened the tie between rural people and their horses. But in the 1990s it became popular again. Rules were codified, an official federation was established and the University of Erzincan, many of whose students grew up in isolated villages on the surrounding prairie, began offering formal training courses for aspiring players. For a time Turks seemed to have forgotten how to ride toward conquest, but they are learning again.

The third of Turkey's great sporting traditions, oil wrestling, was born in the town of Kırkpınar, a few miles from the present-day border with Greece, at the beginning of the fifteenth century. Almost every year since then, boys and men have traveled there from across the country to test their strength and skill. This is the only wrestling tournament in the world at which contestants use three tons of olive oil.

Rules for these matches have changed only slightly over the centuries. In olden times they could go on for hours or even days, since the only way to win was to pin one's opponent to the ground. Some contestants expended so much energy that they died on the field. Now it is also possible to win on points, and matches are limited to forty-five minutes. But wrestlers still fight stripped to the waist, wear specially designed leather trousers and enjoy the boundless admiration of their countrymen. Most important, they begin fighting only after being drenched with olive oil from head to toe.

Once oiled, the competitors skip across the field in lines, slapping their knees and jumping as they move forward. Drummers in Ottoman costume keep a steady beat, and as matches are about to start, announcers sing the praises of "Ye, oh great wrestlers" and recite verses like this one:

> *You cannot get wood from a willow branch.*
> *Every girl cannot be a woman.*
> *Every woman can give birth,*
> *But not every boy can be a wrestler.*

Lovers of this sport say it is psychological as well as physical. Because matches go on for so long, combatants cannot fight without interruption. They spend much time circling, grunting, feinting and trying to intimidate each other. When they sense an opening they charge, grab their opponent, often between the legs, and try to smash him to the ground. Pinning an opponent's shoulders to the ground for three seconds, or throwing him down more often than he can throw you down, is what it takes to win.

The undisputed king of modern oil wrestling is a former factory worker named Ahmet Taşçi. He is an eight-time champion in the heavyweight division, considered a superman because he continues to win even though he is more than forty years old. The only man to have defeated him since he rose to greatness in the 1980s is a whippersnapper in his mid-thirties named Cengiz Elbiye. On the day I saw them face off I realized I was seeing not just a match but the classic confrontation of aging champion versus rising challenger.

The match had been under way for more than half an hour when suddenly, so fast I am not sure I actually saw it, the veteran Taşçi smashed his younger opponent to the ground, pinned his shoulders and was pronounced the winner yet again. Elbiye, his defeated rival, remained on his knees with his face pressed to the ground for several minutes. I thought he was weeping bitter tears, but even if I had been closer I would not have been able to tell if what wetted his face were tears or drops of olive oil. That is certainly as he wanted it.

• EIGHT •

DEATH BY EARTHQUAKE

☪

The soup dumplings at Joe's Shanghai, a wonderful dive hidden on a small street in the heart of New York's teeming Chinatown, have a cult following. They are made with a dollop of meat and broth inside, and you have to be careful how you eat them to avoid having the soup spurt out as you bite. Nothing more serious than that was on my mind as I worked my way through dinner on a sticky summer evening. I took no special notice when the clock passed 8:11.

Half a world away, in Turkey, clocks at that moment read 3:11 a.m. Most people in the industrial boomtowns of Izmit and Adapazarı and the seaside resorts of Gölcük and Yalova were sleeping as calmly as I was eating in New York. But that was the moment when a murderous terror, mean and hateful, ascended suddenly from the depths. The earth began to shake, and for forty-five seconds buildings swayed and fell. Millions of people awoke and fled onto the streets, where they stood and watched in horror as the air around them filled with dust and screams. Thousands were killed as they tried to escape. Many others, most of them elderly and devout, simply pulled blankets over their heads and waited for fate to take its cruel course.

Hours later on that awful day, August 17, 1999, I was at Kennedy Airport checking in for a flight back to Istanbul. A man passing by stopped and stared at the Turkish Airlines sign above the counter where I was waiting.

"My God," I heard him mutter to his companion. "Who would want to go to Turkey now?"

No one yet knew how serious the earthquake had been. Turkish news agencies were reporting a death toll in the hundreds, and that was enough to cast a pall over the passengers on my flight, many of whom were Turks rushing home to search for friends or relatives. After we landed in Istanbul, I was waiting for my luggage when I noticed a young man ambling around the arrival lounge, carrying a clipboard and looking disoriented. He was sizing up passengers and approaching some of them. Soon it was my turn.

"Are you here for the earthquake?" he asked me. I was, of course, but it turned out that he was looking for relief workers. Rescue teams were already arriving, but evidently the authorities had no idea who they were, so the only way to find them was to grab them at the airport.

This was but a taste of what Turkey would live through over the next few days. Prime Minister Ecevit fell into a prolonged state of shock; instead of immediately jumping on a helicopter to survey the disaster area and then ordering his aides into action, he spent days telling whoever would listen that everything was under control and there was no need for concern. Army commanders who might have been expected to deploy thousands of soldiers to the stricken region also sat on their hands. Quickly it became clear that although Turkey lies above some of the world's most dangerous geological faults and is shaken by earthquakes every few years, its government had no plan for dealing with them, no disaster-relief agency, no civil-defense network, not even an official designated to take charge at such moments. In what seemed like a very cruel joke, the government's earthquake-relief fund was found to contain the equivalent of just four dollars and forty-five cents.

The quake's epicenter was barely fifty miles east of Istanbul's city limits, near the shore of a pretty bay at the edge of the Sea of Marmara, and it wrought death and destruction far greater than was first reported. In towns across the region whole blocks of buildings had collapsed, killing thousands instantly and trapping thousands more who died slowly while government officials stumbled aimlessly about, unable to grasp the dimensions of the catastrophe. Prime Minister Ecevit later sought to excuse the government's slow response by saying that roads were too clogged to allow rescue teams to reach devastated towns. Television teams had no such trouble, though, and soon all of Turkey was watching survivors clawing at the rubble with their bare hands and even fighting over shovels and the few available bulldozers. Most television stations dropped their normal programs and broadcast live, day and night, from the disaster zone. Turks by the millions were glued to their screens, watching scenes of heartrending devastation and streams of interviews with enraged survivors, the intensity of whose anger was shocking in a country where exaggerated respect for the state has always been part of the national psychology.

Ecevit and the generals who ran Turkey with him finally responded, but only after a week, and even then they devoted most of their energy to blaming the press. One television station was ordered shut for seven days as punishment for broadcasting reports that vividly conveyed the chaos of the official rescue efforts. The top military commander, General Hüseyin Kıvrıkoğlu, called a handful of Turkish newspaper editors to his office and told them that the main problem had been not the relief effort but irresponsible journalists who emphasized its failures over its successes. He singled out five foreign correspondents as having been especially responsible for feeding these distortions to the world, myself among them, and charged that we had placed ourselves at the service of unnamed subversive "interests." Essentially, his complaint was that we had reported the truth without thinking of what effect it might have on the prestige of the Turkish state.

Earthquake victims, meanwhile, faced a host of horrors. Survivors with loved ones buried beneath rubble bore the most painful burdens. For days, thousands of them could do nothing but sit helplessly before the piles of debris. Power shovels and other heavy equipment, much of it sent voluntarily by private companies, finally arrived in the ruined towns, but only after hopes of finding anyone alive had faded, and they were worked at a pace that survivors naturally found intolerably, heartbreakingly slow. Some nurtured hopes for days, but as time passed most accepted reality and waited only to claim bodies.

On the fifth morning after the quake, I sat among survivors who were maintaining a vigil in front of an apartment complex in the seaside town of Yalova, to which thousands of upwardly mobile Turks had moved in recent years, lured by the prospect of cheap apartments, fresh sea air and proximity to Istanbul. A fifty-foot-high pile of rubble at which they gazed had once been a handsome apartment building. Giant yellow power shovels were clawing at it, ripping away floors and ceilings that had "pancaked" when the quake struck—fallen on top of one another as supporting walls collapsed, crushing scores of victims as they slept. Several bodies had already been pulled from the debris, and the stench that filled the hot, sticky air was a grim signal that more still lay entombed.

As the power shovels worked, the flotsam of human lives tumbled down through the dust—clothes, mattresses, bookshelves, carpets, a television, a washing machine, a radiator, a toilet, a set of the works of Balzac translated into Turkish. The roar of machines found an eerie counterpart in the absolute silence of onlookers, who fixed their gazes on this horrific scene as beads of sweat dripped down their faces.

Shortly before noon, one group of workers cried out. A shovel had broken into a bedroom and they could see a body inside. The big machine backed away, and workers began to pull away slabs of concrete by hand. Half an hour later they freed the bloated body of a young woman, wrapped it in a blanket, zipped it into a green plastic bag and carried it to a waiting ambulance, which sped away with its siren blaring.

A few minutes later one man sitting near me began to turn pale and breathe heavily. He broke into sobs and then suddenly started screaming. "Thirteen years old!" he shouted. "Buried under there! Just a baby! Just thirteen!" With both his hands, he began violently ripping up the grass around him. Relief workers wiped his brow with wet cloths and managed to calm him after a while, but he refused to be led away, preferring to maintain his awful watch.

What made this hellish scene so especially and outrageously tragic was that all around stood buildings that had been damaged either lightly or not at all. These were structures that had been built by responsible contractors using decent materials, and the people who lived in them had survived unhurt while their neighbors had been horribly crushed to death in their beds. Earthquakes are often described as natural disasters, but seismologists like to say that it is buildings that kill people, not the quakes themselves. So it was here. The victims cursed not just the violent earth beneath their feet but also builders like Veli Göçer, who had built the collapsed edifice before which I spent that Sunday.

Lynch mobs tried to find Göçer in the days that followed the quake, but, like other contractors whose buildings had become tombs, he had disappeared. A week later he spoke by telephone with a German newspaper. "There's no reason for me to have a guilty conscience," he said. "Naturally I sympathize with the victims and their families. But I don't understand why they're making me into a scapegoat. I started building the Bahçekent complex in Yalova about six years ago. Naturally I didn't have any idea about construction. I studied literature in school. I'm a poet, not a structural engineer. I remember visiting my first construction site. I saw workers using beach sand to make concrete. When I asked about it, the architects told me that this was completely normal. Only later did I learn that this is a completely wrong and dangerous technique. So I ordered a stop to that disgusting practice. Unfortunately half the complex was already finished."

Several days later Göçer was arrested at a house in Istanbul where he had been hiding. More than a dozen other contractors had already been jailed pending investigations, but Göçer, whom the press had branded "the contractor of death," was the focus of public outrage. Three lines of police officers surrounded the station where he was booked, and when he was brought to prison he had to be isolated to protect him from other inmates, several of whom swore to kill him at the first opportunity.

For weeks after the earthquake, much of northwestern Turkey continued to be shaken by aftershocks, some of which qualified as small quakes in their own right. Dozens of people were injured as they jumped from shaking buildings. In Adapazarı, a town that had been heavily damaged on the first day, a woman died of a heart attack as she rushed from a building she thought was about to collapse. This panic reflected something beyond the culture of exaggeration that traditionally leads Turks to dramatize imminent perils. It showed how unsettled they had become, how deeply their collective psyche had been wounded by the shock of the August 17 disaster and the state's inability to cope with it.

Among journalists it is a truism that covering natural disasters is a colossal waste of time. They take a heavy emotional toll because they force us to confront horrible tragedies, but in essence they are alike; even the most pitiful stories about children dying and families being decimated are almost identical. Worst of all, in the larger scheme of things disasters mean nothing. When the earth stops shaking or the floodwaters recede or the flames are extinguished, people pick up what remains of their lives and go on as best they can. For those interested in the fate of nations, disasters are only distractions.

The Turkish earthquake, however, shattered that cliché just as completely as it devastated towns, cities and human lives. Few natural disasters in modern history have had such a profound political, social and cultural effect. Some Turkish intellectuals went so far as to suggest that when the history of the Turkish Republic is written years or centuries from now, it will be divided into two periods, pre-earthquake and post-earthquake. The quake led millions of Turks to question institutions they had never questioned before, and to accept the necessity of changes they had resisted for years. Survivors saw that thousands had died needlessly—been murdered, some said—because their homes had been built with materials and construction techniques that could not withstand a quake. They knew without being told that this was not simply the fault of contractors like the wretched Veli Göçer but the result of a political system that tolerated corruption and contempt for human life. The self-perpetuating Turkish elite that calls itself "the state" had maintained itself for generations by the fiction that it alone could guarantee people's safety and security. But when the quake struck, this vaunted "state" was nowhere to be seen. Now it blazed in people's consciousness as the institution that allowed unscrupulous contractors to build big housing developments directly above one of the world's most active fault lines.

A flood of images conveyed the Turkish state's failures. Among the most memorable were the white-faced Prime Minister Ecevit, spending the post-earthquake period wandering around as if in a daze; military rescue workers racing frantically to dig out officers lying under the debris of a naval base while ignoring the plight of anguished civilians outside the gates; and the florid President Demirel visiting devastated towns after a very long delay, a trip that turned into a fiasco because all roads in and out of the area were closed to traffic, including relief convoys, for hours before and after his tour, every moment of delay meaning that more trapped victims were dying awful deaths beneath the rubble. No one realized this more than survivors, whose anguish quickly turned to outrage at the institutions they had long considered sacred. When Demirel finally acknowledged the government's failings but warned that "the state is an institution you cannot replace with anything else," he sounded as if he were speaking from another planet.

The official who dominated most news reports in those days was not the president, prime minister or chief of staff. He was one Osman Durmuş, an obscure politician who since the formation of Ecevit's coalition government a few months earlier had been minister of health. Since taking office he had concentrated mainly on the quiet work of dismissing bureaucrats and hospital administrators so that they could be replaced by cronies from his far-right political party, Nationalist Action. Then, in the days after the quake, he showed himself to be one of those narrow-minded nationalists who have done so much over so many years to keep Turkey locked inside its fantasy-world shell. First he declared that Turkey needed no foreign aid for earthquake relief because it could handle everything perfectly well by itself. Then he said that even if aid was accepted, none should come from Armenia; that earthquake victims should be especially careful to refuse any blood sent from Greece; and that there was no need for portable toilets in the devastated region because many mosques had sanitary facilities, and anyway the Sea of Marmara was close by. These comments provoked a fury, including calls for his resignation, but he proudly stayed in office. No senior figure reprimanded him. The closest he came to an apology was to concede that if he were one day on the edge of death, he would be willing to accept blood from a Greek or Armenian donor.

Durmuş's mindless chauvinism did not represent the feelings of most government leaders. But along with many other examples, it conveyed the impression of a government and "state" that were hopelessly out of touch with the needs of its restive people. The earthquake showed Turks that something was fundamentally wrong with the way their nation and political system had developed since the end of military rule in 1983.

Until then, Turks had suffocated under a host of restrictive laws and regulations that effectively cut them off from the world but also insulated their country against corruption. National leaders valued propriety above economic growth, and most ordinary people followed their example. That changed with the emergence of Turgut Özal, a towering political figure and the most revolutionary leader Turkey had seen since Atatürk. As prime minister from 1983 to 1989 and then as president until his death in 1993, Özal lifted hundreds of restrictive rules and urged Turks to ignore those he could not repeal, freeing what proved to be the enormous energies of Turkish entrepreneurs. Within a very few years of his rise to power, this profoundly important campaign brought Turkey into the international mainstream. But as Özal urged Turks to free themselves from the outmoded rules that had held them back for so long, he also sent a not-so-subtle message that rules in general were bad. Some ambitious Turks understood him to mean that getting rich was so important that it didn't matter how one accomplished it.

What sort of business could an unschooled and capital-poor Turk launch that would put him on the road to wealth? Hundreds chose to start construction companies, relying on the help of friends in local politics to win contracts. In a wide-open economy that was growing at dizzying rates, many of these do-it-yourself contractors quickly became rich. The price Turkey paid for their rapid rise to wealth became tragically clear when the earthquake turned many of the apartment blocks they had built into tombs.

If the anger that Turks felt had been directed only at contractors and the inspectors they bribed, if the tragedies of the earthquake had been seen as isolated failures, all might have been slowly forgotten and the country might have returned to its old ways. Instead a new dawn seemed to burst over the country. People of every social class and political persuasion began to understand how dangerous it was to build a country on a social system in which everything is negotiable and *devlet baba*—"daddy state"—is always presumed to know best.

Respect for the state had begun to crumble with the Susurluk scandal in 1996, though with great effort military commanders and political godfathers had managed to put the lid on it before the full truth could emerge. Now they tried frantically to cover up their failures in the earthquake-relief effort. General Kıvrıkoğlu went so far as to demand names of journalists who were not writing glowingly enough about the army's work. But these efforts were fruitless because the relief effort, or what passed for one, had unfolded in full view of an already dubious public. Visceral and intense disgust sparked a civil uprising unlike anything modern Turkey had ever experienced.

Turks correctly saw the state's failures as the logical and even inevitable result of a system in which human life had always been considered a low priority. They learned that the state's traditional relief agency, Kızılay, a local branch of the Red Cross–Red Crescent, had become a dumping ground for incompetent and greedy hacks who spent their budget mainly on lavish trips and stays in luxury hotels. The few tattered old tents it scrounged up when the quake struck quickly became symbols of the government's incompetence and apparent callousness.

While wandering through a waterfront park where several hundred homeless earthquake survivors were living in leaky Kızılay tents, I met a carpenter who told me he had drawn a moral from all this. "I worked as a laborer in Europe, and later I lived in Israel for eighteen months," he said. "That's where I realized that in other countries, protecting human life comes before anything. We don't think like that here. If our leaders cared about human life they would have been ready for this earthquake, but it just isn't a priority for them. That's the main thing that has to change here."

The superb performance of private rescue and relief groups that raced to the earthquake zone to help victims only increased the anger at the state's failure. Twelve hours after the quake struck, a group of mountain climbers and practitioners of extreme sports who had banded together into an emergency-response team were already digging victims out of the rubble, and private charities and individuals were distributing food and blankets to the homeless. They were hard at work while government officials were still giving interviews claiming that their relief columns could not move along jammed or ruined roads to the devastated area. Politicians and generals in Ankara quickly realized that earthquake victims were becoming grateful to the wrong people. They responded by forbidding several religious charities from collecting or distributing relief aid, by urging donors to send their cash only to Kızılay or to an official fund at a government-owned bank and finally by trying to require private groups to transfer their aid to the army so that it could be distributed by soldiers. The cynicism of these maneuvers only emphasized the state's moral blindness.

To this day no one can say with even remote certainty how many people perished in the 1999 earthquake. The authorities stopped counting when they reached eighteen thousand, but thousands more were probably washed into the sea or bulldozed away with wreckage. No definitive list of the dead was ever drawn up.

Even before the pain of the tragedy had faded, another complex of emotions surged across Turkey, beginning with outrage at the government but then moving on to jubilant self-discovery. The generous and effective actions of ordinary people and private groups made millions of Turks realize, many for the first time, that they could take responsibility for their own lives and collective future without guidance from above. This realization introduced a genuine democratic consciousness, not through lectures or theoretical instruction but by events immediately and personally assimilated. It thrilled intellectuals and other reform-minded Turks who had been driven to despair by years of frustration and disappointment.

Private television stations, which Turgut Özal had legalized barely a decade before, rushed to offer exhaustive coverage from the devastated region, broadcasting unforgettable images that made the state's failures undeniable and also gave voice to hundreds of angry survivors whose words were heavy with emotion. Many, weeping openly on camera, talked of friends or relatives still alive under the rubble. The most commonly repeated cries of frustration were *"Devlet nerede?"* and *"Asker nerede?"* Where is the state? Where is the army?

The failure of the army, supposedly Turkey's indispensable institution, was a special shock. In the wake of this disaster, it was nowhere to be seen. Ecevit did not summon it to action and its own commanders did not volunteer troops. Tens of thousands of soldiers who were garrisoned within a few hours' ride of the earthquake zone were not moved from their barracks for days. When they finally did show up in ruined towns, most were assigned to provide security and distribute goods rather than help with rescue efforts. How could this institution defend the state if it was unable to protect the lives of Turkish citizens? The Susurluk scandal had shown that the state's priority was to guard an established order, not to serve individuals, and now it was displaying the same impulses in the earthquake-relief operation.

Had the quake devastated a remote eastern city like Erzincan, where Turkey's worst quake of the century hit in 1939, it might not have struck such a raw nerve. But this one destroyed densely populated towns just a short ferry ride from Istanbul, towns that were built around factories owned by people in Istanbul, towns where Istanbul residents went on their vacations. Hundreds of thousands of ordinary people in the Istanbul area lost friends or relatives, and thousands of them rushed to the region on the first day to try to help. The middle class led the civic uprising that followed, an uprising that was in some ways as shattering as the earthquake itself.

Perhaps the greatest surprise of all was people's response to the work of foreign relief agencies, whose energy and resourcefulness posed such a stark contrast to the Turkish government's paralysis. Teams from abroad appeared almost immediately, flying from their homelands, making their way to devastated towns and setting to work while the Turkish authorities were still lost in slumber. For generations Turks had been taught to believe that they were surrounded by enemies, that at every moment evil forces were plotting against them and their nation. But if more than seventy countries sent rescue and relief workers who saved victims who otherwise would have perished, how could it be true that, as nationalists had long asserted, "The only friend of the Turk is the Turk"?

The Turks' perception of Greece changed most vividly and remarkably, wiping away generations of resentment in a matter of days. Several months before, following the scandal that surrounded the capture of Abdullah Öcalan, Greek leaders had rid their government of powerful Turk-haters. Now, on the very day of the quake, the quick-witted Greek foreign minister George Papandreou telephoned his Turkish counterpart, Ismail Cem, to offer whatever help Turkey needed, and then quickly sent rescue workers, ships and planes loaded with relief supplies, and streams of messages pledging solidarity with the victims. Even more important, Greek television crews rushed to the ruins and began broadcasting live. Countless Greeks shared the grief of parents whose families had been destroyed, the suffering of those who waited tearfully for rescue workers to find their loved ones and the exhilaration of watching victims being pulled alive from the rubble. This was a deeply intimate experience that shook Greeks to their emotional core.

Then, only twenty-seven days later, an earthquake struck in Greece—a smaller one, but powerful enough to give Turks and Greeks a sense of shared fate. Now it was Turkish volunteers who flew to the rescue, and clever Greek officials directed them to help in places where they knew victims were alive and could be helped. Televised pictures of Turks saving the lives of Greek children melted hearts on both sides of the Aegean. Soon the two nations, caught up for years in senseless animosity, found themselves embracing each other with the fervor of lovers who realize they have been separated far too long.

Over the next years suspicion and hostility between Greece and Turkey faded almost completely. Greece not only dropped its opposition to Turkish membership in the European Union but became Turkey's main promoter. Greek leaders came to understand that a stable and friendly Turkey, and the peaceful eastern Mediterranean it would help create, would benefit the entire region. The paradigm that had defined relations between these two countries for generations came to seem like a relic of ancient history.

That was vividly clear when, eight years after the earthquakes, Greek and Turkish leaders met to open a $300 million natural gas pipeline that gave Greece direct access to the rich energy resources of the Caspian basin. At a glittering ceremony beneath the flags of both countries, Greek prime minister Costas Karamanlis said the project would bring "significant benefits to both countries." His counterpart, Tayyip Erdoğan, said it showed how the two neighbors "can live in harmony and both gain from it." Energy specialists welcomed the pipeline, which was to be extended to Italy and thus give southern Europe a welcome alternative to energy sources controlled by Russia. Beyond its economic and strategic value, though, this was a fundamentally political project. It would have been inconceivable a decade before. When it was inaugurated in 2007, cooperation between Greece and Turkey had become so natural that not a peep of protest was heard in either country.

That the 1999 earthquakes had been decisive in creating this new political environment was clear to all. Erdoğan's presence at the opening ceremony, however, hinted at another, less appreciated aspect of the quake's effect. When the quake struck, Erdoğan had just been released from his four-month prison term. He was beginning to conceive the political movement that would ultimately carry him to power. That movement would not have succeeded if Turks had not been fed up with the long-ruling establishment and eager for a new political alternative. The earthquake, and the pitifully inadequate way the government and army responded to it, helped convince millions of Turks that their country needed profound change. That helped create the climate for Erdoğan's astonishing rise.

So the 1999 quake was a seismic event both literally and figuratively. A deeply transformed eastern Mediterranean emerged from its rubble. So did a new national consciousness that reshaped Turkey.

Whenever I told a Turkish friend about my ambition to swim across the Bosphorus, the reaction was the same: "Why?" Each gave me a different warning. The Bosphorus is too dirty, its currents are too unpredictable, the giant tankers and freighters that traverse it are too dangerous. On top of all that, it is illegal to swim anywhere but along the shore.

I was not dissuaded. No one can live near the Bosphorus and see it every day without falling in love with it. I wanted to immerse myself in it, possess it, make it mine.

Istanbul may or may not be the world's most magnificent city, but it is certainly the most magnificently situated. Over the centuries it has been described as the pole to which the world turns, the envy of kings, city of the world's desire. "O city of Istanbul, priceless and peerless!" rhapsodized the eighteenth-century Ottoman poet Nedim. "I would sacrifice all Persia for one of your stones."

This is the only city that straddles two continents, and the Bosphorus is what divides and unites it. Without this strait Byzantium/Constantinople/Istanbul would be unimaginable. It would not have been so enormously important over so many centuries, so eagerly sought after by so many of history's greatest conquerors. Nor would it be nearly so rich, beautiful or romantic.

The Bosphorus is the link between the Black Sea to the north and the Sea of Marmara and Mediterranean to the south, so since time immemorial it has been the key to empires. The sixteenth-century French scholar Pierre Gilles described it as "the strait that surpasses all straits, because with one key it opens and closes two worlds, two seas." It winds and twists for nineteen incomparable miles. I never tire of seeing it, walking along its shores or sailing on it. Every day it has a different color, a different texture, a different mood. It is a world unto itself.

Many scientists now believe that the Bosphorus did not slowly swell to its present size as a river might, but was flooded in a single day seventy-five centuries ago. What a day that must have been! Ten cubic miles of water are thought to have surged northward through what was then a dry valley, and then ten more cubic miles every day for months, coursing into the Black Sea and submerging vast regions along its shores. This cataclysm may well have been the great flood described in the Bible, the Gilgamesh epic and other ancient texts.

The name Bosphorus is said to derive from an ancient Greek word meaning "cow's ford." It was given to this waterway because of the ancient myth about a beautiful maiden, Io, whose love affair with Zeus arouses the anger of his wife, Hera, and whom Zeus then tries to hide from Hera's wrath by turning her into a cow. But Hera discovers the truth and sends a gadfly to torment the cow, which, trying to escape, swims across this waterway.

Some of the first adventurers to sail through the Bosphorus were Jason and his legendary Argonauts, among them Hercules, Theseus and Orpheus, who were on their way to what is now the Black Sea coast of Georgia in search of the golden fleece. In 512 B.C. the Persian emperor Darius built a pontoon bridge across the Bosphorus at its narrowest point, barely seven hundred yards across, so that he could march his army of seventy thousand men into Europe. Overlooking that same spot, Sultan Mehmet II built the breathtaking fortress called Rumeli Hisarı, from which he set out to conquer Constantinople in 1453. It still stands, the most exquisite and delicately shaped piece of military architecture on earth.

Rumeli Hisarı is the crown jewel of the Bosphorus, but its shores are crammed with scores of other extraordinary edifices built directly on the water. The most magnificent among them are ornate Ottoman palaces, most of them designed in the nineteenth century by a gifted family of Armenian architects, the Balians. Each is layered in history.

Beylerbeyi Palace was a favorite summer retreat for nineteenth- and early-twentieth-century European monarchs, among them Empress Eugenie of France, Tsar Nicholas II of Russia, Emperor Franz Josef of Austria and King Edward VII of Great Britain. Çırağan Palace served as a sumptuous asylum and prison for Sultan Murat V, a lunatic who was forced from office after just three months in 1876 and then lived amid its splendor for nearly thirty years. Dolmabahçe Palace, the most overwhelming of them all, is a temple of excess whose construction is said to have bankrupted the empire. It has a marble facade the length of three football fields, two hundred eighty-five rooms, a staircase made of crystal, more than a square mile of handwoven silk Hereke carpets and the world's largest chandelier, which weighs four tons.

Almost as imposing and far more human in scale are the scores of mansions called yalıs that line the shores, set below groves of jacarandas that burst into violet bloom each spring. Classic yalıs are built of wood in styles ranging from neoclassical and baroque to art nouveau and eclectic arabesque, and painted in beautiful pastel colors. Many have been lovingly preserved or restored, either by members of the old upper crust or by the newly rich. Most have docking space for boats. Each has a name: Egyptian Yalı, Snake Yalı, Pink Lion Yalı, Writers' Yalı, even Mad Fuat Pasha Yalı, named for a nineteenth-century Ottoman noble who was bold enough to denounce the repressive rule of Sultan Abdülhamid II. Lord Byron was transfixed by these homes: "Each villa on the Bosphorus looks a screen / New painted, or a pretty opera-scene."

In past eras, sultans, viziers and ambassadors gave grand illuminated parties at their palaces and yalıs. It is still fashionable to be married beside the Bosphorus, and weddings are usually accompanied by fireworks, an old tradition. Often the main dish at these celebrations is fish, because fish caught in the Bosphorus and the nearby seas are as tasty as any in the world. Menus vary with the season since each species has a different temperature tolerance and migrates between the Mediterranean and Black Sea at a different time. My favorite is palamut, a gourmet cousin of the mackerel that appears in late autumn, but others prefer the flaky and delicate lüfer and wait impatiently for sum-

mer because that is when it shows up at markets and on restaurant menus.

The Bosphorus is not only a place of surpassing beauty but also Istanbul's heavily trafficked main street. Ferries cross it and shuttle among its villages a thousand times a day. They and the hundreds of skiffs from which fishermen ply their trade are reminders that a great city depends on this artery for its daily life. It is also the world's busiest commercial waterway. About one hundred fifty vessels, lumbering Russian and Ukrainian rust buckets or giant tankers carrying oil and liquefied natural gas from the rich fields of the Caspian, pass through it each day. Under clauses of the 1923 Lausanne treaty and another signed in Montreux thirteen years later, the Turkish government has no control over them and cannot require them to take on pilots or even to prove that they are insured. Many are not, like a Lebanese freighter that sank in 1992 with a cargo of ten thousand sheep and goats and lies at the bottom to this day.

How much else could be found at the bottom of the Bosphorus! I imagine not just sunken treasures and evidence of a thousand crimes but the weighted sacks into which royal plotters or unfaithful harem women were sewn before being thrown to their watery deaths. Orhan Pamuk once wove a fantasy of the day the Bosphorus dries up and becomes "a pitch-black swamp in which the mud-caked skeletons of galleons will gleam like the luminous teeth of ghosts." Besides fields of jellyfish and soda-pop caps, he expects that "among the American transatlantics gone to ground and Ionic columns covered with seaweed, there will be Celtic and Ligurian skeletons open-mouthed in supplication to gods whose identities are no longer known."

To me, the Bosphorus fantasy that burned most brightly was that of swimming across. After entertaining it for far too long, I finally found a friend with a boat who was willing to accompany me. He advised that we start before dawn, since traffic is lighter then and the waves and currents more predictable.

We set out from near my home in Tarabya, a village near the north end of the Bosphorus, and motored northward toward the entrance to the Black Sea. I wanted to swim westward from Asia to Europe because that is the direction of Turkish history. We found a small inlet below the ruins of Anadolu Kavağı, a twelfth-century Byzantine castle on the Asian side, and there, after waiting for a freighter to glide silently by, I started.

The sun had not yet risen and the waves of the Bosphorus were rippling gently. Its water was warmer and cleaner than I expected. I felt exuberant as I made my way steadily across, thinking of Jason, Darius and Mehmet the Conqueror. Other than my friend's small boat and a couple of jellyfish, I was alone, and grateful to be in this place. To orient myself I focused on a green shape on the shore that I first thought was a yalı *but turned out to be a fishing vessel docked at Yeni Mahalle, the northernmost settlement on the European side. I swam to it and past it. Just thirty-nine minutes after setting out, having covered a distance of slightly more than a mile, I touched the seawall. No moment of my life in Turkey filled me with such rich and complex satisfaction.*

• NINE •

STRATEGIC DEPTH

"Turkey is the bridge between three continents as well as three different religions," a distinguished statesman told the Turkish Parliament in Ankara to much applause at the end of 2007. "We may be saying different prayers, but our eyes are turned toward the same sun and toward the same vision for the Middle East."

Others have recognized Turkey's uniqueness with similar words, but this address carried special weight because of who gave it. The speaker was President Shimon Peres of Israel, the first Israeli leader ever to address the legislature of a Muslim country. More remarkably, the president of the Palestinian Authority was seated at his side.

Only a few days earlier the king of Saudi Arabia had paid an official visit to Ankara. President Bashir Assad of Syria had also left town. Iran's foreign minister and the American secretary of state had been there two weeks earlier, and both received warm welcomes. Foreign ministers from Jordan, France, Latvia, Iraq, Georgia and Afghanistan had recently passed through. Prime Minister Erdoğan had just returned from a meeting in Washington with the president of the United States. He was preparing to leave for the Czech Republic, attend a summit of Turkic leaders in Azerbaijan and then return home to receive the prime ministers of Greece and Italy.

This intense month for Turkish diplomacy was not unusual. It showed how eagerly Turkey is taking on a role it has never before played. For the first time, it has become a force in regional politics, a creative and sought-after contributor to diplomacy in the Caucasus, the Balkans, the Middle East and Central Asia.

In what other country could Pope Benedict have been expected to visit a mosque, remove his shoes, face Mecca and pray? Where else would leaders of all the nations bordering on Iraq have agreed to meet for frank discussions of ways to stabilize that benighted land? Who other than a leader of Turkey could have attracted Prime Minister José Rodriguez Zapatero of Spain, United Nations Secretary General Kofi Annan, Bishop Desmond Tutu of South Africa and former President Mohammad Khatami of Iran to a summit at which they proclaimed a new "alliance of civilizations" aimed at bridging the gap between East and West?

Atatürk's decision to keep Turkey focused on domestic development had never entirely cut off his country from the outside world. During the 1920s he forged a close relationship with the new Soviet Union; in 1934 he helped design a treaty of friendship and mutual assistance with Greece, Yugoslavia and Romania that led President Eleftherios Venizelos of Greece to nominate him for the Nobel Peace Prize. But with those and a few other exceptions, Turkey looked inward for most of its early life. In effect, Turkey spent its first eighty years of national life without an independent foreign policy. After World War II, fearful of Moscow and ever obedient to Washington's wishes, it did no more or less than the U.S.-dominated North Atlantic Treaty Organization wished it to. The only noise it made on the world stage came from its support for ethnic Turks in Cyprus.

The first Turkish leader who set out in a different direction was Turgut Özal, who hoped to make his country the leader of a new Turkic bloc including the Muslim nations that emerged from the wreckage of the Soviet Union. That effort failed, partly because Turkey did not have the resources to support so grand a project and partly because Özal died soon after conceiving it. Necmettin Erbakan's misbegotten campaign to lead Turkey into an alliance with radical Muslim states also came to naught.

Thus it was without a second thought that when the United States decided to invade Iraq in 2003, military planners in the Pentagon assumed there would be no problem in sending part of the invading force through Turkey. The new AKP government had just been elected, but it did not occur to anyone in Washington that Turkey's civic revolution might have weakened its willingness to do America's bidding. Americans were used to the old way of doing things in Turkey: call the generals and rely on them to squeeze whatever necessary out of the ever-obedient government; that had always worked before. They added a sweetener, offering Turkey more than $20 billion in loans to shore up its then exceedingly shaky economy. All Parliament had to do in exchange was allow the United States to build staging grounds in eastern Turkey from which sixty-two thousand soldiers, two hundred fifty-five planes and sixty-five helicopters could strike northern Iraq.

Officials in Washington, along with much of the world, recoiled in shock when, on March 1, 2003, the Turkish Parliament voted to reject this American request. It was the first time Turkey had ever defied the United States on a major security issue. Stunned analysts found a host of reasons. The overconfident United States, used to taking Turkey for granted, had not seriously lobbied for the war in Ankara. Turkey's government was newly elected and still incoherent. Sentiment against the invasion of Iraq was intense in Turkey, and some members of Parliament even hoped they could prevent its occurring. Many Turks were just as horrified by the idea of tens of thousands of foreign troops marching across their territory as most Americans would be. All of them understood that the war would plunge Iraq into chaos and bring a Kurdish regime to power in Iraq's northern provinces.

This vote was the first hint that true democracy might finally be breaking out in Turkey. Members of the newly elected Parliament did not cower before generals as their predecessors had but instead voted to express the will of their constituents. Turks had finally responded to years of pressure from the United States and Europe to consolidate democracy. The first expression of that democracy was a stinging rebuff to Washington.

Relations between Turks and Americans date back to the visit of a U.S. Navy frigate to Istanbul in 1800. After the Civil War, Ottoman rulers bought large amounts of surplus weaponry from the United States. American traders and missionaries, not to mention travelers like Mark Twain and Herman Melville, were part of Turkish life throughout the nineteenth century. In 1952 Turkey joined NATO, and for fifty years it was a faithful ally. Turks feared the Soviet Union and were grateful for the protective umbrella Americans gave them during the Cold War.

Turkish-American relations were never trouble-free, however. Many Turks believe that President Woodrow Wilson's faith in the principle of national self-determination helped to shape the 1920 Treaty of Sèvres, under which their Anatolian homeland was to have been carved into ethnic enclaves. Some were angered when President Dwight Eisenhower used the Turkish-American NATO military base at Incirlik, near the southern port of Adana, as a base to support the 1958 American intervention in Lebanon. Their anger intensified when President John F. Kennedy secretly agreed to remove NATO's Jupiter nuclear missiles based on Turkish soil as part of the deal with Moscow that defused the 1962 Cuban missile crisis. It turned to outrage when, a year later, President Lyndon Johnson warned in an infamous letter that if Turkey sent troops to defend ethnic Turks living in Cyprus—where for three years Greeks and Turks had coexisted under a delicate constitutional arrangement that gave them proportional shares of power—the United States would no longer feel bound by its NATO pledge to defend Turkey against a Soviet attack. After Turkish troops landed in Cyprus a decade later, the United States imposed an arms embargo on Turkey that lasted for four years and led many Turks to view the United States as an unreliable friend.

The two countries enjoyed a rapprochement in the 1980s and early 1990s. They signed far-reaching defense and economic cooperation agreements. Turkey agreed not to block Greece's 1980 reentry into NATO, from which it had been suspended after the military coup of 1967. Turkish forces participated in the American-sponsored Gulf War of 1991. Soon after that war, though, Turkish resentment surfaced again. Turkey lost billions of dollars in trade with Iraq, plunging many families in southeastern provinces into poverty, which in turn contributed to a rise in Kurdish militancy. When the Turkish army stepped up its operations against the burgeoning PKK, Washington responded not with sympathy but instead with condemnations of the army's brutality.

The last high point in Turkish-American relations came in the wake of President Bill Clinton's visit to Turkey in 1999. Clinton happened to arrive soon after the devastating earthquake, and he delighted Turks by visiting survivors in their tents, listening to their stories and even allowing his nose to be tweaked by an infant he scooped up in his arms. His radiant enthusiasm and empathy, so radically different from the sour disdain that Turkish leaders showed toward quake victims, reflected the compassionate side of the American character. It led millions of Turks to look anew at the United States, and to thrill at what they saw.

Clinton also won raves for his skillfully nuanced speech to the Turkish Parliament. He gently urged legislators to move more decisively toward political and social reform, and he predicted that if they did, Turkey would rise to play its "rightful role at the crossroads of the world" and become "critical to shaping the twenty-first century." For weeks after he departed, Turks spoke of little else but his warmth and that of the wonderful country he represented.

The American invasion of Iraq in 2003 radically transformed these attitudes. A public opinion survey taken after Clinton's visit found that 52 percent of Turks had a favorable opinion of the United States; by 2006 the number had fallen to an abysmal 12 percent. When asked in the 2006 poll which countries they believed threatened world peace, 60 percent of Turks named the United States. (Only 16 percent named Iran, which President George W. Bush was then denouncing as part of a global "axis of evil.")

The anti-American sentiment that spread across Turkey after 2003 found expression in a wildly popular book and, soon thereafter, an even more popular film. The book, *Metal Storm*, imagines a scenario in which Turkish soldiers enter northern Iraq to defend the Turkmen minority there and are attacked by U.S. soldiers. The American press, easily manipulated from Washington, falsely depicts the attack as having been initiated by Turks. That gives American troops an excuse to attack Turkey. They capture Ankara, seize rich borax mines and then try to carve up the country so they can give parts of it to Greeks and Armenians. A heroic Turkish agent saves the day by stealing a nuclear bomb and detonating it in Washington.

Metal Storm sold half a million copies in a few months and became the most talked-about book in modern Turkish history. One of the coauthors, Burak Turna, said it was successful because it touched "the subconscious of Turkey." An Istanbul newspaper reported that "the foreign ministry and general staff are reading it keenly" and "all cabinet members also have it."

Turks were still caught up in the visceral emotions set off by this book when *Valley of the Wolves* burst onto their movie screens. It was the most expensive film ever made in Turkey but quickly paid for itself, with an unheard-of 2.5 million people seeing it in the first ten days after its release.

Valley of the Wolves begins with a true-life incident, the arrest of eleven Turkish soldiers in northern Iraq by American troops on July 4, 2003. Washington never explained why it carried out that action, and it offered only a vague apology. In Turkey this episode set off a wave of national outrage, not only because it was seen as a betrayal by a supposed ally but also because the eleven Turkish captives were hooded after being captured. Turks took this as a deep and unpardonable humiliation.

In *Valley of the Wolves* a former Turkish intelligence agent travels to Iraq to avenge the death of one of the eleven, who has committed suicide out of shame. He watches as American troops attack a wedding party on the pretense that it is a terrorist assembly, execute the groom, shoot several guests, including small children, and pack the rest into a shipping container so they can be sent off to the infamous Abu Ghraib prison near Baghdad. Scenes of torture at Abu Ghraib, the first ever depicted on film, add to the horror. In a side plot, an American doctor played by Gary Busey removes organs from dead Iraqi prisoners and ships them off for sale to rich patients in Israel and the United States.

The speaker of the Turkish Parliament, Bülent Arinç, called *Valley of the Wolves* "extraordinary" and said it would "go down in history" because it portrayed the Iraq war "exactly as it happened." Abdullah Gül, then Turkey's foreign minister, said it was "no worse than many of the productions of Hollywood studios." Emine Erdoğan, the prime minister's wife, reportedly broke down in tears after watching it. Audiences in many theaters burst into applause when the fiendish American officer played by Billy Zane was finally killed.

As any visitor to Turkey can attest, the widespread anti-American sentiment that is documented in public opinion surveys and vividly reflected in *Metal Storm* and *Valley of the Wolves* applies only to United States foreign policy, not to individual Americans. Turks have not lost their admiration for the American "way of life." During the presidency of George W. Bush, though, many of them came to deplore the U.S. policy of unilateral intervention in the Middle East. They were deeply alienated by America's refusal to accommodate Turkish concerns in the region, by its uncritical support of Israel and by what they saw as its global campaign against Muslims. They watched with alarm as the United States plunged Iraq into chaos and then encouraged the establishment of a Kurdish regime in northern Iraq that gave sanctuary to PKK guerrillas. This produced a broad national consensus that Turkey needed to break out of Washington's orbit and pursue an independent foreign policy—something Turkish leftists had been urging for years without success.

The first Turk to articulate this idea in detail was Ahmet Davutoğlu, a pious scholar who was educated in English and German, had chafed under his professors' insistence that he revere European culture above that of his own country, and went on to head the international relations department at Beykent University in Istanbul. During the 1990s he emerged as something of a guru to Islamic politicians. In 2000 he published a thick, dense tome entitled *Strategic Depth*. It went largely unnoticed outside of academic circles, but it caught Tayyip Erdoğan's attention. After becoming prime minister, Erdoğan, who considered the Turkish foreign ministry a hotbed of militant Kemalism and therefore mistrusted it, hired Davutoğlu as his personal adviser on foreign affairs. Soon the onetime professor became Turkey's chief foreign policy strategist. While ambassadors and foreign ministers did the day-to-day diplomatic work, Davutoğlu conceived long-term strategies.

One evening in the lobby bar of the Ankara Hilton, Davutoğlu and I demurely sipped tea as other guests drank and flirted the hours away. I sat transfixed as he delivered a cogent monologue explaining what "strategic depth" means for Turkey. It begins, he told me, with a fundamental principle: "Zero problems with neighbors." Turkey's generations of trouble with Greece had been largely overcome by the time Davutoğlu rose to power, but on his watch its relations with other nearby countries also improved dramatically. He arranged for Prime Minister Erdoğan and President Vladimir Putin of Russia to exchange state visits that produced a remarkable thaw in relations. Inviting Israeli and Palestinian leaders to visit Ankara together was his idea. After the former Lebanese president Rafik Hariri was assassinated in 2005, the United States strongly pressured Turkey to respond by breaking off relations with Syria and Iran, but following Davutoğlu's advice the government refused to do so.

"Strategic depth," Davutoğlu continued, also means that Turkey should take an active part in resolving regional conflicts that fester near its borders. Countries on different sides of Turkey, like Georgia and Bulgaria, should be encouraged to use Turkey as a diplomatic bridge. Rejecting the old Kemalist view that Turkey has broken completely with its Ottoman history, Davutoğlu believes that the Ottoman example of cultural tolerance has great relevance in the modern age, and that Turkey should be active throughout what was once Ottoman territory and even beyond. No longer, he insists, can Turkey be pigeonholed as simply a "flank country" guarding southeastern Europe, a country with "strong muscles, a weak stomach, a troubled heart and a mediocre brain."

The policy of strategic depth has steadily expanded Turkey's horizons. In 2005 a Turk was elected president of the fifty-seven-nation Organization of the Islamic Conference. That same year Turkey signed a "framework agreement" with the Gulf Cooperation Council that is expected to be a precursor to a free trade accord. It has become an active leader of the Economic Cooperation Organization, which groups ten countries in and around Central Asia, and wants to join the sixteen nations that comprise the East Asian Summit. Istanbul is the permanent headquarters of the Organization of Black Sea Cooperation. There are Turkish embassies in more than ninety countries from Austria to Australia, Vietnam to Venezuela and South Africa to South Korea. If the United Nations ever decides to expand the number of permanent Security Council members, Turkey will almost certainly press for one of the new slots.

Not everyone in Washington is pleased by this new assertiveness. When Turkish leaders welcome their Syrian counterparts to Ankara, or hail Hamas as a democratically elected movement that deserves respect in Palestine, or sign energy deals with Iran, or strengthen their friendship with Russia, people in Washington ask a question that was never heard there before: Who lost Turkey?

One answer might be that American influence in Turkey ebbed because American leaders charged ahead with radical plans to remake the Middle East without considering Turkey's advice. The larger reason, though, is simply that Turkey matured into independent nationhood. It is still an active NATO member, eager to join peacekeeping missions in places like Bosnia and Afghanistan and fundamentally supportive of policies that embody what Atatürk called "universal values." Turkey finds itself estranged from the United States only when American leaders look for quick rather than long-term solutions to world problems, confront unpleasant regimes militarily rather than diplomatically and find rivals and enemies in places where Turks look for friends and partners. The news commentator Hüseyin Bağci, searching for a metaphor to describe the new Turkish-American relationship, compared it to that of "a married couple that sleeps in the same bed but has different dreams."

Among all of Turkey's international ambitions, one is most tantalizing: to join the European Union. Its path to membership has been strewn with obstacles, many of its own making. In the early 1970s, after Greece emerged from military dictatorship and applied to join, EU leaders quietly decided that if they were to accept Greece, they should also accept Turkey. When this message reached Ankara, however, Prime Minister Bülent Ecevit replied that Turkey was not interested. He was at that time a left-wing nationalist—an ideological species rare in the world but common in Turkey—and he viewed the EU as a project of imperialist capitalism. Turkey's business elite, terrified of the competition and ethics rules that come with EU membership, supported him. In an act of supreme irresponsibility, this odd coalition rejected an overture that could have radically reshaped modern Turkish history.

The idea of Turkish membership in the EU, dormant for years thereafter, once again became popular during the 1990s. In 1995 Turkey and d a "customs union" that greatly reduced trade barriers. ss in economic cooperation was not, however, matched po- ırkish prime ministers gave speech after speech insisting that re determined to lead their country into the EU, but they did ke enough of the steps that were prerequisites for membership. nomic restructuring and abolition of the death penalty were not ıough. As long as jailhouse torture was common and the armed forces maintained a veto over government policy, no one in Europe took Turkey's application seriously. The older generation of European leaders, represented by figures like Helmut Schmidt ("The Turks belong to a completely different cultural domain") and Valéry Giscard d'Estaing ("Accession by Turkey would change the nature of the European project"), found little opposition to their anti-Turkish views. In 1999 the EU left Turkey off its list of desirable new members. Turks were indignant, but much of the fault was their own.

It took the rise of Tayyip Erdoğan and his AKP to breathe real life into Turkey's European ambition. The sweeping reforms Erdoğan pushed through Parliament made Turkey more democratic and more economically open than it had ever been. It came steadily closer to meeting EU membership criteria. In 2004 the EU, recognizing Turkey's progress, scheduled a vote of member states on whether to open talks that would lead to its accession.

As the vote approached, Chris Patten, then the EU's commissioner for external affairs, gave a speech in which he reflected at length on the challenges and opportunities that Turkey and the EU offered each other. He praised Erdoğan for launching "a program of constitutional reform designed to entrench democracy, promote the protection of minorities, and limit the role of the military in government." The upcoming vote, he said, would be "the main test of the European Union's commitment to a pluralist and inclusive approach to Islam." He continued:

> The case that this is a pivotal moment in the EU's relationship with the Islamic world can be, and is, overstated. But our approach to Turkey does matter. It says a great deal about how we see ourselves, and want to be seen, in terms both of culture and geopolitics . . . Is Turkey Euro-

> pean? If aspiration is any guide, the answer would have to be a resounding yes. Turkey has resolutely steered a European course since the end of the Sultanate in 1922. The feeling runs deep, and is promoted with unrelenting vigor by successive Turkish governments . . . How much interest should we take in the fate of our southern neighbor and ally, bordered by Iraq, Iran, Syria and the southern Caucasus? How welcoming should we be to a neighbor that has demonstrated the falsity of the case that Islam and democracy do not mix? When we do take an interest, should we recognize Turkey as a respected partner or as a difficult pupil? . . . At one time, particularly when Western Europe was a more savage place, Turkey and the Turks were the very incarnation of the outsider. But that was when "Europe" and "Christendom" were synonyms. We've moved on from that . . . We cannot help but be conscious of the symbolism, at this time, of reaching out a hand to a country whose population is overwhelmingly Muslim.

Patten's appeal, and others like it, convinced European leaders. At their summit in December 2004, in a step that thrilled most Turks, they agreed to begin accession negotiations with Turkey. Every country that has ever begun this process and maintained its wish to join the EU has ultimately been admitted.

Negotiations between Turkey and the EU—a one-sided process in which the applying country must overhaul its legal codes to comply with ninety thousand pages of EU regulations—seemed likely to take a decade or longer, but Turkey plunged into the job. It gave shape and form to the country's democratic aspirations. Each step Turks took toward fulfilling the conditions of EU membership represented progress toward the freedom, prosperity and stability that embodied their national ambition.

"While the hard power of the United States is destroying Iraq, the soft power of the EU is transforming Turkey," an insightful commentator marveled during a lunch we shared at a seaside restaurant near his home in the Aegean town of Ayvalik.

The process of bringing Turkey and the EU together did not proceed without trouble. Every time a Turkish intellectual was prosecuted for violating old taboos still enforced by law—especially when he happened to be Orhan Pamuk—Europeans shook their heads in disbelief. Turks, for their part, were increasingly frustrated by what they saw as the EU's refusal to acknowledge their reforms and its constant hectoring and criticism. Still, younger European leaders, from Tony Blair ("To send an adverse signal to Turkey, I think, would be a serious mistake for Europe") to Daniel Cohn-Bendit ("Europe is witness to a miracle on the Bosphorus"), accepted the idea of Turkish membership.

Then, at a decisive summit in Brussels in December 2006, Europe changed its mind. In a turgid declaration full of diplomatic euphemisms, EU leaders announced that they were suspending talks with Turkey on eight key "chapters" of its membership application. They also insisted that future talks would be "an open-ended process, the outcome of which cannot be guaranteed beforehand." In other words, even if Turkey fulfilled every qualification for membership, it might still not be admitted. No other applicant had ever been told this.

The EU officially based its decision on a dispute over the right of vessels from the Republic of Cyprus to use Turkish ports, which in 1987 Turkey had forbade them to enter. It was correct to insist on this point, and Prime Minister Erdoğan, who feared a nationalist backlash if he compromised on any issue related to Cyprus, was short-sighted in his obstinate refusal to discuss it. All understood, however, that far larger issues were also involved. Turks believed they had to do with prejudice against Islam. Europeans argued that the EU had expanded so quickly that people in member nations had developed "enlargement fatigue" and were no longer ready to accept a country as large, poor and culturally different as Turkey.

The idea of Turkey joining the EU had always been a project of European elites. Those elites had failed to persuade ordinary people of its value, and European politicians found it expedient to oppose rather than support Turkish accession.

Whatever the true reasons for Europe's about-face in 2006, it led many Turks, and many Muslims around the world, to conclude that if Europe treated the world's most democratic and secular Muslim country like this, its proclaimed desire to bridge the gap between East and

West could not be taken seriously. The turnabout also undermined Turkey's democratic movement, thrilled its nationalists and xenophobes, fueled fires of anger that were burning throughout the Muslim world and strengthened the hand of those who preach "identity politics," which holds that religious and cultural differences among groups of nations are eternal and immutable. It also boded ill for Europe. In decades to come, Turkey will have a young, vibrant and well-educated population, open to innovation and eager to work for moderate wages. Europe, by contrast, will seem old and encrusted, with no one to pay the pensions of its graying population.

With Turkey as a member, the EU could truly aspire to global power. It would have the raw material to build a security force that could project the power of democratic ideals around the world. Instead it chose to retreat into its shell, leaving global leadership to the overwhelmed United States, to China and to emerging blocs of radicals who cackled with glee over this breakup.

For two generations, the mighty force now known as the European Union had been pursuing a single ideal: the expansion of a community of shared values that would stabilize a continent torn for centuries by war. During that period, Turkey was adrift, unable to make a decisive choice in favor of democracy. By 2006 Turkey had finally made its choice and was hurtling toward freedom, but Europe had fallen into an identity crisis of its own. By falling victim to its insecurities, its fear of the changing world and its perception of being threatened politically, economically and above all culturally, Europe seemed to say that, at least for the moment, geography mattered more than ideals.

Many Turks had already been losing faith in the EU. They were mightily vexed when the Republic of Cyprus was admitted without first reaching an accommodation with the island's Turkish minority, a decision that gave eight hundred thousand Greek Cypriots a permanent veto over the efforts of seventy-five million Turks to join Europe. Then, at the same summit in Brussels at which it took back its offer to Turkey, the EU welcomed Romania and Bulgaria as new members. These decisions led many Turks to believe the EU was irredeemably prejudiced against them. A goodly number would have been happy if their leaders had told Europe to drop dead.

Although Prime Minister Erdoğan shared that bitterness, in public he remained calm. He called the EU decision "unacceptable" and "unfair to Turkey" but insisted that it was merely a temporary setback, which Turks should expect during such a complex process. His nation's determination to join the EU remained undiminished, he said, because the democratization that the EU demands was precisely what most Turks wanted. Instead of denouncing the EU for freezing talks on eight of the thirty-five "chapters" in the accession process, he chose to emphasize that talks on the other twenty-seven remained active. When confronted by opposition to Turkish membership from European leaders like President Nicholas Sarkozy of France, he said simply that it was Turkey's job to proceed resolutely on its reformist course and then, once it fulfilled all conditions for EU membership, to see how Europe responded.

"Despite the EU's crude rebuff, Turkey's multi-faceted modernization will continue," the political scientist Soli Özel predicted. "A widening sphere of freedom and democratic engagement brings forth demands from long-suppressed groups—from Kurds to environmentalists—and, as in all such cases, triggers a reaction. Yet these are all the birth pangs of a more modern Turkey that will remain European while modernizing itself, even if Europe cannot yet grasp this process and its significance."

Decoupled from both its longtime ally (the United States) and the ally it wished to embrace (Europe), Turkey is for the first time a truly independent actor. No longer do Turks feel the need to check with other world capitals before making their moves on the global chessboard. If they could so dramatically reshape the paradigm of their own domestic politics, many of them concluded, they should also be able to change the way they approached the world.

The second reason that Turkey found itself able to strike an independent course was the shattering series of changes that reshaped global politics after the Cold War. Turkey is located between three especially volatile regions: the Balkans, the former Soviet Union and the Middle East. Slowly Turks realized that, if only to assure their own long-term stability, they could not stand idly by as these regions were consumed by constant political upheavals. Then they became more ambitious. Turks now believe that history and geography have given them a role no other country can play. They are enthusiastic democrats; heirs to a multicultural empire; masters of a large, dynamic and resource-rich country and believers in a noncoercive brand of Islam. Many sense that their country's golden moment has finally come, that it has not simply a valuable message for the world but also the ambition and means to spread it.

Earlier Turkish governments were reluctant to offer their success as an example to other Muslim countries, but that changed as the Islamic world plunged into turmoil. Politicians and thinkers in many Muslim countries, as the Syrian scholar Sadik Al-Azm wrote in 2005, "have come around to a new and different look at present-day Turkey."

> Both the Arab world and Islam in general are in dire need right now of a reasonably free, democratic and secular model that works in a Muslim society. Turkey is at the moment the most likely place for such a model to develop and mature . . . In other words, what we need here is a credible, functioning counter-example to the failed Muslim Taliban instance that the Americans left us with in Afghanistan not so long ago, with all its horrors and deformations.

To transform the Islamic world is an almost unfathomably grand project, but it is only part of what Turkish visionaries hope their nation can achieve in the twenty-first century. They approach the emerging new world with a remarkable combination of assets and interests. Although Turkey is not a world power, it has become a strong second-division player with ambitions comparable to those of India, Brazil, Indonesia and South Africa.

Turkey is friendly with Israel but also highly sympathetic to the Palestinian cause. It sees Russia and China as potential partners, and views neither Iraq nor Iran as a demon. In turbulent Muslim countries like Lebanon and Pakistan, Turks enjoy good relations with both government and opposition. Turkey seeks peaceful, gradual solutions to global problems, and it opposes the use of violence as a means to short-term ends. Most Turks still feel sympathetic to European values and culturally comfortable with the United States, but their horizons are now broader than they have been at any time since the end of the Ottoman era.

"Both developments inside Turkey and Turkish policy will be consequential over a wide area in diverse ways," the American geopolitical analyst Ian Lesser predicted in 2007. "Turkey is important for what it is or could become, rather than simply because of where it sits."

Atatürk summed up his vision for Turkey with the motto *Yurtda Sulh, Cihanda Sulh*—"Peace at home, peace in the world." During his lifetime and for three generations after his death, "peace in the world" meant staying out of it. Now it means active engagement with it. The decades ahead will see the emergence of a new multipolar world. Turkey will be one of its poles.

My favorite Turkish writer is everyone's favorite, Nazım Hikmet. By universal agreement he is the greatest literary figure the Turkish Republic has produced. Poet, playwright and novelist, extravagantly gifted and fervently patriotic, he was also a Communist who spent much of his life in jail and died in exile in 1963 after having been stripped of his Turkish citizenship. Every Turk knows his name, but to this day his works may not be taught in public schools. His life and literary creations exemplify Turkey's glories and frustrations, its audacious beauty and its paralyzing fears.

Nazım—his admirers always call him by his first name—was born in 1902 in Salonika, the same city where Atatürk had been born twenty years earlier. Unlike Atatürk he came from a well-to-do family, but like the Great Man he decided as a youth that he could best serve his country by making a career in the military. When illness forced him to leave the naval academy, he chose to follow his other passion, poetry. On a trek across Anatolia in his late teens he met several Turkish Communists. Impressed with their idealism and fascinated by the promise of bolshevism, a conviction that deepened after he visited Moscow in 1922, he joined the Communist Party. He saw no contradiction between his love of Turkey and his Marxist convictions, but the authorities did. His talent proved no defense against persecution, and he spent the rest of his life in trouble with the law.

Turkey shared a tense border with the Soviet Union, and for years Soviet leaders plotted to bring it into their sphere of influence or even to seize it and incorporate it into their empire. In this climate it was too much to hope that a Turkish poet could get away with writing rhapsodic elegies to Marxism and bitter condemnations of oppression in Turkey. Nazım was in and out of prison on a variety of charges, but at the same time he flowered as a poet. His style was as revolutionary as his politics. Until he picked up a pen, Turkish poetry had for centuries been heavily stylized and effete. He was the first writer to produce poetry in conversational, colloquial Turkish, and although his books were banned for years, he was the first to touch the hearts of ordinary Turks. In his approach to literature and life he was comparable to Walt Whitman, a poet of the common man who scorned conventional patriotism but still insisted that he loved his country beyond all reason. The heroes in Nazim's poems, he once wrote, were not "generals, sultans, distinguished scientists or artists, beauty queens, murderers or billionaires; they were workers, peasants and craftsmen, people whose fame had not spread beyond their factories, workshops, villages or neighborhoods."

At another time he explained his ambition this way: "I want to write poems that both talk only about me and address just one other person and call out to millions. I want to write poems that talk of a single apple, of the plowed earth, of the psyche of someone getting out of prison, of the struggle of the masses for a better life, of one man's heartbreaks. I want to write about fearing and not fearing death."

The works Nazım produced in the 1930s have lost none of their freshness. Today they speak to Turks as poignantly as ever, like this one written in the Istanbul House of Detention:

> *I love my country:*
> *I've swung on its plane trees,*
> *I've slept in its prisons.*
> *Nothing lifts my spirits like its songs and tobacco . . .*
> *My country:*
> *goats on the Ankara plain,*
> *the sheen of their long blond silky hair.*

The succulent plump hazelnuts of Giresun.
Amasya apples with fragrant red cheeks,
olives,
  figs,
    melons,
and bunches and bunches of grapes
          all colors,
then plows
and black oxen,
and then my people,
    ready to embrace
        with the wide-eyed joy of children
anything modern, beautiful and good—
my honest, hard-working, brave people,
half full, half hungry,
          half slaves. . . .

Nazım was strongly attracted to the epic form, and he first embraced it in a long elegy to Sheik Bedreddin, a fourteenth-century mystic whose egalitarian ideals led him to foment an ill-fated rebellion against the Ottoman sultan. When military cadets were found to be reading it in secret, Nazım was arrested and sentenced to twenty-eight years in prison on charges that he was inciting the army to rebel. He spent the next thirteen years in jail, producing not only a stream of poems but also translations of Italian librettos for the Ankara State Opera. This was a wonderful example of how the Turkish state worked and sometimes still works; while one branch of government was imprisoning him, another was paying him to help bring masterpieces of European culture to eager Turkish audiences.

As Nazım's health deteriorated, leftists organized a worldwide campaign for his release that was supported by admirers including Sartre, Picasso, Robeson, Yevtushenko and Neruda. After Adnan Menderes won his shocking victory at the polls in 1950 and became Turkey's first democratically elected prime minister, he decreed a general amnesty under which the poet was finally freed. The army, however, was not through with him. Soon after his release he was ordered to report for military service despite the fact that he was forty-eight years old and sick. Sur-

mising that he would never survive his service, he fled across the Black Sea to the Soviet Union, where he lived for the rest of his life. There he was embraced by Communist leaders and wrote crass poems in homage to Lenin and Stalin. After the Turkish authorities stripped him of his citizenship, though, he alienated his hosts by turning down their offer of Soviet citizenship and accepting a Polish offer instead, honoring a Polish ancestor who had fought in anti-Russian uprisings during the eighteenth century.

In his prison poems, Nazım had often reflected on the possibility that he would one day be sentenced to die and summarily executed:

Death—
a body swinging from a rope.
My heart
  can't accept such a death.
But
you can bet
  if some poor gypsy's hairy black
    spidery hand
      slips a noose
        around my neck,
they'll look in vain for fear
                in Nazım's
                  blue eyes!

As it turned out, however, he died in Moscow, never having been allowed to return home to the land he loved. Admirers have started a campaign to bring his body back, but not every Turk likes the idea.

"Let him stay there!" my friend Altemur Kılıç, a fierce nationalist whose father was a compatriot of Atatürk's, once spat at me. "Hikmet was our evil genius. He was no doubt a very good poet, a very good wordsmith and not a negligible man. I would even admit that he was a patriot in his own way. His poems about our War of Liberation are magnificent. But he wanted Turkey to become liberated so it could become a satellite of Soviet Russia. He did great harm to Turkey. I cannot consider him a hero of democracy, as some people do today."

During the 1960s Nazım's poetry books, which had already been translated into dozens of foreign languages, began to reappear in Turkey. Today new editions of his works stream off the presses, theater companies present his plays to sold-out houses and pop stars turn his poems into hit songs. The Nazım Hikmet Foundation, based in Istanbul, organizes exhibitions related to his life and work and publishes a thick pocket calendar each year filled with pictures of him and excerpts from his writings. But the fact that the education ministry still forbids schoolteachers to present his poems to their students reflects a lingering bitterness toward him in some circles. Staunch Kemalists, those who believe the Republic still faces dire threats, consider him to have been a traitor and do not want to see him turned into more of a hero than he already is. They see a sinister and subversive hand behind the campaign to rehabilitate him.

Nazım Hikmet called himself "a child of the twentieth century, and proud of it." His admirers are to be found wherever people read books. Denise Levertov has described him as "a supremely confident, energetic, passionate and powerfully imaginative poet." Raymond Carver called "Human Landscapes," his seventeen-thousand-line epic masterpiece, "one of the great works of modern literature." Tristan Tzara, who translated several of his works into French, said that his poetry "exalts the aspirations of the Turkish people and articulates the common ideals of all nations." In death his renown has spread, and no one now doubts the strength of his creative genius. Surely it will take no more than another generation for Turkey's ruling elite to embrace him, probably with the same tormented uncertainty that shaped his own feelings for his homeland:

You are my imprisonment and my freedom,
my flesh,
burning like a summer night,
you are my country.
You, with your green spots in golden-brown eyes,
you are my great one, my beauty, my triumphant desire
that slips ever further away
the closer one comes to it.

• TEN •

THE PRIZE

An attractive and vivacious Turkish woman I know lived at home with her parents until she was in her mid-twenties. She liked the arrangement, not just because Daddy paid her credit card bills but also because her family is close-knit and loving. Her parents thought they were guarding her virtue by keeping her close at hand. In fact, she had been sleeping with boyfriends since she was in high school.

This arrangement perfectly mirrored the way Turkish society functioned during the 1980s and 1990s. A vibrant new generation had emerged, full of energy and determined to enjoy everything the world has to offer. The country's political regime, though, remained stuck in a bygone era. Trapped in denial, it insisted against all evidence that nothing had changed and that rules everyone had obeyed for generations could be enforced forever.

In 2002 my friend finally moved into her own apartment. That was the same year Tayyip Erdoğan led his AKP to victory and started tearing down the rigid structures that had defined the Turkish Republic since its founding. Although this was no more than coincidence, it was wonderfully symbolic. My friend's parents were forced to admit, most reluctantly, that their baby had grown up and would now live as she wished. Turkey's old elite, also against its will, is being forced to admit the same thing.

Generations of Turks grew up learning that there was no virtue more perfect than obedience. They never questioned either their leaders' wisdom or their legitimacy. More than simply dutiful subjects, they were genuinely grateful for the privilege of being ruled. The revolution that replaced sultans with zealous modernizers wiped away many traditions, but not this one. Atatürk found it invaluable because it allowed him to impose his revolution from above. Many Turks accepted him and his regime simply because he was in power. When sultans told them to fear God and scorn the European infidel, they did so because they knew instinctively that the man in power must be right. When Atatürk told them to do the opposite, they submitted just as willingly and for the same reason.

Turks have a vivid collective memory of the chaos out of which their nation emerged. Over the years they have watched several nearby countries—Yugoslavia, the Soviet Union, Lebanon, Afghanistan, Iraq—dissolve into fratricidal conflict. These experiences convinced them of the supreme value of stability. Atatürk's heirs insisted for generations that democracy was the enemy of stability. They shaped a political system based on the principle that Turkey faced a unique array of threats and therefore needed a special kind of democracy. Limits on freedom were deemed necessary because national security could not be guaranteed without them.

"You in the West also had long periods of backwardness and intolerance," a Turkish diplomat told me once as we walked along a quiet corridor in the foreign ministry in Ankara. "You had dictatorships, civil wars, religious fanaticism, the Inquisition, all kinds of horror. Then, over a period of centuries, you climbed out of that hole. You had the Enlightenment. You had philosophers who wrote books about democracy. Very slowly, people started to understand and accept these new ideas. You began to have governments based on democratic principles. Now, because you went through all of that, you can give your people complete freedom. Your societies are stable enough to handle it. But it's not the same here. Our Enlightenment began only seventy-five years ago. It's too soon to lift every restriction. The risk is too great. We could lose everything."

When I asked my diplomat friend how long he thought it would take before Turks grew wise enough to assume the responsibilities of freedom, he stopped in his tracks and turned to me, a deeply serious expression on his face. Obviously he had pondered this question before. "It's been three-quarters of a century since this process started," he said. "Maybe after a century has passed we'll be far enough along." Then, after another pause, he repeated the key word with emphasis: *"Maybe."*

Over the course of its first seventy-five years, the Turkish Republic succeeded in creating a democratic space in a part of the world where there has traditionally been very little democracy. That was a historic achievement for which Turks and people everywhere owe Atatürk an eternal debt. By the end of the twentieth century, however, that achievement was still incomplete. Shapers of the state, like the diplomat I met in Ankara, liked to say that it would take a long time for Turks to reach their promised land. Then, suddenly, in a way no one had anticipated, they began racing there.

By the time the new century dawned, the face of Turkey and the consciousness of Turks had been reshaped by social, technological, educational and demographic revolutions. The rise of Tayyip Erdoğan's new regime was the political expression of those revolutions. By the time his AKP came to power in 2002, two-thirds of Turks were under the age of thirty-five. Free thought and open inquiry had replaced obedience as supreme virtues.

For generations the Turkish state spoke with a single voice. That voice has been replaced with a dazzling cacophony issuing from more than three hundred television channels and a thousand radio stations. Forces set in motion by an open economy and an invigorated democracy have greatly weakened the power of old elites. Turkey is today a more open society than it has ever been.

For many years Turkish leaders were justifiably obsessed with the twin dangers of separatism and religious fundamentalism. Movements aimed at tearing Turkey apart, as the long Kurdish rebellion showed, bring only blood and tears, and if one were ever to succeed, it would probably be devastating to all parties. And fundamentalism is as great a danger as the most radical Kemalists believe it to be, since it would rob Turks of their freedom and their future. It is not only appropriate but necessary for the state to combat these threats. For years it did so by suppressing people's identities and their cultural and spiritual longings.

The old idea of "Turkishness" was based on the fiction that Turks are an ethnically united people rather than a richly diverse mosaic. To be proud of one's ethnic heritage, or even to acknowledge it, was considered a treasonous form of separatism. Turgut Özal's statement in the mid-1980s that he had a Kurdish grandmother was a bold challenge to this taboo. The next Turkish leader to defy it was Prime Minister Erdoğan, who announced during a visit to Georgia in 2004 that his ancestors had arrived in Anatolia during the nineteenth century from the Georgian town of Batumi. With this admission, he was encouraging Turks to rise from the Procrustean bed on which their state had tried to make them lie for generations.

None wish more fervently to grasp this chance than Turkey's tens of millions of Kurds. For decades the state fiercely refused to hear their cries or acknowledge their pain. It spoke to them only in the language of force, and the PKK responded just as brutally. Prime Minister Erdoğan seemed to want to break this cycle, but his loss of support from Europe and the emergence of a Kurdish ministate in northern Iraq made change exceedingly difficult.

Those who fear that Kurdish militants and the Turkish state are either politically or psychologically incapable of resolving their conflict find no shortage of arguments. A quarter-century of war and terror spilled rivers of blood and left a legacy of unfathomable pain. Nonetheless, those who look desperately for glimmers of hope believe they see some. Within weeks of taking office in 2007, President Abdullah Gül declared that resolving this long, devastating conflict would be a priority. Then, just a few days after he said this in public for the first time, the journalist Fikret Bila published a compilation of astonishing interviews with retired generals who prosecuted the Kurdish war. With the wisdom of hindsight, they admitted to great mistakes.

General Kenan Evren, who during the period of military rule in the early 1980s decreed a sweeping ban on the use of the Kurdish language, lamented having done so. "On the contrary," he added, "Kurdish should have been made a requirement for civil servants sent to the southeast."

General Doğan Güreş, who as chief of the general staff in the mid-1990s ordered the burning of hundreds of Kurdish villages, said he had come to believe that there is "nothing wrong" with Kurds who want to express their cultural identity. General Aytaç Yalman, a former army commander also known for his scorched-earth tactics, admitted that he and his fellow commanders had failed to appreciate the "social aspect" of the conflict.

Some consider these men heroes who fought to defend the survival of the Turkish nation. Others consider them war criminals. All recognize them as pillars of the state. The revelation that they have come to regret the way the state treated Kurds during the 1980s and 1990s caused a national sensation. It undercut the position of militants who equate Kurdish nationalism with treason, and it electrified Kurds and others who dream of peace in southeastern Turkey. Whether it might be met with an equivalent round of soul-searching from leaders of the PKK, who also bore a great measure of guilt for the horrors of this long war, remained tantalizingly unclear.

The election of 2007 brought more than twenty Kurdish nationalists into Parliament. Some wanted them arrested as accomplices to terror. Others saw them as proof that Turkish democracy offered a peaceful alternative to rebellion and hoped they could serve as a bridge between two worlds that had for years refused to understand each other. Only optimists dared to believe that Turkey was on its way to resolving this most brutally urgent of all its challenges. But against the background of a conflict that dragged on for so long, broke so many hearts and destroyed so many lives, the mere fact that optimism could rear its head suggested that there was at least some basis for hope.

How to reconcile the state and its long-suffering Kurdish citizens is among the greatest conundrums facing modern Turkey. It is part of a greater dilemma the nation has never managed to resolve: how to treat minorities. Despite the changes that have reshaped Turkish life, not simply Kurds but Christians, Arabs, Alewite Muslims, ethnic Armenians and others know they must not assert their identities in ways the state finds threatening. The regime that emerged to rule Turkey in the first decade of the new century could rightly claim to represent the will of the majority more fully than any in recent history. Democracy is only complete, however, when the majority guarantees the rights of minorities. Turkey still fails that test.

If developing a new respect for Kurds and other minorities is Turkey's most pressing need, repealing laws that restrict free speech is hardly less urgent. The sight of journalists and writers being forced to defend themselves in court for the crime of expressing their opinions is nothing less than scandalous. Until the laws that make those prosecutions possible are repealed, Turkey will not be able to claim that its society is truly free or open.

The new regime must also prove, not just by promise but in action, that it is truly committed to maintaining the secular essence of the Turkish Republic.

A new debate now dominates public discourse in Turkey. It is not about Kurds or democracy or the European Union, but rather about the nature of the regime dominated by Prime Minister Erdoğan and President Gül. Is this regime truly committed to democracy, or has it been using democracy to cover a hidden agenda that aims to wipe away the secular order and turn Turkey into an Islamic state?

Those who believe the latter have found enough evidence to terrify them. They leaped to denounce Erdoğan when he tried to open universities and government jobs to graduates of religious schools, and to women who wear head scarves. When one of his cabinet ministers proposed criminalizing adultery, and another suggested that female university students be given virginity tests, their outrage grew. They saw more proof in the threatening policies of AKP mayors who tried to impose prohibitions on alcohol and establish separate beaches for men and women. Even more disturbing were cases in which applicants for high government posts, like governor of the central bank, seemed to be ruled out of contention if their wives did not wear head scarves.

Erdoğan caters to all the factions in the AKP, including those that want to see a greater religious influence in public life. Yet when he called an election in 2007, scores of fundamentalist-leaning AKP deputies in Parliament found that he had excluded them from his list of candidates. The list offered more female candidates than any other party, and none who wore head scarves.

Meeting people who have been elected to office as AKP candidates is a good way to appreciate the party's big-tent character. I found a fine example in Gaziantep, a booming industrial city in a region of eastern Anatolia that is rich in Hittite, Assyrian, Persian and Roman history. For fifteen years the mayor of Gaziantep had been Celal Doğan, an old-style political boss from the fiercely secular Republican People's Party. Nothing could happen without him; he built parks, laid water and sewer lines and even ran the city's soccer team. Even though he became increasingly isolated, and despite accusations of extravagant corruption, he so dominated Gaziantep that many considered him invincible. Yet in the local election of 2004 he was overwhelmingly defeated by a little-known physician named Asim Güzelbey, whose main qualification was his affiliation with the AKP.

"I don't consider myself especially religious, and my wife doesn't wear a head scarf," the new mayor told me when I visited him at City Hall. "If I have a political identity, it is simply as a democrat, which I take to mean that the law is above all and applies equally to all. I come from a conservative family, and this party is conservative. It is also a party dedicated to honesty and transparency. Turks are thirsty for that because we're so fed up with corrupt politics."

Mayor Güzelbey conceded that there are "some extremists" in the AKP who sympathize with Islamic political goals. There are actually more than just "some." Many of the party's leaders appear moderate, open-minded and fully aware of how much Turkey's success has depended on its secular ethos. Its base, however, is more conservative and at times more resentful of the secular state. That makes Prime Minister Erdoğan's role even more important, and his deepest beliefs even more intriguing.

"Our prime minister has changed and improved," Mayor Güzelbey assured me. "What he said five or twenty years ago doesn't mean he is incapable of adapting to the contemporary world. I'm convinced that he truly believes in democracy. Look at what he is doing—what more proof could you want? This man is leading us into Europe. There's no danger of him taking us toward Islamic radicalism."

Meeting AKP supporters like Asim Güzelbey is reassuring. A few hours after our chat, though, I was sitting in a charming Gaziantep inn with my friend Aykut Tuzcu, a visionary businessman who publishes the local newspaper and is active in many civic causes. When I asked him about what was happening in Turkey, he winced with almost physical pain.

"I don't know what to say," he told me. "I see a contrast. These people are pushing hard for Turkey to join the EU, but they're also pushing for a more religious society at home. I don't understand what Erdoğan is doing. I worry a lot, and I'm not the only one."

Is this new regime spreading true democracy, or are people right to worry about it? Both. Never since the early days of Atatürk's rule has Turkey moved so quickly toward new levels of freedom. The same regime, however, is led by men who fervently embrace Islam and calmly accept and even cater to ultra-nationalism. It is good for Turkey that this new regime has come to power. It is also good that many mistrust it.

"These people need to be watched," one of my Turkish friends, an American-educated university professor, told me when I asked him what he thought of his country's new leaders. "But secular Turks like me had no real alternative. We would have preferred that someone more like us would lead this transformation, but the civilians we elected in the 1990s all turned out to be disasters. Now we finally have a leader who's taking us where we need to go. It's not exactly the way we had hoped history would unfold, but this is the option we have."

One remarkable result of Turkey's transformation has been the evolution of the Islamist movement. For generations Turks who were traditional Muslims understood that their state feared, hated and wished to repress them, that they had no place in the Turkish Republic. Some of these believers flirted with truly subversive notions, even the idea of overthrowing the Republic. Now, with Turkey under the rule of elected leaders who are unabashed believers, devout Muslims feel included rather than excluded. Many seem to have moderated their views. In 1999 21 percent of Turks told public opinion surveyors that they wanted *sharia* law based on the Koran to replace Turkey's civil code; by 2007 the number had fallen to 9 percent. Fundamentalism's appeal has faded as Prime Minister Erdoğan has persuaded believers that they have a place in the Turkish Republic.

The new regime has also managed to moderate the views of some—

though by no means all—militant secularists. These are men and women whose great dream is to see Turkey integrated into the Kantian, post-Enlightenment world represented most fully, they believe, by the European Union. They admit, often grudgingly, that Prime Minister Erdoğan has done more to bring Turkey closer to the EU than any previous Turkish leader. Many were pleasantly surprised when, after the EU brusquely turned its back on Turkey in 2006, he responded not with outrage but by insisting that Turkey would continue on its reform process regardless. Turkey's key goal, he repeatedly insisted, was to fulfill the political and economic conditions for EU membership—not simply because Turkey wants to join but because these reforms are good for Turkey.

Prospects for eventual Turkish membership in the EU remain highly uncertain. Perhaps a realistic goal would be for Turkey and Europe to consummate their relationship in 2023, when the Turkish Republic celebrates its centenary.

Prime Minister Erdoğan has won over some skeptics with his willingness to pursue at least some European-style reforms. Others are impressed by his successful economic policies. The basis for these policies was laid by the previous regime's brilliant finance minister, Kemal Derviş, who went on to head the United Nations Development Program, but Erdoğan embraced and deepened them. The results have ranged from impressive (like annual growth rates of 7 to 8 percent) to spectacular (like the rise in foreign investment from $1 billion in 2002 to $20 billion in 2006). During that same period, the gross domestic product jumped by more than 50 percent and export income doubled. In the mid-1990s inflation galloped out of control, with rates approaching 100 percent annually. A decade later the rate had fallen to the comfortable single digits. Achievements like these would appeal to voters in any country.

No transaction more vividly symbolized the international reach and ambition of Turkish companies than the successful bid by Ülker, the country's largest snack food producer, for the high-end Godiva chocolate company, founded by a Belgian gourmet in 1926. Ülker paid $850 million for Godiva, making this a substantial transaction but not an earth-shattering one. The symbolism, though, was as richly delicious as a

Godiva truffle. A generation ago, it would have been unthinkable that a Turkish company could take over such a prize. Now transactions like this hardly raise an eyebrow. Europe may not be ready to accept Turkey politically, but Ülker's purchase of a company whose products the public instinctively associates with European refinement shows that Turkey's economic power has become difficult to resist.

Even all of this progress has not been enough to turn every Turk into an admirer of the new regime. That is as it should be. Prime Minister Erdoğan, for all his successes, has had his share of monumental failures. He has been unwilling or unable to resolve the continuing Kurdish crisis, and his efforts to wipe away restrictions on free speech have been half-hearted at best. Nor has he been able to reassure nervous secularists that he accepts Atatürk's fundamental principles.

The new regime has also stood by as ultra-nationalist ideas have spread alarmingly in the Turkish body politic. These ideas far exceed patriotic pride, going so far as to insist that "nation" and "Turkishness" are abstractions so central to life that anyone who seems to violate their traditional meanings is a traitor. That category has broadened steadily from those who criticize the army or question Atatürk's legacy to anyone who speaks out for Kurdish rights, seeks more freedom for Christians or offers alternative views of the Armenian tragedy. The fact that the government thinks it must assign bodyguards to some of the country's most brilliant writers and thinkers shows the seriousness of the threat of extreme Turkish nationalism.

Repeated rejections from the European Union and perceived snubs by the United States add to this atavistic nationalism. The mass press irresponsibly feeds it. It has become a potent force—and large voting bloc—in Turkish society. Political leaders, including Prime Minister Erdoğan, pander to it in ways that damage the cause of democracy instead of challenging it and trying to change it. Why has Turkey not accepted the principle of Kurdish rights, granted more protection to minorities or wiped away restrictions on free speech? One good reason is that to do so would alienate the steadily growing pool of these ultra-nationalist voters. The regime seems less interested in neutralizing this reactionary bloc than in adjusting its program to assure that it wins a good number of its votes.

Creeping corruption, always an acute danger in one-party governments, is also infecting this regime. Sons of leading figures have become extraordinarily rich. One of Prime Minister Erdoğan's sons-in-law has bought a media conglomerate in a deal that dangerously blurs the line between press and government. This trend is not new in Turkey, but many voters hoped it would end when they elected a party as publicly committed to good governance as the AKP had been.

Some Turks who were at first sympathetic to the new regime sense that the old intolerance is being replaced by a new, more dangerous kind. "Nationalism is becoming so strong, and so influenced by fascist and racist ideas, that I am more scared now than ever," one told me. Another wrote in an anguished email, "Many democratic figures, artists, intellectuals and scholars who suffered greatly under army regimes are anxious and desperate. We feel the fear everywhere."

This chilling climate has led a growing number of educated Turks to choose to live abroad. Some, like the son of the murdered editor Hrant Dink, left because of direct threats and a conviction that the state was uninterested in protecting them. Others simply fear that angry intolerance is becoming too strong a part of national life and prefer to live elsewhere.

"I don't believe this preference is based on economic factors," Murat Belge, a relentless campaigner for democracy, wrote in a newspaper column.

> In Turkey there is no suffocating poverty like in India, and there never has been. But there are other things that do count as "suffocating," especially for people who are well educated and enlightened. Is it necessary to discuss what suffocates us when a street thug can shout "Smarten up!" at a Nobel Prize–winning author and the entire establishment and legal system lines up on the side of that thug? Yes, it is. It is necessary to discuss it continuously.

Despite the new regime's decidedly incomplete commitment to democracy, though, it has taken epochal steps. Most Turks realize that, and have responded with a burst of hope. Turkey is a more dynamic place than ever in its modern history. Nowhere is that more visible than in Istanbul, its pulsating heart. Istanbul is exploding with energy, a perfect symbol of the excitement the new regime has brought to a nation long trapped in torpor and pessimism.

The old Istanbul, as Orhan Pamuk wrote in his memoir, was shrouded in the sad and wistful melancholy Turks call *huzun*. It was populated by people who had little concept of individual worth and mindlessly accepted a way of life that encouraged them "to be content with little, honoring the virtues of harmony, uniformity, humility." That Istanbul no longer exists. Instead of being lost in lassitude and *huzun*, it is now, as a gushing cover story in *Newsweek International* proclaimed in 2006, "the coolest city in the world."

> After decades of provincialism, decay and economic depression—not to mention the dreary nationalism mandated by a series of governments dominated by the military—Istanbul is re-emerging as one of Europe's great metropolises. Signs of renewed self-confidence are everywhere. The city is still thickly atmospheric, with bazaars, Byzantine churches and Ottoman mansions pretty much everywhere. But that faded grandeur has recently been leavened with new energy. Stock markets are surging. Young, Western-educated Turks are returning home to start businesses. Foreigners are snapping up choice real estate. Turkish painters, writers, musicians, fashion designers and filmmakers are increasingly in the international spotlight . . . Reforms pushed by the EU—from its insistence that the military step back from politics to human-rights and free-speech liberalizations—have reshaped Turkey's political and social landscape . . . Europe may yet balk at admitting Turkey to its Union. Yet the world won't end if it does. All signs suggest that Istanbul will continue to re-create itself, perhaps even more energetically. Remember the sounds of Istanbul's streets—European and Turkish and Balkan and Middle Eastern, all coming together in a strange but beautiful harmony.

For generations Turks agreed with their leaders that no sacrifice made in the name of stability was too onerous. They no longer believe that. Youthful, vigorous and boundlessly enthusiastic, they are trying to turn their country into a modern democracy. In the process, many have become happier and more prosperous than they have ever been.

Modern Turkey is a land of rising prosperity and declining conflict. It has not shaken off all its crippling fears but is nonetheless buoyed by limitless hopes. Many of its people are seeking to shape a new way of life, one that balances tradition with modernity, secularism with religious freedom, and unity with diversity. If they succeed, they will not only immeasurably enrich their country but also allow it to play the global role to which history and geography entitle it. That would make Turkey a model for developing countries, a beacon in the Islamic world and an invaluable ally of all who work for peace and freedom.

Every Saturday night for three years, radio listeners in Istanbul could hear a voice speaking in heavily accented Turkish that welcomed them to another evening of blues music. "Yalnız gerçek *blues* çalıyorum," *the voice would say as each show began. I play only real blues.*

That voice was mine. I got a great kick out of being the "blues baba," *or blues daddy, on Turkey's hippest radio station. Mine was hardly the first or only blues show in the country, but as far as I know I was the first American to host one, the first disc jockey in Turkey who not only featured artists like Lightnin' Hopkins, Alberta Hunter, Roosevelt Sykes, Big Joe Turner and Muddy Waters but had actually had the privilege of hearing them perform live.*

A generation of Turks grew up hearing blues-influenced musicians like Eric Clapton, Johnny Winter and the Blues Brothers. But I never played their music. I was interested only in "real blues," music that many Turks had never heard before.

When I first planned the show, I resolved that any artist I featured would have to fit two categories: black and dead. I eased up on the second restriction a bit but never allowed myself to cross over into blues-rock or other derivative styles. The reason for this was not any kind of exclusionary elitism. My mission was to broaden the knowledge and taste of my audience. I wanted to let them know that Mick Jagger did not write "Little Red Rooster" and that "Hound Dog" was not an Elvis Presley original.

In my bilingual commentary I always tried to tell something about the lives of the artists whose music I played. I also explained the rudiments of blues history, working under the assumption that many Turks liked this music but didn't know much about it. Listeners sometimes told me they loved my show and then asked, "What is blues anyway?" To help orient them, I often talked about the southern roots of blues music and how it moved north and went electric. Most of my listeners had probably never heard phrases like "Jim Crow" or "Parchman Farm," nor could they understand why so many blues songs are about leavin' home and ramblin'. I tried to present the cultural background against which blues music emerged, explaining how the forces of poverty and racism produced such rich musical expression.

After a while, I began to sense that many Turks found my explanations remote and hard to grasp. What I really needed to do, I realized, was to explain this music in terms Turks could easily understand. After all, African-Americans are hardly the only people in the world who feel the blues. They developed a richly evocative way to express those emotions, but the emotions themselves are universal.

I didn't want my radio station—which was always skirting the edge of the law anyway—to find itself in trouble because of something I broadcast, so I never delivered my imagined monologue on the air. If I had, it would have gone something like this:

You say you're a Kurd living in southeastern Turkey. One of your uncles was arrested and tortured during the 1990s, and you have a cousin who has gone "to the mountain" as a PKK fighter. You're happy the terror war is over but worried that it might start again. Protesters stage regular demonstrations in your town, and when they hold up pictures of the PKK leader and shout pro-PKK slogans, the police attack. You'd like to break out of the cycle of protest and resistance, but the government remains unwilling to allow you to live with your Kurdish identity. Like most of your friends, you have little hope of finding a job. The "miracle on the Bosphorus" might as well be happening on the moon. What's the matter? Blues got you.

You say you're a thinker who has decided there are things you don't like about your country. You believe the government is too religious, or too irreligious. People are unwilling to confront ugly aspects of their national past. Military service is compulsory. Minorities are not free. Generals meddle in politics. Maybe these complaints are valid, maybe not. But as a patriotic citizen you believe you have the right and even the obligation to express them. When you do, you find yourself under indictment for insulting Atatürk, the army or "Turkishness." What's the matter? Blues got you.

You say you're an ambitious young woman who revels in the freedom Turkey offers to those of your sex. You enroll in medical school, but on your first day you find a guard standing outside the classroom. He won't let you enter because you're wearing a head scarf. Despite Turkey's promise of gender equality, you find yourself in a predicament like those facing women in Yemen or Saudi Arabia. What's the matter? Blues got you.

You say you're a Turk who wants your country to complete its long march toward democracy. The first decade of the twenty-first century brought it closer to this goal than you ever dreamed possible. Much of the credit goes to the European Union, which gave Turkey a road map for reform. At the end of the reform process lay the prospect of EU membership, which is as close as this world offers to a permanent guarantee of stability and prosperity. Then suddenly the EU withdrew its offer. The great outside dynamic pushing Turkey toward modernity seemed to evaporate. You feel abandoned and recall the classic Robert Johnson verse: "I went down to the crossroads, tried to flag me a ride / But nobody seemed to know me, everybody passed me by." What's the matter? Blues got you.

You say you're a worldly woman who grew up under the protection of Atatürk's secular republic. Without his vision, you realize, Turkey would probably have become an unhappy country like Iran or Iraq or Syria. Wherever you look, you see evidence of how spectacularly successful his revolution has been. Yet now a group of pious Muslims has been elected to run Turkey. Their wives wear head scarves, and when you are on the street you cannot help noticing that the head scarf is more common than ever in your lifetime. You worry that the nation you love may fall into the darkness of religious rule. What's the matter? Blues got you.

You say you're an intellectual who hated the old Turkish paradigm of military-dominated government. Now times are changing, but as your fear of generals has faded, new fears have taken their place. You see centralization of power in the hands of people whose commitment to freedom and secularism you doubt. Around you, you see nationalism rising and respect for minority groups as limited as ever. Your motto is "No army, no sharia,*" but when you proclaim it, you feel lonely. What's the matter? Blues got you.*

These fears are real and deeply felt. They do not, however, outweigh the remarkable progress Turkey has made toward liberation. It is not only escaping from its crippling fears but emerging to play a uniquely valuable role in the world. Blues music now speaks to its condition in a new way.

Blues songs are not, as some mistakenly believe, all about pain and suffering. In fact, they are often about freedom and redemption. They chart the loneliness of the human soul and the endless frustrations of life, so they fit Turkey during the days when it was torn by conflict. Ultimately, though, they celebrate survival and triumph. That makes them ideal anthems for today's Turkey. A vibrant nation has emerged from generations of victories and defeats. Its people are thriving. They can now face the world exultantly and cry out, with Muddy Waters, "I'm here! Everybody knows—I'm here!"

INDEX

A

Abduction from the Seraglio (Mozart), 7
Abdülhamid II, Sultan, 35, 209
Abdullah, King of Saudi Arabia, 213
Abdülmecid, Caliph, 40–42
Abu Ghraib prison, 218
Achilles, 51, 52, 53, 109, 111
Adana, 165
Adapazarı, 193, 197
Adrasan, 165
Afghanistan, 59, 79, 95, 221, 236
Agamemnon, 52
Ağca, Mehmet Ali, 98
Agos, 104, 105
Ahlat, 112
Akçam, Taner, 156
Akhtamar Church, 88, 108
Akmeşe, Hamza, 187
AKP (Justice and Development Party): democracy and, 162–63, 181, 222; as dominant political party, 186; in election of 2002, 22, 24, 77, 81, 215, 235, 237; in election of 2007, 183–84; founding of, 77; fundamentalist factions in, 162, 186; Islamism and, xiv, xv, 18, 181, 240–42, 251–52; judicial challenge to, 185; pluralist ideology of, 21, 58, 240–43
Alevis, 62–63
Alewites, 239
Alexander the Great, 52–53, 111
Algeria, 119
amnesty, for PKK, 139, 140, 141, 155
Anadolu Kavağı, 211
Anatolia, 16, 30, 37, 38, 39, 76, 77, 107, 113, 216; old elite's contempt for, 21; pre-Islamic history of, 109–13
Ani, 112–13
Ankara, 10, 34, 42, 65, 73, 189; Cankaya neighborhood of, 70
Ankara Hilton, 219
Ankara Symphony Orchestra, 73–74
Ankara University, 60–61
Anna Karenina (Tolstoy), 152
Annan, Kofi, 214
Antalya, 37, 111
Anti-Terror Law (1991), 154–55
Arabic script, 43

Arabs, 3, 239
Ararat, Mount, 112
archaeology: of Troy, 51–52, 53; of Zeugma, 109–10; *see also* ruins
Argentina, 93
Argonauts, 208
Arinç, Bülent, 218
Armenia, Republic of, 87, 101, 104, 107, 118, 180, 199
Armenian massacre (1915), 11, 17, 88–93, 100–104, 155, 157, 180, 244; Armenian-Americans and, 101–104; Kurds and, 89–90; 2005 conference on, 100–101, 107
Armenians, 87–88, 104, 107–108, 112, 239; Sèvres Treaty and, 37, 39
Armstrong, H. C., 45
Artvin, 113
Assad, Bashir, 213
Assad, Hafez al-, 117–18, 124–25
Assyrians, 87
Atatürk, Mustafa Kemal, 33–49, 79, 93, 106, 155, 228, 237; assassination attempt on, 44; birth of, 35; cult of, 48–49, 154; death of, 27–28, 46; democracy opposed by, 10, 44, 153; as dictator, 44–45, 236; European ideals of, 34, 36, 39–40, 46, 221; freedom of the press and, 45; as hero of Gallipoli, 36, 37, 55; isolationist policies of, 166, 214, 228; mausoleum of, 34, 91; military career of, 35–36; political parties under, 44; polygamy outlawed by, 160; progress as key belief of, 47–48; religious garb banned by, 42–43, 60, 160; religious power opposed by, 60, 160; secularism of, 17, 58, 251; statues and images of, 48–49, 122; surnames of, 35, 46; Turkish Republic founded by, 10–11, 14, 24, 37–39, 40, 242
Ateş, Atilla, 125
Athena, 52
Athens, 4
Austen, Jane, 5
Australians, in Gallipoli assault, 54–55
Austria, 141
Azerbaijan, 107, 213
Azm, Sadik Al-, 227

B

"bad Turks," xv, 180
Bağci, Hüseyin, 221
Baghdad, 4
Bagheri, Mohammed Reza, 73
Bahçeli, Devlet, 140–41
Balian family, 209
Balkans, xiv, 214, 226
Baski, Lutfi, 135
Batman, 146–47
Batumi, Georgia, 238
Bayburt province, 189
Baydar, Yavuz, 101
Baydemir, Osman, 136
Bayraktar, Hasrettin, 121
Bayraktaroğlu, Arın, 84
Baysal, Nurcan, 139
Bedreddin, Sheik, 231
Belge, Murat, 245
Belgrade, 4
Benedict XVI, Pope, 214
Berkan, Ismet, 106, 157–58
Berlin Wall, 47
Beykent University, 219
Beylerbeyi Palace, 209
Bible, 208
Bila, Fikret, 238
Black Sea, 36, 54, 55, 208
Blair, Tony, 224
blues: as applied to life in Turkey, 250–52; author's radio program of, 249–50
Blues Brothers, 249
Bodin, Jean, 6
börek, 29–30
Bosnia, 119, 221
Bosphorus, 37, 54, 207–11; author's swim across, 207, 210–11
Bosphorus University, 100
Boysan, Aydın, 30–31

Britain: in Gallipoli assault, 54; Kenya and, 103; Malaya and, 119
Brothers Karamazov, The (Dostoevsky), 5–6
Bucak, Sedat, 97
Buda, 4
Bulgaria, 92, 220, 225
Burdur, 178
Busey, Gary, 218
Bush, George W., 142, 217, 219
business, expanding role of, xv, 16–17, 243–44
Büyükanit, Yaşar, 99, 182
Byron, Lord, 7, 209
Byzantine Empire, 4

C

cadets, 175–76, 231
Caesar, Julius, 53
Cairo, 4
calendar, replacement of Muslim with European, 43
caliphate, abolition of, 40, 42
camel fighting, 187–88
Çankaya, 70, 181
Carver, Raymond, 233
Çatlı, Abdullah, 97–98
Caucasus, xiv, 214
Cem, Ismail, 203
Central Asia, xiv, 39, 214, 220; origin of Turks in, 3, 30, 188, 189
Cevdet, Abdullah, 14
Chechnya, 119
China, 225, 227
Christians: as Turkish minority, 24, 239, 244; Turks as viewed by, 3–4
Churchill, Winston, 36, 38, 54, 55
CIA, 128
Çiçek, Cemil, 100, 182
Çıldıroğlu, 112
Çiller, Tansu, 67, 118, 174
Çırağan Palace, 209
cirit, 189–90
Clapton, Eric, 249
Clinton, Bill, 217
Cohn-Bendit, Daniel, 224
Cold War, 216
Commandos of the Armenian Genocide, 90
Committee of Union and Progress (Young Turks), 14, 36, 60
Communism, Communists, 44, 47, 153, 229, 232
Congress, U.S., Armenian massacre and, 102–104
conscription, 177–78, 179
Constantine I, Roman Emperor, 53
Constantinople, 53; fall of (1453), 4, 37, 53, 208; *see also* Istanbul
constitution (1982), 33; free speech restricted in, 154; military imposition of, 14–15
Constitutional Court, 182
contractors, 1999 earthquake and, 196–97, 200
corruption, xv, 17, 65–66, 100, 174, 198, 200, 241, 245
counter-elite, 16–17, 20–21, 76
coups, military, 14, 173; of 1960, 61; of 1971, 61; of 1980, 14, 16, 63, 93–94, 117; of 1997, 74–75
Crusades, 4, 53
Cuban missile crisis (1962), 216
Curio, Augustino, 5
Cyprus: Greeks as majority on, 225; Ottoman conquest of, 4; Turkey and, 214, 216, 224, 225

D

Dadrian, Vahakn, 156
D'Alema, Massimo, 125, 126
Damascus, 4
Dardanelles (Hellespont), 36, 37, 38, 52, 54, 55
Darius I, Emperor of Persia, 208, 211
Davutoğlu, Ahmet, 219–20
Dede, Mercan, 162–63

"deep state," 12, 18, 22, 99, 105, 138, 156, 159
Demirel, Süleyman, 15, 62, 67, 68, 74, 152, 168, 198–99
Demirtaş, Selahattin, 140
democracy: AKP and, 162–63, 181, 222; Alevis and, 62; Atatürk's opposition to, 10, 44, 153; Erdogan's commitment to, 20, 21, 24, 78, 82, 134, 162–63, 181, 182, 222, 226; EU as fostering of, 136, 142, 185; evolution of, xiii–xiv, 10–11, 12, 15–16, 21, 152, 153, 162, 169, 174, 181, 215, 222, 225, 226, 227, 237, 239, 245, 247, 251; Islam and, 20, 59, 77, 162, 227; Kemalism as antithetical to, 13, 15, 72, 77, 160, 183, 236; Kurds and, 134, 136, 140; military rule vs., 172, 182; 1999 earthquake and, 202; political parties and, 46; secularism and, 184
Dereli, Toker, 79–80
Derviş, Kemal, 243
devlet ("state"), 25–26, 132–33
devlet baba ("daddy state"), 200
Dimitrov, Philip, 92
Dink, Hrant, 104–105, 245; murder of, 105–107, 157
Disraeli, Benjamin, 7
divorce, 43
Diyarbakır, 44, 115–16, 120, 134–36, 138, 139–40, 145
Doğan, Celal, 241
dolma, 29
Dolmabahçe Palace, 209
domestic violence, 161
Dörpfeld, Wilhelm, 53
Dostoevsky, Fyodor, 5–6
Durmuş, Osman, 199

E

earthquake of August 17, 1999, 193–205, 217; contractors and, 196–97, 200; democracy and, 202; Ecevit and, 194–95, 198; foreign relief agencies and, 203–204; government failures in, 194–95, 197, 198–99, 201; Greece and, 199, 203–204; media coverage of, 195, 197, 201, 202, 203–204; military failures in, 194, 200–201, 202–203; old elite and, 198–99; political and social effects of, 198, 201–205; private relief groups and, 201–202
East Asian Summit, 220
Ecevit, Bülent, 77, 127, 130, 134, 168; EU membership rejected by, 221; 1999 earthquake and, 194–95, 198
Economic Cooperation Organization, 220
education: Kemalist control of, 78, 100, 159, 233; religious schools and, 59, 60–61, 63–64, 70; of women, 78–80
Egypt, mufti of, 42
Eisenhower, Dwight, 216
Elbiye, Cengiz, 191
elections: of 1950, 61; of 1983, 64; of 1995, 65–67, 174; of 2002, 22, 24, 77, 81, 215, 235, 237; of 2007, 183–84, 239; military and, 14
elites, *see* counter-elite; old elite
Enlightenment, 34
entrepreneurs, 200
Enver Pasha, 36
environmentalists, xiv, 226
Ephesus, 110, 187
Erbakan, Necmettin, 61–62, 63, 64; anti-European views of, 71–72; in election of 1995, 65–67; Iranian visit of, 68; Islamism of, 66, 68, 70, 74, 80, 174, 214; on Kurdish War, 72; Libyan visit of, 68–69, 76; as prime minister, 67–74, 174, 214
Erdoğan, Ermine, 218
Erdoğan, Recep Tayyip, 47, 64, 75, 102, 106, 153, 185, 204, 213, 224, 238; Davutoglu as advisor to, 219; on

"deep state," 105; economic policies of, 243; elected prime minister, 22, 24, 77, 235, 237; EU membership as goal of, 22, 77, 82, 143, 222, 225–26, 241–42, 243; human rights and, 162; imprisonment of, 18–20, 76, 174; Islamism of, 19, 22, 81, 240–42; as Istanbul mayor, 18–19, 21, 64, 76, 82; journalists sued by, 156–57; Kurdish problem and, 99, 134, 142–43, 244; military challenged by, 180–81, 182, 183, 184–85; pluralist views of, 20, 21, 58; police torture ended by, 160; pro-democracy policies of, 20, 21, 24, 78, 82, 134, 162–63, 181, 182, 222, 226; ultra-nationalist campaign against, 158
Erdoğan, Tülay, 79
Ertep, Ismet, 83
Erzincan, 203
Erzincan, University of, 190
Erzincan province, 189
Erzurum, 49
Euphrates River, 109, 124
Europe: as Atatürk's model for Turkey, 34, 36, 39–40, 46, 221; dual image of Turks in, 5, 6–7; Erbakan and, 71–72; Islam and, 3–4; Ottoman threat to, 4–6; postwar economic rebirth of, 168; Turkey's relationship with, xiv, 139, 187, 188, 227; Turkish "guest workers" in, 169, 201; Turkish territory in, 39
European Parliament, 126
European Security Initiative, 161
European Union (EU): anti-Turkish sentiment in, 141, 186, 224, 226, 244, 251; democracy fostered by, 136, 142, 185; Ecevit's rejection of membership in, 221; Islam and, 222–23, 224; Kurds and, 135, 140, 180; Pamuk's arrest and, 155; Turkey's proposed membership in, 22, 77, 82, 135, 136, 141, 142–43, 158, 178, 185–86, 204, 221–26, 241–42, 243, 251
Evren, Kenan, 94, 106, 238
ezan (call to prayer), 44, 61

F

Feast of Sacrifice, 59
feminists, xiv, 73
fez, banning of, 42
Firat, Dengir Mir Mehmet, 162
fish, 209–10
France, 38; Algeria and, 119; anti-Turkish sentiment in, 141; Armenians in, 102, 104; Syria and, 124–25; in Turkish War of Liberation, 38; "zone of influence" of, 37, 39
Frederick II, King of Prussia, 5
freedom of religion, 5, 13, 59
freedom of speech, xiv, 13, 20, 46, 75, 80, 106, 135, 152–54, 160, 237, 240, 244, 251
freedom of the press, 45, 75, 154, 240

G

Gagik I, King of Armenia, 88
Gallipoli, battle of, 36, 54–55
Gaziantep, 49, 241–42
gendarmerie, 147
genocide, definition of, 102–103
Genocide Museum, Yerevan, Armenia, 91
Georgia, Republic of, 113, 220, 238
Germany, Federal Republic of: anti-Turkish sentiment in, 141; economic boom in, 168
Germany, Imperial: Versailles Treaty and, 37; in World War I Turkish alliance, 36, 166
Gilgamesh epic, 208
Gilles, Pierre, 208
Giscard d'Estaing, Valéry, 222
Göçer, Veli, 197, 198
Godiva, 243–44

Gölcük, 193
Great Britain, *see* Britain
great flood, 208
Greece, 180; democracy in, 136, 185; independence struggle of, 7; NATO membership of, 216; 1999 earthquakes and, 199, 203–204; PKK supported by, 118, 127–28; in "population exchange" with Turkey, 39; in Sèvres Treaty, 37, 39; Turkey's relationship with, 203–204, 214, 220; in Turkish War of Liberation, 38–39
Greece, ancient, 110–11
Greeks: Constantinople and, 4; as Cypriot majority, 225; exodus from Turkey of, 11, 39; in Trojan War, 51–54, 55
Gül, Abdullah, 76, 80–81, 181–82, 218; as president, 181–82, 184–86, 238, 240
Gulf Cooperation Council, 220
Gulf War (1991), 17, 216
Gümüşsorgü, 146
Güreş, Doğan, 239
Güzelbey, Asim, 241

H

Hakkari province, 137
Halicarnassus, 110
harems, 6
Hariri, Rafik, 220
Hasan (translator), 145–46, 149–50
hashish, 86
Hatay province, 124–25, 180
head scarves, 18, 24, 35, 58, 70, 73, 78–80, 81, 176, 181, 240, 241, 251–52
Hector, 51
Hellenic ruins, 110–11
Hellespont (Dardanelles), 36, 37, 38, 52, 54, 55
Hera, 208
Herodotus, 52, 110
heroin smuggling, 118, 178–79
Hikmet, Nazım, 229–33
Hindemith, Paul, 43
Hitler, Adolf, 91
Hobbes, Thomas, 36
Homer, 51–52, 54, 110
"honor killings," 161
Hopkins, Lightnin', 249
horsemanship, 189–90
"Human Landscapes" (Hikmet), 233
human rights, 12, 46, 72, 80, 153, 156, 160, 162, 169, 180; Kurds and, 24, 115, 117, 132, 135, 138, 149, 160, 226, 238–39, 244
Human Rights Watch, 148–49
Hunter, Alberta, 249
huzun, 246

I

Iliad (Homer), 51–52
Imam Bayıldı, 29
imam hatip, 63–64
imams, 58, 59, 60
Imperial Reckoning (Elkins), 103
Imrali island, 130–31
Incirlik military base, 216
independence courts, 44
India, 85
Indonesia, 119
inflation, 17
Ingres, Jean-Auguste-Dominique, 7
intellectuals, exodus of, 245
Interpol, 97, 128
Io, 208
Iran, 85, 87, 217; Erbakan in, 68; 1979 revolution in, 63; religious fundamentalism in, 58, 68, 80, 251; Turkey and, 180, 220, 227
Iraq, 87, 236, 251; Kurds in, 134, 142–43, 180, 215, 219, 238; PKK backed by, 118; Turkey and, 214, 227
Iraq War, 103, 142, 223; Turkey and, 215, 217, 219

Ishak Pasha castle, 112
Islam: Alevi, 62–63; Alewite, 239; Atatürk's opposition to, 42–43, 60, 160; caliphate of, 40, 42; democracy and, 20, 59, 77, 162, 227; EU and, 222, 224; Europe and, 3–4; fundamentalist, 58–59, 61, 68, 80, 153, 237–38, 242, 251; as political force, 61–65, 251–52; *see also* AKP; Sunni, 62–63; *see also* Muslims
Islamic world, Turkey as model for, 227
Islamism, 20, 65, 162; AKP and, xiv, xv, 18, 181, 240–42, 251–52; of Erbakan, 66, 68, 70, 74, 80, 174, 214; of Erdogan, 19, 22, 81, 240–42
isolationism, 166–69, 225; of Atatürk, 166, 214, 228
Israel, 125, 128, 201, 213, 220, 227
Istanbul, 4, 16, 37, 42, 77, 82, 165, 189, 203, 207; Armenians in, 104; Disraeli's description of, 7; Erdogan as mayor of, 18–19, 21, 64, 76, 82; *huzun* and, 246; Kasimpasa district in, 18; as melting pot, 9–10; *see also* Constantinople
Istanbul University, 78–80
istiklal ("freedom"), 9, 25–26
Istiklal (boulevard), 9–10, 70
Italy, 204; in Turkish War of Liberation, 38, 39
Izmir (Smyrna), 25, 37, 44
Izmit, 193

J

Jagger, Mick, 250
James I, King of England, 5
Janissaries, 49, 179
Jason, 208, 211
Jerjian, George, 156
"Jerusalem Day," 72
Jews, 5
Johnson, Lyndon, 216
Johnson, Robert, 251
journalists, 120, 131, 148, 198; Atatürk and, 45; 1999 earthquake and, 195, 197, 201; prosecution of, 13, 156–57, 174
Justice and Development Party, *see* AKP

K

Kahramanmaraş, 62
Kanlı, Yusuf, 25
Karamanlis, Costas, 204
Karatepe, Şükrü, 76
Kars, 49, 108, 112
Kasimpaşa district, 18
Kayseri, 16, 76, 130, 181
Kemal, Mustafa, *see* Atatürk, Mustafa Kemal
Kemal, Namık, 35
Kemalism, 11, 13, 24, 34, 78, 219, 220, 233; democracy vs., 13, 15, 72, 77, 160, 183, 236; education system controlled by, 78, 100, 159, 233; isolationism of, 166, 168, 214, 225; military support for, 33, 61, 173, 175, 176, 182, 184; nationalism as basic tenet of, 13, 21, 137, 154, 176, 237; as reactionary ideology, 46–48, 49, 66, 81, 173, 182, 186; as religion, 33–35; secularism as basic tenet of, 13, 20, 58, 70, 237; Sunnis and, 62
Kennedy, John F., 216
Kenya, 103, 127–28
Khatami, Mohammad, 214
Khomeini, Ayatollah, 63, 72
Kılıç, Altemur, 232
Kinzer, Steven (author), 156; arrest and interrogation of, 145–50; blues program of, 249–50; Bosphorus swum by, 207, 210–11
Kırıscı, Kemal, 95
Kırkareli, 20
Kırkpınar, 190
Kıvrıkoğlu, Hüseyin, 195, 201

Kızılay, 201
Klose, Hans-Ulrich, 126
Kocadağ, Hüseyin, 97
Konya, 63
Koran, 60, 79
Korean War, Turkey in, 165–67
Korelis, 165–69
Koru, Fehmi, 80
Kurdish War (1984–99), 17, 72, 95–96, 118–24, 134, 141–42, 145, 151, 153, 174, 178, 216–27; Army's scorched earth policy in, 118–19, 121, 122; military admissions of mistakes in, 238–39; ultra-right gunmen in, 119, 137
Kurdistan, 69, 116, 135, 145
Kurdistan Workers Party, *see* PKK
Kurds, 87, 115–43, 153, 155, 250–51; and Armenian massacre, 89–90; democracy and, 134, 136, 140; insurgencies of, 11, 24, 44, 95, 115, 116; in Iraq, 134, 142–43, 180, 215, 219; nationalism of, 95, 116, 119, 134, 154, 238; Özal's recognition of, 17; in Parliament, 80, 239; racism and, 141; rights of, 24, 115, 117, 132, 135, 138, 160, 226, 238–39, 244; Sèvres Treaty and, 37, 39; terrorist attacks on, 99, 137, 138–39, 178; *see also* PKK
Kuwait, 79

L

Language of Suffering, 156
Latin alphabet, 43
Lausanne, Treaty of (1922), 39, 210
Lebanon, 216, 227, 236
leftists, 93–94
Leninism, 123
Lesser, Ian, 228
Levertov, Denise, 233
Lewis, Bernard, 45
Libya, Erbakan's visit to, 68–69, 76
Lice, 120–23
Lloyd George, David, 37
lüfer, 209–10
Luther, Martin, 4, 60
Lycian League, 111–12

M

Mağden, Perihan, 157
Mahçupyan, Etyen, 159
Mahmut II, Sultan, 179
Malatya, 16
Mamak Military Prison, 94
Mardin, 16
Marlowe, Christopher, 5
Marmara, Sea of, 130, 179, 194, 199, 208
Mars, 109
Marthoz, Jean-Paul, 148–49
Marxism, 62, 117, 229–30
Mater, Nadire, 95
Mecca, pilgrimages to, 61, 62
Medes, 87
Mediterranean Sea, 208
Mehmet II ("the Conqueror"), Sultan, 37, 53, 208, 211
Mehmet's Book (Nadire), 96
Mehmet VI Vahidettin, Sultan, 40
Melville, Herman, 84, 216
Menderes, Adnan, 61, 231
Mersin, 16
Mesopotamia, 116
Metal Storm (Turna and Uçar), 217–18, 219
meyhane, 29–31, 74
meze, 29–30, 184
Middle East, 125; Turkey's expanding role in, xiv, 213–14, 220–21, 226; U.S. unilateral policies in, 219, 221, 223
migrants, in Istanbul, 9–10
military: Atatürk in, 35–36; authoritarian rule of, xv, 14, 17, 21, 63–64, 141, 142, 162, 174, 180, 222, 252; bunker mentality of, 180; cadets in, 175–76,

231; civilian control of, 172; conscription and, 177–78, 179; constitution imposed by, 14–15; coups led by, *see* coups, military; democracy opposed by, 172, 182; elections and, 14; Erdogan's challenges to, 180–81, 182, 183, 184–85; heroin smuggling and, 178–79; Kemalist ideology of, 33, 61, 173, 175, 176, 182, 184; Kurdish War of, *see* Kurdish War (1984–99); 1999 earthquake and, 194, 200–201, 202–203; officer corps of, 171–72, 176–77; Özal's challenges to, 17, 64, 173–74; populace distrusted by, 16; as reactionary institution, 180

Mill, John Stuart, 36

minorities, xiv, 24, 239–40; *see also specific minorities*

MIT, 80

Mitterrand, Danielle, 125

Montagu, Lady Mary Wortley, 6–7

mosaics, Roman, 109–10

mosques, 57, 59, 70

Motherland Party, 68

Mozart, Wolfgang Amadeus, 7

Mudanya, 131

mufti, 42

Murad IV, Sultan, 85

Murat V, Sultan, 209

Muslims: Bulgarian attacks on, 92; call to prayer (*ezan*) of, 44, 61; head scarves of, 18, 24, 35, 58, 70, 73, 78–80, 81, 176, 181, 241, 251–52; religious practices of, 18, 42–43, 44, 48, 58, 60; *see also* Islam

N

Nagorno-Karabakh, 107

Nairobi, 127–28

Nakşibendi, 17

nargile salons, 83–86

National Assembly: Atatürk's creation of, 38; Atatürk's dictatorship supported by, 44; caliphate abolished by, 40, 42; Ottoman monarchy abolished by, 40; secular status of Turkey affirmed by, 43

nationalism, xv, 13, 153, 225, 244; as basic tenet of Kemalism, 13, 21, 137, 154, 176, 237; of Kurds, 95, 116, 119, 134, 154, 238; *see also* ultra-nationalists

Nationalist Action party, 199

National Order party, 61

National Salvation party, 63

National Security Council, 15, 17, 74, 75, 76, 181; Islamic organizations closed by, 76–77

NATO: Greece's membership in, 216; Turkey's membership in, 69, 167, 177, 214, 216, 221

Nazim Hikmet Foundation, 233

Nedim, 207

Netherlands, 119

Newsweek International, 246

New Zealanders, in Gallipoli assault, 54–55

North Atlantic Treaty Organization, *see* NATO

O

Öcalan, Abdullah, 117, 118, 120, 123–24; capture of, 127–29, 141–42, 203; imprisonment and trial of, 129–34; reconciliation urged by, 132–33, 141; in Rome, 125–26; Syria and, 117–18, 124–25

Odysseus, 52

oil wrestling, 190–91

old elite: Armenian massacre and, 158–59; cultural diversity feared by, 10, 21; diminished power of, 237; education system controlled by, 78, 100; in election of 2002, 24, 235; in election of 2007, 183; Islamic fundamentalism feared by, 58–59, 181, 186; Kurdish

old elite (*cont.*)
problem and, 158–59; loyalty to *devlet* as tenet of, 25; militant secularism of, 21, 58, 181–82, 183, 243; nationalism of, 21; and 1999 earthquake, 198–99; reactionary impulses of, xiii, 12–14, 15, 25, 46–48, 49, 162; *see also* Kemalism
opium, 86
Oran, Baskin, 158
Organization of Black Sea Cooperation, 220
Organization of the Islamic Conference, 220
Osman, Sultan, 4, 5, 40
Othello (Shakespeare), 3
Ottoman Empire, 3–8, 39, 179; abolition of, 40; absolutism of, 14; Armenian massacre by, *see* Armenian massacre; cavalry of, 189; collapse of, 10, 14, 35, 37, 60, 166, 172, 223; cultural and political autonomy in, 5, 220; Europe threatened by, 4–6; palaces of, 208–209; religious freedom in, 5; in World War I German alliance, 36, 166
Özal, Turgut, 76, 168; background of, 16, 18, 238; counter-elite mobilized by, 16–17, 20, 200; military challenged by, 17, 64, 173–74; as prime minister, 16–17, 19–20, 64, 202, 214
Özcan, Gül Berna, 184
Özel, Soli, 226

P

Pakistan, 227
palamut, 209
Palestinian Authority, 213
Palestinians, 220, 227
Pamuk, Orhan, xiv–xv, 151–53, 210, 224; Nobel Prize of, xv, 157; prosecution of, xv, 155
Papandreou, George, 203
Parliament, 10, 24, 46, 181, 213; Clinton's address to, 217; Iraq War and, 215; Kurds in, 80, 239; military control of, 15
Patten, Chris, 222–23
Pecevi, Ibrahim, 85
Pelosi, Nancy, 103
penal code: free speech restrictions in, 155; women's rights in, 161
Peres, Shimon, 213
Pergamon, 110
Persian Gulf states, 58–59
Persian War, 52
Peter of Bracheaux, 53
Phaselis ruins, 111
PKK (Kurdistan Workers Party): amnesty for, 139, 140, 141, 155; democracy and, 140; formation of, 117–18; in Iraq, 134, 219, 238; in Kurdish War, 118–24, 133–34, 148–49, 216–17; Marxist-Leninist ideology of, 117, 123, 137; popular support for, 136–40, 143; postwar attacks by, 135, 142–43, 250; as terrorist organization, 120, 137, 138–39, 140, 238, 239
police, 123, 147; torture used by, 94, 119, 160, 222
political parties: autocratic nature of, 16; banning of, 15, 44, 63, 75, 174; democracy and, 46; 1950 introduction of, 46; under Atatürk, 44; *see also specific parties*
politicians, prosecution of, 13
polygamy, 160
Portugal, 136, 185
Poseidon, 51
poverty, 160
presidency, powers of, 181
Presley, Elvis, 250
press: freedom of, 45, 75, 154, 240; Kemalist control of, 159; nationalism promoted by, 244; and 1999 earthquake, 195, 197; *see also* journalists
provincialism, 10

Pusan, Korea, 167
Putin, Vladimir, 220

Q

Qaddafi, Muammar el-, 69

R

racism, 141
radio, 237
rakı, 27–31, 65, 89, 145, 184
Ramadan, 18, 62, 70
Red Cross-Red Crescent, 201
Religious Affairs Directorate, 59
Republican People's Party, 60–61, 241
"repudiation," 43
Rhodes, 4
Rize, 165
Roman Empire, 4, 109, 111
Romania, 214, 225
Rome, Öcalan in, 125–26
Rousseau, Jean-Jacques, 36
ruins: Byzantine, 112; Hellenic, 110–11; Roman, 111; *see also* archaeology
ruling elite, *see* old elite
Rumeli Hisarı, 208
Russia, 55, 88, 118, 119, 125, 204, 220, 227

S

Sabah, 69
Safranbolu, 117
Salonika (Thessaloniki), 35, 229
Samast, Orgün, 105–107
Sanlı, Selahattin, 169
Sarkozy, Nicholas, 226
sarma, 29
Saudi Arabia, 79, 213
Savaş, Vural, 76
Saving Private Ryan (film), 151
Say, Fazil, 162
Schliemann, Heinrich, 51–52
Schmidt, Helmut, 222
schools, religious, 59, 60–61, 63–64, 70
secularism: of Atatürk, 17, 58, 251; as basic principle of Turkish Republic, 11, 20, 43, 57, 182, 240, 252; as basic tenet of Kemalism, 13, 20, 58, 70, 237; democracy and, 184; of old elite, 21, 58, 181–82, 183, 243; women's rights and, 79; *see also* Kemalism
Selçuk, 187, 188
Şemdinli bombing, 99–100, 106, 138
separatism, 154, 237, 238
Serbs, 119
Sèvres, Treaty of (1920), 37, 39, 44, 180, 216
Sezer, Ahmet Necdet, 157, 181–82
Shakespeare, William, 3
sharia law, 73, 81, 242, 252
Silk Road, 145
Silvan, 137
Silvestrini, Achille Cardinal, 126
Sincan, 72–73
sipahi cavalrymen 189
Sirnak, 138–39
Sivas, 62–63
Smyrna (Izmir), 25, 37, 44
Soviet Union, 11, 39, 44, 125, 214, 216, 226, 230, 232, 236
Spain, 136, 185
strategic depth, 219–20
Strategic Depth (Davutoglu), 219
subsidies, 16
Sufis, 17
Sunnis, 62–63
surnames: of Atatürk, 35, 46; requirement for, 45–46
Susurluk scandal, 97–99, 100, 106, 200, 203
Switzerland, Erbakan's exile in, 61, 63
Sykes, Roosevelt, 249
Syria, 117–18, 124–25, 127, 180, 213, 220, 251

T

Tabriz, 4
Tamburlaine the Great (Marlowe), 5
Tarabya, 210
tariffs, 16
Taşçi, Ahmet, 191
Taşgan, Ali, 165, 167, 168–69
Taurus mountains, 112
Taylan, Orhan, 94
television: free speech and, 237; and 1999 earthquake, 195, 201, 202, 203–204
terrorists: government sponsorship of, 99, 138–39, 178; PKK as, 120, 137, 138–39, 140, 238, 239
Thessaloniki (Salonika), 35, 229
Thetis, 109
Thucydides, 52
tobacco, 83–86
Toprak, Dagistan, 139–40
torture, 94, 119, 160, 222
tourism, 107–108, 168
Trabzon, 44, 105
Treatment of Armenians in the Ottoman Empire, 156
Tripoli, 4
Troy, Trojan War, 51–54, 55
Truth Will Set Us Free, The (Jerjian), 156
Tugan, Rojbin, 137–38, 141
Turkey, Republic of: anti-Americanism in, 217–19; anti-religious policies of, 57–60; arms embargo and, 216; Atatürk as founder of, 10–11, 14, 24, 37–39, 40, 242; as centralized state, 11; counter-elite in, 16–17, 20–21; cultural diversity of, 21, 29, 30, 220, 227; Cyprus and, 214, 216, 224, 225; as "deep state," 12, 18, 22, 99, 105, 138, 156, 159; democracy in, *see* democracy; *devlet* in, 25–26; economic boom in, xiii, 11–12, 16–17, 21, 160, 181, 200, 243–44; embassies of, 220; EU membership as goal of, 22, 77, 82, 135, 136, 141, 142–43, 158, 178, 185–86, 204, 221–26, 241–42, 243, 251; as European, xiv, 139, 187, 188, 227; European territory of, 39; expanding regional role of, xiv, 213–14, 220, 226–28; founding of, xiv, 7–8, 10–11, 14, 24, 37–39, 40, 95, 172; Greece's relationship with, 203–204, 214, 220; immigrants in, 101–102; Iran and, 180, 220, 227; Iraq and, 214, 227; Iraq War and, 215, 217, 219; military in, *see* military; minorities in, xiv, 24, 239–40; *see also specific minorities*; as model for Islamic world, 227, 247; modern reinvention of, xiii, 11–12, 24, 25–26; NATO membership of, 69, 167, 177, 214, 216, 221; old elite in, *see* old elite; in "population exchange" with Greece, 39; racism in, 141; secularism as basic principle of, 11, 20, 43, 57, 182, 240, 252; strategic depth as policy of, 220; Syria and, 124–25, 127, 220; unrealized potential of, 8, 28, 247; U.S. relationship with, xiv, 215–19, 226, 228, 244
Turkish Airlines, 75
Turkish Communist Party, 44
"Turkishness," fiction of, 238, 251
Turkish Olympic Committee, 159
Turkish Peace Committee, 94
Turks: "bad," xv, 180; as epitome of evil, 3–4; horsemanship of, 189–90; origins of, 3, 30, 101–102, 113, 188, 189, 238
Turna, Burak, 217–18
Turner, Big Joe, 249
Tutu, Desmond, 214
Tuzcu, Aykut, 241–42
Tzara, Tristan, 233

U

Ülker candy company, 18, 75, 243–44
ultra-nationalists, xiv, 24–25, 97, 107,

155, 157, 158–59, 177, 242, 244–45, 252
ultra-right gangs, 93–94, 119, 137
United Nations: genocide defined by, 102–103; Security Council of, 220; Turkey as founding member of, 166
United States, 167; Armenians in, 101–104; and capture of Öcalan, 128–29; Iraq War of, 103, 142, 215, 217, 219, 223; Turkey's relationship with, xiv, 215–19, 226, 228, 244; Turkish arms embargo of, 216; Turkish popular opinion of, 217–19; unilateral Middle East policies of, 219, 221, 223
Urartu, 87, 89
Urban II, Pope, 4

V

Valley of the Wolves (film), 218–19
Van, 87–88
Van, Lake, 87, 89, 108, 112
veil, banning of, 42–43
Venizelos, Eleftherios, 214
Vienna, 4
Vietnam War, 95
Virtue party, 76–77
Voltaire, 5, 36

W

War of Liberation, 38–39, 44, 60
Waters, Muddy, 249, 252
weddings, 209
Welfare Party, 64–67, 70; banning of, 75; grass-roots organizing by, 64; Islamists in, 65
Wilson, Woodrow, 216
Winter, Johnny, 249
women: education of, 78–80; head scarves of, 18, 24, 35, 58, 70, 73, 78–80, 81, 176, 181, 241, 251–52; rights of, 24, 44, 160–61; veils of, 42–43, 160; violence against, 161; *see also* feminists
World Economic Forum, 161
World War I, 34, 36, 54, 60, 166
World War II, 166
writers, prosecution of, 13, 153, 158, 240

X

Xenophon, 117
Xerxes, 52

Y

yalıs, 209
Yalman, Aytaç, 239
Yalova, 193, 196–97
Yayla, Atilla, 157
Yeltsin, Boris, 125
Yeni Mahalle, 211
Yerevan, Armenia, Genocide Museum in, 91
Yılmaz, Mesut, 67, 68
Young Turks, 14, 36, 60
Yugoslavia, 214, 236

Z

Zaman, 69
Zane, Billy, 219
Zapatero, José Rodriguez, 214
Zarakolu, Ragip, 156
Zeugma, 109–10
Zeus, 208
Zübeyde Hanim, 33, 35, 48